THE
ISAIAH FOUNTAIN
CASE

*Outrage and Jim Crow Justice
on Maryland's Eastern Shore*

JOSEPH KOPER

SECANT PUBLISHING
Salisbury, Maryland

THE ISAIAH FOUNTAIN CASE:
Outrage and Jim Crow Justice
on Maryland's Eastern Shore

Secant Publishing, LLC
P.O. Box 4059
Salisbury, MD 21803

www.secantpublishing.com

ISBN 978-1-7359957-9-3 (hardcover)
ISBN 979-8-9851489-0-9 (paperback)
ISBN 979-8-9851489-1-6 (ebook)

Library of Congress Control Number: 2022914479

Contents

To Jackie—for everything.

ACKNOWLEDGMENTS

There is nothing like writing a book to make a first-time author feel humble. I am very grateful to supportive friends and family members who were beta (early draft) readers for this manuscript. A huge "thank you" goes to Dee Fratus, Marion Jackson, Frank Koper, Jackie Koper, Wayne Layfield, and Norval Toms. All of them contributed valuable suggestions and unique insights for improving *The Isaiah Fountain Case*, based on their life experiences and individual viewpoints, and I am in their debt.

My editor, Christine Doran, did a wonderful and perceptive job of copyediting and provided additional great suggestions to improve the manuscript. I knew I was "on to something" with *The Isaiah Fountain Case*, when—using a wonderfully colorful British expression—Christine reacted to the book's Epilogue by saying that she was "duly *gobsmacked* by the twist in the tale." I hope my readers share Christine's reaction.

The Talbot County Free Library—one of the treasures of Talbot County—and the staff of the library's Maryland Room provided invaluable guidance and assistance in assembling research materials and photos for this book. I extend my gratitude to Becky Riti and Monique Gordy for their enthusiastic support and cooperation.

Likewise, the staff of the Talbot Historical Society was most helpful in providing additional photos for the book. In a series of emails during the COVID shutdown of the Historical Society, Cathy Hill provided me with an especially unique insight for the book with her revelation of the "lost" diary of Alice Gale Reddie, the sixteen-year-old Easton girl who documented her thoughts about Isaiah Fountain's execution.

Thank you to Ron Sauder of Secant Publishing who, after reading the first chapter of *The Isaiah Fountain Case*, commented that he was "mightily intrigued" and wanted to read more. His enthusiasm about this book validated my belief that Isaiah Fountain's story is compelling and important and should be known by more people.

Most importantly, I want to thank Jackie Koper, my amazing wife of fifty-four years, for her selfless patience and understanding while I sat at my computer keyboard writing multiple drafts for this book. During the process I often neglected her and many domestic tasks that I should have attended to. What a wife! We'll always be thankful for the Ides of March!

PREFACE

A powerful reckoning on racism and
inequality was upon us.

—BOB WOODWARD, *RAGE*

Controversy on the Courthouse Grounds

When I began writing this book in the spring of 2020, the COVID-19 pandemic had just begun to explode in the United States. By the end of May, George Floyd had been killed by a police officer in Minneapolis. In the following months, Floyd's gruesome choking death was followed by several other Black fatalities—all involving the actions of various police departments throughout the country. This string of deaths escalated racial tensions all over the country, and Black Lives Matter and other racial justice movements exploded everywhere. Talbot County, on Maryland's pastoral Eastern Shore, did not escape this widespread national debate about race.

The long-simmering issue of the "Talbot Boys" Confederate statue, located on the Talbot County Courthouse lawn (where enslaved people were sold and much of this story took place), was again resurrected. The statue was dedicated in 1916 to commemorate eighty-four county residents who served with the Confederacy in the Civil War, but the more than 300 county Union veterans are not memorialized.[1] This issue of the "Talbot Boys" had caused much contention and division. The local *Star-Democrat* newspaper published letter after letter debating the pros and cons of keeping or removing the statue—the only one of its kind remaining on public property in Maryland. News outlets across the country added their opinions at a time when municipalities throughout the nation were removing similar Confederate monuments. Front lawns throughout the county displayed yellow-and-black "MOVE TALBOT'S CONFEDERATE MONUMENT" signs or blue-and-white "PRESERVE TALBOT HISTORY" signs. In May 2021, a lawsuit was filed in federal court to have the Talbot Boys statue removed from the courthouse property. The plaintiffs were the Talbot County branch of the NAACP and the Maryland Office of the Public Defender.[2] The reader will soon find that this was not the first time that these courthouse grounds would be the epicenter of controversy.

Richard Potter, president of the Talbot County NAACP, filed a sworn declaration to accompany the federal lawsuit. In his declaration, he asserted that the monument "celebrates inequality, glorifies violence and disregards the dignity of Black people."[3]

He added:

> I am disappointed in our elected officials as we are still fighting for the removal of a Confederate monument on the courthouse lawn; a place where all individuals can go to seek a fair and just trial. I am frustrated with the Council because in 2015 when this issue first came up, the NAACP presented our stance and recommendations and

I believe it was not taken seriously because it was viewed as only a "Black person issue" and the opposition outnumbered us.[4]

Potter declared that the Talbot County government sanctioned "systemic racism of the highest form" by continuing to allow the statue to remain. Its presence, he said, "gives license to and encourages racial division in Talbot County."[5]

Despite his scathing denunciation of the council, Potter stated that the ". . . members of our community overwhelmingly support the removal of . . . the Talbot Boys statue and want Talbot County to be a place where inclusivity is a hallmark and bedrock foundation. . ."[6]

On September 14, 2021—following years of debate, protests, and the federal lawsuit—the Talbot County Council reversed a previous vote and passed a resolution to move the monument to a private battlefield park in Harrisonburg, Virginia. Councilman Frank Divilio, a former supporter of keeping the statue, proposed the resolution, stating: "The Talbot Boys issue has divided our community for too long and has sidelined many other important things the county council and county government needs to address." Another council member, who voted against the resolution, said the statue's removal would leave "scars" in the county.

Historical Contrasts

In many ways, the story told in this book about the events of a century ago is in stark contrast to today's Talbot County. In fact, I was amazed to learn during my research for this book about the overtly racist attitudes and events that were prevalent in the county a hundred years ago. In 2022, Talbot presents itself as a welcoming and diverse place. Easton, the county seat, is a picturesque town with art galleries, fine restaurants, museums, live theater, and many active and productive charitable organizations. The town of Easton is considered by many to be the cultural capital of the Eastern Shore. Talbot County's beautiful scenery and rich cultural climate inspired the local tourism board to describe it as "The Hamptons of the Chesapeake." It is a favored weekend getaway spot and retirement mecca for many in the greater Baltimore-Washington, DC area.

Still predominantly White (77.4 percent), Talbot is now home to multicultural communities that include African Americans (12.8 percent), Latinos (7.2 percent), Asians (1.4 percent), and other ethnic groups (1.2 percent).[7] The institutionalized racism of the Jim Crow era[8] is gone, although tensions and racial incidents may flare from time to time. As the NAACP and the public defender's office phrased it in their 2021 lawsuit:

> . . .while race relations in Talbot County have improved significantly since the end of the Jim Crow era, there have been intermittent instances of hatred and violence, remnants of Talbot County's segregationist past. Black people also remain severely underrepresented in county government and excluded almost entirely from positions of prominence in the county's power structure."[9]

Cited in the lawsuit were an unexploded bomb on the lawn of a Black family during school desegregation in the 1950s, a cross burning on Tilghman Island in the 1980s, racial discrimination in the county's roads department in the

1990s, and Ku Klux Klan leafleting in the waterfront town of St. Michaels in 2019. Moreover, in the 360 years that Talbot County has existed, it has had only one Black member of the County Council, Corey Pack, who was elected in 2007 and reelected several times since. There has never been a Black county manager.[10]

Historical Similarities

Obvious similarities between the present and Isaiah Fountain's era are their global pandemics. Both the Spanish flu of 1918-1920 and the COVID-19 virus of 2020-2022 seriously affected the United States' health system and resulted in the loss of hundreds of thousands of lives. Both pandemics overwhelmed the nation's economy and triggered the failure of many businesses and the resulting loss of jobs.

A century ago, the nation was in the clutches of the Jim Crow era and was experiencing the Great Migration of African Americans from the rural South to the industrial North to seek better-paying jobs.[11] Many of these jobs were created by the absence of White workers who were engaged in the Great War in Europe. When the war ended, the soldiers returned and immigrants from Europe flowed to the United States. The resulting competition for jobs between African Americans and Whites became acute and contentious. This competition created widespread racial tensions in the South and North alike,[12] spawning the notorious "Red Summer" of 1919. During that summer and beyond, White supremacist terrorism, including lynchings and race riots, occurred in more than three dozen cities across the country.[13]

In 2020 and 2021, the United States experienced similar health and economic conditions resulting from the COVID-19 pandemic. As 2020 was a presidential election year, the nation also experienced rampant political, racial, and social divisiveness. Such widespread racial unrest—intensified by George Floyd's death that May—had not been experienced since the race riots of the 1960s. Protests and riots occurred regularly in cities throughout the country, many involving property damage, injuries, and deaths.

Author Bob Woodward commented on the 2020 unrest in his book, *Rage*. In words that could also have applied to the events of a century earlier, he concluded: "A powerful reckoning on racism and inequality was upon us. There seemed to be no end in sight, and certainly no clear path to get there."[14]

Woodward's concerns were prophetic: more turmoil *was* on the horizon. On January 6, 2021, a mob of thousands, seeking to overturn the results of the Electoral College and the 2020 presidential election, violently stormed the Capitol of the United States. This vicious assault on the US Congress resulted in death, injury, property destruction, and the interruption of the business of Congress. Some members of the mob carried Confederate battle flags in the Capitol's rotunda, and some rioters wore clothing with Nazi symbols. The *New York Times* wrote that the sight was "a piercing reminder of the persistence of white supremacy more than 150 years after the end of the Civil War."[15] The storming of the Capitol was a shocking, almost unbelievable example of United States citizens rebelling against their government while exhibiting racist symbols and Lost Cause sympathies.

Not long after the Capitol insurrection, I happened to read the book *Robert E. Lee and Me: A Southerner's Reckoning with the Myth of the Lost Cause.* The book examined the causes of an earlier rebellion—the Civil War. It also explored the many myths about the Lost Cause and discussed why some of our country's oldest wounds from slavery and Jim Crow have never healed.[16] Many of the book's observations about the Confederacy, its supporters, and the proponents of the Lost Cause myth struck a note of familiarity when compared to the January 6 insurrection at the Capitol. A similar note was struck by the controversy over the Talbot Boys monument at the Talbot County Courthouse. Pandemics, political controversies, racism, and violent behavior—separated by a century—once again created division and wrath throughout the nation and in Talbot County, Maryland. It was déjà vu!

Many of the events described in this book took place on the same Talbot County Courthouse grounds where the Talbot Boys Confederate statue was erected in 1916—just three years before the Isaiah Fountain case began. In 2021, the Talbot Boys controversy galvanized and outraged the citizens of Talbot County, not unlike the Isaiah Fountain case of a century earlier.

Echoes of the Past

Although many things have changed in Talbot County and the United States over the past century, including our outlook on civil rights, these recent local and national events show that echoes of the past endure. Casey Cep, a native daughter who became a Rhodes Scholar and acclaimed biographer of Harper Lee, wrote in a 2013 essay that: "Talbot County, like so much of America, has an uneasy relationship with its past…"[17] Much of the county's uneasiness may be due to Maryland being a border state during the Civil War, with many of the residents being Confederate sympathizers or combatants against the Union. Even after the Civil War, Talbot's plantation owners had a vested interest in preserving slavery and keeping Blacks in submission with racist Jim Crow laws. The various civil rights laws of the 1960s ended the overt and abusive discrimination of the Jim Crow era by imposing legal boundaries and restrictions that changed our social and behavioral norms. In spite of these laws, there are still some who scratch, peel, and scrape at the fabric of our society to defy these norms and laws.

In some areas of Talbot County and elsewhere on the Eastern Shore, Confederate flags still fly from residential flagpoles or are attached to vehicles as decals or bumper stickers. During a demonstration in the summer of 2020 to keep the Talbot Boys Confederate monument, a group of supporters surrounded the statue. One of the demonstrators waved the red and white pro-Confederate flag that was flown by some Marylanders during the Civil War.[18]

To the chagrin of many residents, Talbot County's controversies have attracted the attention of the national news media. In a 2020 article in *The New Yorker*, Cep recalled how she learned in school about the Talbot Boys, Admiral Franklin Buchanan, and other local Confederate personalities. However, she learned nothing about the Black Union veterans, who later founded the nearby enclave of Unionville, along with freed Blacks. Nor was she taught about the Easton neighborhood called The Hill, thought by some to be the oldest free Black settlement in the country. She did learn about the "necessary and heroic" events of the national Civil Rights Movement, but local integration efforts in Easton and nearby Cambridge were portrayed as "dangerous and thuggish."[19]

Cep wrote that such omissions in her education gave her and other White residents a "distorted vision of life on the Eastern Shore." She goes on to say: "More troublingly, some have suggested that, despite our history of enslavement and Confederate sympathies, we have not merely developed but have somehow always possessed a kind of local immunity to the racism that afflicts every other community in this country."[20]

Reminiscent of a century ago, the COVID pandemic is still with us after two long years, with over 1,000,000 Americans dead. Infection rates seem to be declining, but we've heard about that before. Millions of people are out of work—many by their own choosing, others due to COVID-related issues. Incidents of racial violence continue—not only against African Americans, but also Asians. Other types of shocking violence have become prevalent in our society and now represent a new kind of terrorism. In these respects, it appears that not much has changed from a century ago.

Many of our ancestors took part in or tolerated racist acts and events that would shock us today. Many such incidents of institutional racism, outrage, violence, and threats of violence have been lost in the fog of history. The Isaiah Fountain case is just one such incident. While I am confident that the majority of today's citizens would reject the hostile attitudes and actions that threatened Isaiah Fountain a century ago, the purpose of this book is to tell his story in full to a modern audience for the first time in the hope that we can learn from our history.

On March 14, 2022, the Talbot Boys Confederate Monument—a symbol of racism for many—was removed from the Talbot County Courthouse grounds. After standing for 106 years, the monument's removal was heartily cheered by most of the spectators. A few of the onlookers expressed their disappointment.

Endnotes

1 Dickson J. Preston, *Talbot County: A History* (Centreville: Tidewater Publishers, 1983), 280. Although Preston lists eighty-four names listed on the base of the monument, other sources give different counts. However, the author has counted a total of ninety-six names.

2 Maryland Office of the Public Defender, *et al* v. Talbot County, Maryland (1:21-cv-01088-ELH Document 1), Complaint, May 5, 2021. ACLU of Maryland. Accessed February 8, 2022, at 1. https://www.aclu-md.org/sites/default/files/field_documents/opd_et_al_v._talbot_county.pdf.

3 Maryland Office of the Public Defender, *et al* v. Talbot County, Maryland (1:21-cv-01088-ELH Document 11-3), Declaration, August 13, 2021. ACLU of Maryland. Accessed February 8, 2022, at 2-3. https://www.aclu-md.org/sites/default/files/doc._11-3_declaration_of_r._potter.pdf.

4 Maryland Office of the Public Defender, *et al* v. Talbot County, Maryland, Declaration, at 3.

5 *Id.* at 4.

6 *Id.* at 6.

7 Census.gov, accessed January 25, 2022, https://www.census.gov/quickfacts/fact/table/talbotcountymaryland/RHI125219.

8 Becky Little, "Who Was Jim Crow?" *National Geographic*, August 6, 2015, https://www.nationalgeographic.com/history/article/150806-voting-rights-act-anniversary-jim-crow-segregation-discrimination-racism-history. In the 1830s, Thomas D. Rice, a White theatrical performer, began performing a blackface act called "Jumping Jim Crow." As part of the act, he did a song and dance he patterned after an enslaved man he had observed. Rice's character became known as "Jim Crow" and appeared as a caricature in various cartoons. The term "Jim Crow" began to be used as a term to denigrate African Americans. The term was later applied to the various restrictive laws that mostly Southern states passed to restrict the liberties of African Americans.

9 Maryland Office of the Public Defender, *et al* v. Talbot County, Maryland, Complaint, at 21.

10 *Id.* at 22.

11 "Conclusion: The Legacy of WWI," Boundless US History, World War I: 1914–1918, Lumen, accessed June 25, 2021, https://courses.lumenlearning.com/boundless-ushistory/chapter/conclusion-the-legacy-of-wwi/

12 "Conclusion: The Legacy of WWI."

13 Wikipedia, s.v. "Red Summer," last modified March 4, 2005, https://en.wikipedia.org/wiki/Red_Summer.

14 Bob Woodward, *Rage* (New York: Simon & Schuster, 2020), 386.

15 Maria Cramer, "Confederate Flag an Unnerving Sight in Capitol," *New York Times*, January 9, 2021 (updated January 14, 2021), https://www.nytimes.com/2021/01/09/us/politics/confederate-flag-capitol.html?searchResultPosition=1.

16 Ty Seidule, *Robert E. Lee and Me: A Southerner's Reckoning with the Myth of the Lost Cause* (New York: St. Martin's Press, 2021), 29–41.

17 Casey Cep."Shallow-buried Stories of Slavery Still Haunt My Home County." Aeon Essays. Aeon, last modified 28, 2013. https://aeon.co/essays/shallow-buried-stories-of-slavery-still-haunt-my-home-county.

18 Lydia Woolever, "Turning Tides: After Decades of Silence, the Eastern Shore Begins to Reckon with Its Difficult History." *Baltimore Magazine*, February 2021. Last modified September 14, 2021. https://www.baltimoremagazine.com/section/historypolitics/eastern-shore-begins-to-reckon-with-difficult-history-racism-slavery/.

19 Casey Cep, "My Local Confederate Monument," *The New Yorker*, last modified September 12, 2020, https://www.newyorker.com/news/us-journal/my-local-confederate-monument.

20 Cep, "My Local Confederate Monument."

INTRODUCTION

The Fountain case is one of the most noted
in the State's annals.

—*EASTON STAR-DEMOCRAT*

The Isaiah Fountain case was arguably the biggest and most enduring news "event" ever to occur in Talbot County, Maryland. Lawyer and author Sherrilyn Ifill wrote that the Fountain case "was one of the most notorious on the [Eastern] Shore during the early part of the twentieth century." She added that the case also involved Talbot County's largest incident of mob violence in its history.[1] The case involved rape, racial bias, lynch mobs, armed troops, manhunts, death, and a surprise ending—with each element provoking high emotions. The Fountain case and its many derivative stories generated hundreds of newspaper articles in Maryland and elsewhere for more than two and a half years during the core of the Jim Crow era. The case was conspicuous due to the remarkable levels of public outrage that were generated by and on behalf of the various involved parties: the victim, the accused, the community, the justice system, and the news media. The blatant and institutionalized bias of the Jim Crow era against African Americans only aggravated the outrage and helped to propel the case to its long-lived notoriety.

The Fountain case was a headline-maker, with local and regional newspapers publishing hundreds of related dramatic news banners and spirited articles. The coverage was often contentious, with the *Easton Star-Democrat* at odds with the "big city" publications. This antagonistic journalistic jousting often became its own story, so that time and again, the reporting of the Fountain case was almost an afterthought. Some newspaper articles became tools for indignant tirades, name-calling, and threats of legal action.

Isaiah Fountain became a media sensation. Had television, radio, the Internet, and social media been around a century ago, Isaiah Fountain would have been as well known as Monica Lewinsky, O.J. Simpson, Charles Manson, or George Floyd. His story might have been made into a major motion picture or a Netflix series. However, despite its notoriety and longevity in the media, the Fountain case eventually faded into the obscurity of Talbot County's forgotten, but fascinating, past.

I first learned about Isaiah Fountain when I read *On the Courthouse Lawn: Confronting the Legacy of Lynching in the Twenty-First Century* by Sherrilyn Ifill. The book's abbreviated account of Fountain took up only seven pages and—I later discovered—was incomplete. Nevertheless, Ifill's compelling account piqued my curiosity and prompted me to learn more. I uncovered only brief references in a few local histories of Talbot County but discovered many more fascinating details in newspapers of the time. Especially helpful were the *Easton Star-Democrat*, the *Baltimore Sun*, the *Baltimore Evening Sun*, the *Baltimore Afro-American*, and the *Wilmington* [Delaware] *News Journal*. These five newspapers alone had published hundreds of articles about the Fountain case from April 1919 through November 1921 and supplied much of the detail of Isaiah Fountain's story.

Initially, I was confident that the court records and trial transcripts would be useful in telling Fountain's story.[2] Unfortunately, the official trial transcripts and most other legal records relating to Fountain's court proceedings have been lost. Following Fountain's trials, the Talbot County and Baltimore County Circuit Court trial documents were sent to the Maryland State Archives for permanent storage but were later lost or destroyed. Only some local circuit court ledger entries and some Maryland Court of Appeals records now remain. The Maryland Court of Appeals records (including briefs, motions, and some other documents) remain at the Maryland State Archives in Annapolis. These digitized records provided primary source material and some very helpful insights into the Fountain case.

Using the surviving Court of Appeals records, brief accounts from local histories, and the reporting from the newspapers mentioned above (and others), I was able to compile facts and details about the Fountain case. Microfilm copies of the *Easton Star-Democrat* from the Maryland Room at the Talbot County Free Library in Easton were my source for many local details. The *Star-Democrat* was the closest local news source[3] and probably the most in-the-know, due to its local, on-site access to the events. However, the *Baltimore Sun* and *Baltimore Evening Sun*, along with the dailies from Wilmington, Delaware, had the most complete, and probably the most factually reliable, coverage.[4] The *Baltimore Afro-American* supplied rich and detailed coverage from the perspective of the African American community as it struggled for racial equality within the Jim Crow system.

In the absence of the official trial transcripts, I relied on the various newspaper articles for details about witness testimonies and other happenings in court. The various different newspapers often reported different witnesses' testimonies and attorneys' comments, and I have attempted to weave together the various reports about the court sessions as accurately as possible.

Many other Eastern Shore publications also reported on the Fountain case, as well as newspapers in New York, New Hampshire, Pennsylvania, Washington, D.C., Kansas, Oklahoma, North Dakota, and elsewhere. Most of those papers were getting their news reports second- or third-hand, and in many instances they were simply word-for-word copies of the more on-the-scene newspapers. Other times some of the details and facts were changed and sensationalized into obviously inaccurate articles.

In the early twentieth century, the *Easton Star-Democrat* was a weekly paper, published only on Saturdays, while the Baltimore and Wilmington newspapers were published daily. At times, the fast-moving events of the Fountain case outpaced the once-a-week publication schedule of the *Star-Democrat*. This publication delay caused some events not to be covered, as they were overtaken by newer events before the paper went to press. The Baltimore and Wilmington dailies filled this gap in the local coverage.

The *Star-Democrat* (and other Eastern Shore papers) often showed strong local favoritism in their reporting of Fountain's story.[5] Like other local publications of the time, the *Star-Democrat* tried to portray its community, readership, and local leaders in the best possible light. In doing so, the newspaper often showed bias against the defendant and provided explanations and excuses for the behavior and actions of the local White populace, as well as some of the local government officials in the stories. The Black population of Talbot County was largely ignored in most local reporting, except when mentioned as possibly aiding Isaiah Fountain to escape or otherwise evade the authorities.

The three Baltimore dailies often provided balance to the local perspective, but not always. These "big city" publications often showed their own biases against some of the attitudes and actions of their rural Eastern Shore cousins. Throughout the duration of the Fountain case, the competing biases of the *Star-Democrat* and the Baltimore papers resulted in an ongoing war of words. The cosmopolitan, "sophisticated," more liberal Western Shore publications and the more conservative and parochial Eastern Shore papers were almost constantly at odds over how the Fountain case was reported. I have included examples of these journalistic squabbles throughout the book. In the absence of official court transcripts, I hope that my choice and interpretation of key newspaper reports presents a balanced and accurate narrative of the Isaiah Fountain case.

Isaiah Fountain's experiences of a century ago and the related events that occurred during the Jim Crow era may shock and surprise many readers, but they did, indeed, happen. Today, the Fountain case is unknown to most people and gets brief mention (if any) in local history books. A century ago, however, the case of Isaiah Fountain provoked outrage in Talbot County and was notorious across the Eastern Shore, throughout Maryland, and beyond. In fact, in 1919, the *Easton Star-Democrat* wrote: "The Fountain case is one of the most noted in the State's annals."[6]

Endnotes

1 Sherrilyn A. Ifill, *On the Courthouse Lawn: Confronting the Legacy of Lynching in the Twenty-First Century* (Boston: Beacon Press, 2018), 9–10.

2 The *Easton Star-Democrat* boasted about the very detailed and voluminous record of the case of State of Maryland v. Isaiah Fountain that had been prepared by the Talbot County deputy clerk. The article continued: "This is the first record of this kind made up in Talbot County since the early 1870s." "Record of Fountain Case Prepared," *Easton Star-Democrat*, December 20, 1919, 2. (This reference to the 1870s may be about an earlier case involving a Black man accused of raping a White girl.)

3 The *Easton Star-Democrat* was then located just a few buildings east of the Talbot County Courthouse on the north side of East Dover Street (now the Prim Salon & Boutique at 9 East Dover Street).

4 Some of the Baltimore newspapers' articles were submitted by the Fountain defense team in their appeal to the Maryland Court of Appeals because of the reporters' apparent eye-witness accuracy in reporting the events from Fountain's first trial.

5 The *Easton Star-Democrat* often described the White victim using diminutive terms that emphasized her frailty and helplessness, such as "little," "little white girl," "gentle young girl," etc., while describing her African American assailant as "negro fiend" or "negro brute."

6 "Fountain to Baltimore," *Easton Star-Democrat*, November 29, 1919, 1.

CHAPTER 1

Isaiah Fountain:
A Jim Crow Era Black Man

. . . we will realize more and more how fortunate
we are in having no race questions.

—JOSEPH B. SETH

Villain or Victim

For some, Isaiah Fountain was a villain and scoundrel of the worst sort; for others, he was a martyr and handy victim. This conflicting public persona existed because Fountain was accused of raping a White girl. More significantly, Fountain was also an African American, and the alleged rape occurred during the Jim Crow era in Talbot County on Maryland's Eastern Shore. The Eastern Shore was an area where Jim Crow and racial segregation were as prevalent at the time as many places in the Deep South.[1]

When Isaiah Fountain awoke on Tuesday, April 1, 1919, he surely had no idea how the day's events would change his life forever and make his name a household word throughout

Maryland and beyond. Before the day ended, Fountain would be accused of rape and become the subject of a multistate manhunt. He'd later be arrested and face lynch mobs—several times. He would be tried twice, found guilty, and sentenced. He'd escape jail and be recaptured. Finally, he'd be sentenced and punished for rape. The story of his boldness and resourcefulness, though, didn't end with his sentencing and punishment. The final act of the Isaiah Fountain story is both remarkable and unexpected. It will leave the reader wondering about Isaiah Fountain's guilt or innocence, and whether he was truly a villain or simply a victim of Jim Crow justice.

Isaiah Fountain

Isaiah Fountain lived on his family farm near the tiny Black hamlet of Williamsburg,[2] situated about four miles south of Easton, Maryland, the county seat of Talbot County. Fountain was a rather successful farmer—especially for a Black man of the Jim Crow era living on Maryland's Eastern Shore. He owned his own house and farm (probably with his father, Isaac) in the rural Trappe district of southern Talbot County. According to the *Baltimore Afro-American*, "Fountain owned his two-story whitewashed house with some 14 acres of fertile land on the Trappe Road, minded his own business, had money in the bank, and asked odds of nobody." The paper added that "For these reasons he was a good person to accuse of rape." The same article stated that Fountain wouldn't take any "sass" from White people, and his independence and relative success did not sit well with the "lower element."[3] The *Easton Star-Democrat* reported that, in addition to the house and acreage, he also possessed "One mare and colt, one dark bay horse, sow and pigs, one Berkshire shoat, one wagon, one top carriage, one walking cultivator, one riding cultivator, chain harness, four sets of rope harness, two sets carriage harness; interest in wheat, peas and other crops."[4] Furthermore, Fountain had a savings account in an Easton bank.[5]

By the standards of the day, Fountain was a successful and self-reliant Black man. However, as this was the Jim Crow era, his relative success and independence would have been difficult for some Whites to accept. Some of Fountain's White neighbors likely harbored feelings of jealousy and resentment toward him.

An article in the *Baltimore Afro-American* reported that Fountain was nicknamed "Bully," had a good reputation, and was a law-abiding citizen. The newspaper stated that he had been employed by some well-off White people in the county, who spoke positively about his character and reputation.[6] The *Baltimore Sun*, however, reported that Fountain "did not have a good reputation."[7]

Another *Afro-American* article noted that Fountain had an earlier brush with the law in 1917. The paper said that he was unjustly imprisoned for driving an unshod horse. A local justice of the peace sentenced him to two years in prison for cruelty to an animal. Fountain's lawyer, however, "sued out a writ of *habeas corpus*," and Fountain was ordered released from his sentence. The paper reported: "The judge, after listening to argument in the case, freed Fountain, saying that he looked like an honest, respectable man."[8]

The *Afro-American* stated that Fountain's release from his sentence angered Talbot County State's Attorney Charles J.

Butler, who then maintained an ongoing interest in Fountain. Butler—the paper said—was out to "get" Fountain.[9]

The 1900 Federal Census indicated that Fountain was born in March of 1890, making him twenty-nine years old in 1919.[10] He was married and had two small children—a boy, Preston (six years old at that time) and a girl, Myrtle (eight years old).[11] Census records show that he lived on the farm with his parents, Isaac and Fanny, and had three sisters and five brothers. A daughter-in-law named Margaret is also listed as residing in the household. However, it's unclear if Margaret was Isaiah Fountain's wife or the wife of one of his brothers.[12] Later newspaper reports said that Fountain and his wife were experiencing some problems in their marriage. They noted that his wife no longer wanted to live on the Fountain farm in Williamsburg and wanted, instead, to return to her family in Camden, New Jersey.[13]

There is some confusion about Isaiah Fountain's education. The 1900 census showed that he attended school and could read and write.[14] The Easton paper reported that he could not read.[15] It's likely that Fountain's education fell somewhere in the middle and was incomplete. He probably attended the local Black school when his farm chores allowed and learned just enough to get by.

No full-length photos of Fountain survive. A later police description listed him as "About 28 years old; 5 feet 7 1/2 or 8 inches in height; weight, between 170 and 175 pounds; full, round face with brown skin."[16] A front- and side-view "mug shot" photograph, taken after he was first arrested, was published in the *Baltimore Sun*.[17] A realistic side-view drawing made during his second trial was published in the *Towson Jeffersonian* newspaper.[18] Both sets of images show him with a prominent, full jawline and what might be described as a slight smile or even a smirk. A description of Fountain by one of his trial judges states: "he was a large man, dark, and he bore a distinguishing and striking characteristic, a peculiar facial expression, which has been described in the case as 'a grin,' or as 'a funny grin,' or as 'a silly grin,' but a 'grin.'"[19] This unique facial feature would be a liability to Fountain at trial.

The Time and the Place

Isaiah Fountain and his White and Black Talbot County neighbors were affected and shaped by the time and place in which they lived, including the physical environment, culture, attitudes, history, and legal system. To better understand the time and place of early-twentieth-century Talbot County, it's worthwhile to note some of the important and interrelated elements that influenced the lives of all its residents. These elements were: Jim Crow laws, the "Lost Cause" in Talbot County, and the culture of lynching.

Jim Crow Laws

Jim Crow laws were state and local laws established to enforced racial segregation. The laws were passed in the late nineteenth and early twentieth centuries, primarily in Southern states by White, Democrat-controlled legislatures. The purpose of the laws was to negate the political and economic gains made by Blacks during the Reconstruction period following the Civil War.[20] Jim Crow laws mandated separate accommodations for Blacks and Whites on trains,

5

steamboats, and other transportation; separate schools, housing, and hospitals; poll taxes and voting tests; and separate rest rooms and water fountains, among many other ways of denying equality to African Americans at local and state levels. More informal practices were also a part of the Jim Crow culture: For example, Blacks knew not to be on the same sidewalk as a White person, they knew not to look a White person in the eye, and they knew not to talk to or otherwise engage a White female—especially in any conduct relating to sex. Transgressions of informal rules of behavior could land a Black person in serious trouble just as easily as breaking a formal law.

Jim Crow laws were enforced in the various states until the mid-1960s. President Lyndon Johnson signed the federal Civil Rights Act in 1964, ending the institutionalized segregation that had been mandated by the Jim Crow laws. A year later, the Voting Rights Act ended the most egregious efforts to keep Blacks from voting, although some efforts of voter suppression still occur in less obvious forms. In 1968, the Fair Housing Act ended legalized discrimination in the renting and selling of apartments and homes to Blacks and other minorities.[21] These three federal laws officially ended the era of Jim Crow, although they could not totally put an end to racism and discrimination in every aspect of United States culture.

Talbot County and the "Lost Cause"

Talbot County and the rest of the Eastern Shore was a physically isolated region, separated from the rest of Maryland by the Chesapeake Bay and a poor road system. According

6

to author John Wennersten, "the white population of the agricultural Eastern Shore was proud of the region's plantation heritage."[22] Many of these same Whites were former Southern sympathizers and slaveholders who affirmed the ideology of the "Lost Cause." They believed that the Confederate cause was just and heroic. Most of them tended to look back with nostalgia and fondness on the Confederate cause and the days of institutional slavery. The Lost Cause sentiment had plenty of advocates in Talbot County, as noted by historian Dickson Preston:

> This myth was fostered by the former slave-holding families who were still Talbot's social leaders in the early 1900s. The legend was reinforced by the negative attitudes exhibited by most of the county's whites toward the North on the issues of black freedom and black civil rights.[23]

The Lost Cause movement intensified with the fiftieth anniversary of the end of the Civil War. At that time, advocates began to agitate for monuments to be erected to memorialize the Confederate cause. Preston wrote about the "angry debate" that ensued, with the "unreconstructed rebels" of Talbot County having their way over the Confederate monument. The "rebels" ignored the service of three hundred Talbot County Union veterans—many of them Black—and built the monument to Confederate veterans. Preston noted that a proposal to dedicate the monument to both sides was turned down.[24]

Joseph B. Seth was one of Talbot County's "unreconstructed rebels." He also was one of its leading advocates of the Lost Cause movement and the construction of the Talbot Boys monument. Seth served in the Maryland House of Delegates and the Maryland Senate and later as mayor of Easton from 1914 to 1916.[25]

Seth was born in Talbot County in 1845 to a well-to-do slaveholding family. In 1926, he published a nostalgic memoir in which he looked back on the untroubled time of growing up on the Eastern Shore. He wrote about his near-idyllic childhood, the natural beauty of the Chesapeake Bay, changes in agriculture, and the "happy" and "devoted" enslaved people who were owned by his family. His memoir contains many anecdotal examples about his own longing for the "good old days" of institutional slavery. Seth's sentiments are glaringly clear when he writes that "It has been frequently said that the golden period of the social life of this country was between the years 1750 and 1850."[26] His statement epitomizes the Lost Cause sentiment held by many of his contemporaries.

Joseph Seth made many references to the enslaved people that his family owned and his family's benevolence toward them. Seth reflected: "They were happy under the kindly rule of their masters and were fresh enough after the day's work to put wonderful life into their dancing."[27] Seth was convinced of their happiness under slavery when he commented:

> The bulk of the slaves were devoted to their masters and their families, taking great interest in everything concerning them. They considered themselves a part of the family and their devotion was so great that they would run any risk to protect them. The families were equally devoted to the slaves and with the whole Southland had the tenderest affection for the faithful old Mammies and Uncles.[28]

Referring to a particular enslaved man of the family, Seth wrote: "Charlie said he realized the great benefits and advantages he and his family had received by being brought up under a humane master, even though in slavery."[29] Seth even described some of his family's enslaved people as "happy-go-lucky"[30] and seemed convinced that in Talbot County, "we will realize more and more how fortunate we are in having no race questions."[31]

In the same memoir, Seth also mentioned the Talbot County favorite son, the formerly enslaved Frederick Douglass, with some disdain. He noted that Douglass came from the area and was "notorious" before and after the Civil War. He added, "He ran away from his home in Talbot County when a young man. Today he is practically unknown."[32]

The prominent Lloyd family of Wye Plantation in Talbot County owned Frederick Douglass during his early years as an enslaved man. In discussing the Lloyds, one author wrote in 1944: "Today the old families of the Shore are likely to dwell on slave days with nostalgic regret. It is one of their pet articles of belief that slaves were never treated cruelly in that delectable country—or hardly ever." The author added that family descendants would often say defensively: "My grandfather never sold a slave." Such grand families conveniently "forgot" about the whippings, family separations, sales to traders, or uses of "slave breakers." Such "disagreeable" activities were usually performed by others, out of sight of the slaveowners and their plantation homes.[33] Thus, many Lost Cause believers never fully realized or acknowledged the bitter truths about slavery.

As noted above, Joseph Seth was the driving force in Talbot County for raising funds for the Talbot Boys monument that until March 2022 stood in front of the Talbot County Courthouse. Seth began his campaign for a monument in 1914 when he enlisted the aid of influential lawyer Colonel David G. McIntosh of Towson, Maryland.[34] As a native North Carolinian and former Confederate officer, McIntosh moved to Maryland after becoming dissatisfied with the process of Reconstruction in the South.[35] McIntosh had maintained his sympathies to the Lost Cause and was influential in Maryland in promoting the movement and helping to raise funds for Talbot County's Talbot Boys monument. He was another "unreconstructed rebel."

After a successful fundraising effort, a stone monument was erected on the Talbot County Courthouse grounds in July 1914, listing the names of eighty-four Talbot countians who had served the Confederacy. This was at a time when "wartime passions were still strong and the county was dominated by persons of Southern sentiment."[36] Not long after the monument was dedicated, Seth decided that it should be topped with a statue. He wanted one different from other statues that had been erected throughout the country. Seth proclaimed: "It is my desire to get away from the conventional soldier figure which is found on all of the monuments North and South, and to get an allegorical figure representing youth and courage." The result was a bronze statue of a boy soldier, holding the Confederate flag draped over his shoulder. The completed "Talbot Boys" monument was dedicated on June 5, 1916.[37] The monument was one of hundreds that were erected throughout the country in the early part of the twentieth century as part of the Lost Cause movement and, until recently, was one of the few remaining on public property.

Seth would be surprised, if not shocked, to learn that Frederick Douglass—the local man he derided in his memoirs—had earned great fame and success. Today, Douglass's larger-than-life bronze statue stands alone in front of the Talbot County Courthouse.

Lynching

Many of us first encountered portrayals of lynching when we were kids, watching cowboy movies and TV westerns. Such shows often featured posses or vigilante groups that administered swift, "Wild West" justice to cattle rustlers, horse thieves, and other "bad guys." The culprits were usually captured and summarily hanged without benefit of a trial. Such extrajudicial executions are lynchings. They were relatively common across the Western frontier, where most of the victims were White.[38]

Today, lynchings usually involve racially based killings by mobs. Although most people associate lynching with hanging, lynchings can also involve shootings, burnings, beatings, beheadings, or any combination of violent acts that end in the death of the victim.

Lynching is generally defined as a premeditated extrajudicial killing by a group. "It is most often used to characterize informal public executions by a mob to punish an alleged transgressor, punish a convicted transgressor, or to intimidate a group. It can also be an extreme form of informal group social control, and it is often conducted with the display of a public spectacle. . . for maximum intimidation."[39]

On the physically isolated and politically conservative Eastern Shore, lynchings were not unknown. According to

Sherrilyn Ifill, more than any other Jim Crow law or practice, "lynching and the threat of lynching helped regulate
and restrict all aspects of black advancement, independence,
and citizenship in many small towns for half a century."[40] In
addition, "on the Shore, as in the South, sex was a driving
force behind lynchings during this period. Headlines rang
loudly of another black 'brutal beast' who had committed
an 'outrage' upon a helpless white female from a 'prominent'
local family."[41] This constant threat of being lynched influenced the lives of Black people in Talbot County and their
relationships with White Talbot countians.

John Wennersten has noted that the White population
of the Eastern Shore (including Talbot County) "defended
violence as a necessary means of 'keeping niggers in their
place.'"[42] This violence often included lynching.

Many Whites might have agreed with using lynching
to keep African Americans "in their place." However, some
Whites of the "better class" denounced the practice—not
necessarily because of any moral convictions, but because of
appearances. They were concerned with the public image of
their towns or counties and thought that lynchings and other
displays of racial violence weren't worthy of their gentility
and social status. Also, many Whites thought that lynchings
diminished the authority of the legal system and law enforcement within their jurisdiction.

No lynchings ever occurred in Talbot County.[43] Nevertheless, local African Americans were acutely aware of the
very real judicial and nonjudicial dangers that could await
them for even the suspicion of crimes against White society—especially those involving White females. Talbot
County Blacks knew that other parts of the Eastern Shore

had a history of lynching that extended from the nineteenth into the early twentieth century. [44]

Even without lynchings, the White-dominated legal system often treated Blacks with sometimes fatal harshness. Easton experienced three sensational "legal" hangings of Blacks in the 1870s, "each of which brought a morbid, carnival spirit to the small town." These hangings caused Easton's population to swell with thousands of curious onlookers.[45] However, despite the negative racial attitudes in the county and the three "legal" hangings, Talbot County somehow avoided having any lynchings.

According to C. Christopher Brown, author of *The Road to Jim Crow*, Blacks throughout the Eastern Shore recognized that the local legal systems were dominated by White male judges, jurors, prosecutors, lawyers, sheriffs, and police. These White officials decided how things were to be done and when to apply the death penalty. Black people also knew that if the local White population became unsatisfied with how the White-dominated justice system operated, or if it operated too slowly, they could usually resort to mob violence (that is, lynching) with little fear of legal consequences.[46]

With the challenges brought by Jim Crow laws, the constant threats of lynching, and the Lost Cause sentiment that permeated much of Talbot County society, one can appreciate the anxiety, fear, and even terror that must have weighed on the minds of Black people of the time. Certainly, they all knew the formal and informal boundaries that they were expected to live within and the consequences if they strayed. This was Isaiah Fountain's Talbot County in 1919.

Fountain—The Day of the Crime

It's likely that Tuesday, April 1, 1919, started out like any other day for Isaiah Fountain on his small farm in Williamsburg, located between Easton and Trappe. It was early spring, and Fountain had already planted his crops of wheat and peas, but other farm chores vied for his attention.

The *Baltimore Sun* reported that on this day, Fountain sent his wife to the Talbot Bank in Easton to withdraw some money to pay for a "shoat" (a baby pig) he had bought from a neighbor the previous day. While his wife drove their ragged farm horse and shabby buggy to Easton, Fountain took care of his farm duties. He later said that he was splitting wood from 9:00 a.m. until about 2:00 p.m. By this time, his wife had not returned from Easton, and Fountain started to worry. He decided to walk the four miles to town to look for her.[47]

On the road to Easton, he met two local people. The first was a Black man named Morris Bannon. Fountain asked him if he had seen his wife driving the carriage. Fountain told Bannon that he was concerned for his wife because the horse was skittish. Next, Fountain met a White neighbor, Mr. Theodore "Swanaker" (most likely spelled "Schwaninger"), who offered him a ride into Easton on his buggy.[48] Fountain climbed aboard, and they arrived in Easton about 3:25 p.m.[49]

Fountain went to the Talbot Bank and found that his wife had withdrawn ten dollars from their account. He then searched the town but couldn't find her. Suspecting that she had run away with the money to her family in New Jersey, Fountain went to Easton Chief of Police William R. Stoops and asked him to go to New Jersey to bring her back. Chief Stoops told him to come back the following Monday to see what could be done. Fountain also spoke to the teller at the Talbot Bank and an official at the county courthouse. He searched the town again and found his horse and buggy in a nearby shed. Fountain didn't leave Easton until after 4:15 p.m., when he drove his horse and buggy back to his farm—without his wife.[50]

The next morning, concerned about his wife's abrupt departure, Fountain left his Williamsburg house for Camden, New Jersey, to try to patch things up with her. The *Baltimore Afro-American* reported that prior to arriving home on Tuesday, Fountain had "told neighbors and several persons in Easton of his intended trip."[51] From his farm, it was an easy half-mile walk to the Llandaff station of the Philadelphia, Wilmington & Baltimore Railroad.[52] There Fountain purchased a ticket to Philadelphia and caught the train that originated in Oxford, Maryland and traveled through Easton, then northeast to Clayton, Delaware. From Clayton, another line carried him north to Wilmington, Delaware, and Philadelphia, Pennsylvania. Fountain arrived in Philadelphia before noon, then crossed the Delaware River to Camden, New Jersey.[53]

Arriving in Camden, Fountain found his wife staying with her parents and tried to convince her to return with him to Maryland.[54] She told him that she didn't want to live on a farm anymore, but he was not interested in giving up his farm. Evidently, the couple reached some agreement, and she agreed to return home in a week. Fountain then went to Philadelphia and took the trolley to West Chester, Pennsylvania, to visit his brother John. He arrived there on Sunday and stayed until Monday morning.[55] On Monday, April 7,

Isaiah Fountain's life was suddenly changed due to an event that had occurred less than a week earlier.

Endnotes

1   Dickson J. Preston, *Talbot County: A History* (Centreville: Tidewater Publishers, 1983), 281.

2   The enclave of Williamsburg is in the vicinity of what is now Old Trappe Road (MD Route 565) and Llandaff Road.

3   "Good People in Easton Outnumbered by the Bad," *Baltimore Afro-American*, June 25, 1920, 3. ProQuest.com.

4   "O'Dunne's Pay," *Easton Star-Democrat*, May 3, 1919, 2.

5   "Death Decree for Fountain," *Baltimore Sun*, April 25, 1919, 3. Newspapers.com.

6   "Farmers Crowd Courthouse," *Baltimore Afro-American*, April 18, 1919, A1. ProQuest.com.

7   "To Try Fountain Again," *Baltimore Sun*, July 18, 1919, 18. Newspapers.com.

8   "Afro Reporter Not Wanted," *Baltimore Afro-American*, October 24, 1919, 2. ProQuest.com.

9   "Fountain May Be Reprieved," *Baltimore Afro-American*, May 14, 1920, 2. ProQuest.com.

10 1900 Federal Census, Trappe, Talbot, Maryland. Page: 11; Enumeration District: 0091; FHL microfilm: 1240628. Ancestry.com. (Accessed July 27, 2020.) The 1910 and 1920 censuses list Fountain as being born in 1889 and 1892, respectively. Viewing copies of the early twentieth-century census forms show that the reports were not always accurate, consistent, or complete with the information recorded by the census-takers. Because the 1900 census listed Fountain's month and year of birth ("Mar, 1890") and the 1910 and 1920 censuses listed only the year of birth, I used what I considered the more accurate birth date—March 1890.

11 "Still Denies His Guilt," *Easton Star-Democrat*, July 17, 1920, 1.

12 1920 Federal Census, Trappe, Talbot, Maryland; Roll: T625 662. Page: 1B; Enumeration District: 146. Ancestry.com. (Accessed July 27, 1920.)

13 "Death Decree for Fountain," *Baltimore Sun*, 3.

14 1900 Federal Census.

15 "Still Denies His Guilt," *Star-Democrat*, 1.

16 "Police at Baltimore Throw Out Dragnet," *Baltimore Sun*, June 16, 1920, 1. Newspapers.com.

17 "All Talbot in Manhunt," *Baltimore Sun*, April 23, 1919, 8. Newspapers.com.

18 "Fountain Escapes," *Towson Jeffersonian*, June 19, 1920, 1. Maryland State Archives. https://mdhistory.msa.maryland.gov/msa_sc3410/msa_sc3410_1_63/html/mdsa_sc3410_1_63-0164.html.

19 "Court Gives Reasons," *Easton Star-Democrat*, May 22, 1920, 1.

20 Wikipedia, s.v. "Jim Crow Laws," last modified November 13, 2001, https://en.wikipedia.org/wiki/Jim_Crow_laws.

21 Editors, "Civil Rights Act of 1964," History.com, last modified January 4, 2010, https://www.history.com/topics/black-history/civil-rights-act.

22 John R. Wennersten, *Maryland's Eastern Shore: A Journey in Time and Place* (Cornell Maritime Press/Tidewater Publishers, 1992), 146.

23 Preston, *Talbot County*, 280.

24 Preston, *Talbot County*, 280.

25 "Joseph B. Seth, MSA SC 3520-1707," Maryland State Archives, accessed November 17, 2021, https://msa.maryland.gov/msa/speccol/sc3500/sc3520/001700/001707/html/msa01707.html. "Easton Mayors, Talbot County, Maryland," Maryland State Archives, accessed July 18, 2021, https://msa.maryland.gov/msa/mdmanual/37mun/easton/html/emayors.html.

26 Joseph B. Seth and Mary W. Seth, *Recollections of a Long Life on the Eastern Shore* (Easton, Maryland: The Star-Democrat Press, 1926), 11.

27 Seth and Seth, *Recollections*, 13.

28 Seth and Seth, *Recollections*, 28.

29 Seth and Seth, *Recollections*, 17.

30 Seth and Seth, *Recollections*, 12.

31 Seth and Seth, *Recollections*, 8.

32 Seth and Seth, *Recollections*, 33.

33 Hulbert Footner, *Rivers of the Eastern Shore* (New York: Little and Ives Company, 1944), 284–285.

34 Teri West and Kirstyn Flood, "Legacy of Slavery, Segregation Influences Debate over Removing Confederate Statue in Maryland," Capital News Service Maryland, last modified June 15, 2020, https://cnsmaryland.org/2020/06/15/legacy-of-slavery-segregation-influences-debate-over-removing-confederate-statue-in-maryland/.

35 "David Gregg McIntosh—A Civil War Colonel & His Son, Part I," Baltimore County Small and Solo Atty's Blog, last modified November 8, 2010, https://baltimorecountysmallandsoloatty.wordpress.com/2010/11/07/david-gregg-mcintosh-a-civil-war-colonel-his-son-part-i/. McIntosh was such a staunch Confederate that he refused to surrender his unit with Lee at Appomattox and slipped through Union lines to continue the fight. He surrendered a month later with the final surrender of all Confederate forces.

36 Preston, *Talbot County*, 222.

37 West and Flood, "Legacy of Slavery, Segregation Influences Debate over Removing Confederate Statue in Maryland."

38 "Lynchings & Hangings of America," Legends of America website, accessed July 18, 2021, https://www.legendsofamerica.com/ah-lynching/.

39 Wikipedia, s.v. "Lynching," last modified October 7, 2002, https://en.wikipedia.org/wiki/Lynching.

40 Sherrilyn A. Ifill, *On the Courthouse Lawn: Confronting the Legacy of Lynching in the Twenty-First Century* (Boston: Beacon Press, 2018), xvii.

41 C. Christopher Brown, *The Road to Jim Crow: The African American Struggle on Maryland's Eastern Shore, 1860–1915* (Baltimore, Md.: Maryland Historical Society, 2017), 159.

42 Wennersten, *Maryland's Eastern Shore, 146.*

43 Preston, *Talbot County*, 281.

44 Ifill, *On the Courthouse Lawn*, xiv.

45 Brown, *The Road to Jim Crow*, 153.

46 Brown, *The Road to Jim Crow*, 150.

47 "Death Decree for Fountain," 3.

48 "Negro Assailant of White Girl to Hang," *Wilmington Evening Journal,* April 25, 1919, 3 and 24. Newspapers.com. "Swanaker" is undoubtably meant to be "Schwaninger," the name of a local family and nearby road.

49 "Death Decree for Fountain," 3.

50 "Death Decree for Fountain," 3.

51 "Fountain's Case to Be Appealed," *Baltimore Afro-American,* May 2, 1919, A1. ProQuest.com.

52 John C. Hayman, *Rails Along the Chesapeake: A History of Railroading on the Delmarva Peninsula, 1827–1978* (Marvadel Publishers, 1979), 44. This Pennsylvania Railroad branch line had previously been owned by the Chesapeake & Delaware Railway Company and, before that, the Maryland & Delaware Railroad.

53 "Clayton, DE to Easton and Oxford, MD," Abandoned Rails website, accessed July 18, 2021, https://www.abandonedrails.com/clayton-to-easton-and-oxford.

54 "Fountain Has Small Chance for Justice," *Baltimore Afro-American,* April 25, 1919, 4. ProQuest.com.

55 "Death Decree for Fountain," 3.

CHAPTER 2

The Victim and the Crime

Negro fiend . . . little white girl.

—EASTON STAR-DEMOCRAT

In the spring of 1919, as Talbot County was recovering from the Spanish flu pandemic and just before the notorious "Red Summer" of racial violence, a rape occurred in the Trappe district of Talbot County, Maryland. The crime took place on Tuesday, April 1, 1919, and involved a young White girl living near Trappe. The girl accused a local African American man of sexually assaulting her, but initially could provide no other details about the man.

The very first newspaper account of the crime appeared two days later, on Thursday, April 3, in the *Baltimore Sun*. The first local newspaper article about the crime was published in the weekly *Easton Star-Democrat* on Saturday, April 5. The *Star-Democrat's* article made liberal use of inflammatory racist language, referred to the perpetrator as a "Negro fiend," and mentioned the "probabilities" of "the Lynch law." The town of Trappe and the entire county were euphemistically described as showing "intense feeling" over "the outrage."[1] In future reporting, the *Star-Democrat* would continue to use other euphemisms such as "indignation," "excitement," and "boisterous" to describe other similar gatherings that were, really, angry mobs bent on racial violence.

Bertha Simpson

On Tuesday, April 1, 1919, while Isaiah Fountain was on his way to Easton to search for his wife, a teenage White girl was attending classes at Trappe High School, approximately eight miles south of Easton, "as the crow flies." The small town of Trappe had a population of about 240 people,[2] and the high school was located on its Main Street.[3]

The girl's name was Bertha Simpson, and she had just turned fourteen in March. Bertha's parents, Robert and Ida Simpson, had three sons and three daughters, Bertha being the third oldest.[4] Robert Simpson was employed as a farm manager, and the family lived in the Royal Oak district of Talbot County on the west side of the Tred Avon River, just across from Oxford. According to the *Washington Times*, Bertha Simpson was living near Trappe with her grandparents, Mr. and Mrs. Henry Diffenderfer, so that she could attend school there.[5] The Diffenderfers lived about two miles northwest of Trappe in the Island Creek Neck area of the Trappe district of Talbot County.[6] It was Simpson's routine to walk to and from the school, about two miles each way.

Various newspapers noted that Simpson looked physically larger and more mature than her actual age. The *Baltimore Sun* described her as "exceptionally good looking. She is large for her age, but she does not look older than her years."[7] In a published letter to the *Sun*'s editor, Dr. Charles Davidson from Easton wrote, "Bertha Simpson is no little, undeveloped child with a dull and cloudy mind. . . she is developed, mind and body, far beyond her years."[8] The *Baltimore Afro-American* described her as "a big strapping girl weighing from 125 to 130 pounds. Witnesses for the State, who have known her since she was a baby told a representative for the *Afro-American*, that she is at least 17 or 16 years of age."[9]

The *Easton Star-Democrat* often described Simpson using diminutive terms such as "little" or "little white girl," while it described her African American assailant as "negro fiend," "ignorant negro,"[10] or "negro brute."[11] During the Jim Crow era, this type of reporting was all too common, especially in cases involving the sexual assault of a White female by a Black male. The local newspaper reports tended to emphasize the innocence and purity of the White victims while demonizing the Black perpetrators. Such reporting tended to reflect the feelings of many White Talbot countians.

The Crime (Tuesday, April 1, 1919)

The *Baltimore Sun* reported that classes were dismissed at Trappe High School at 3:30 p.m. on Tuesday, April 1, 1919, where Bertha Simpson was a student. Simpson promptly left school at dismissal time and headed home. On her way, she stopped three times: at the Trappe post office, a local store, and her aunt's house. She then walked north on Trappe Road toward her grandparents' home, located about two miles northwest of Trappe.[12] Her walk would have taken her on a country road bordered by woods and farm fields.

The *Sun* reported that while Simpson was walking along Trappe Road, a buggy driven by a Black man passed her without stopping. The report claimed that he drove down the road about a mile from Trappe, pulled the buggy off the road, and hid in the woods. When the teenager approached, he grabbed her and pulled her into the underbrush. When she tried to run away, he caught her. He threatened to kill her if she made any noise, threw her to the ground, and raped her. The *Sun* stated that the assault took place approximately one mile north of Trappe, "on the public road leading from Trappe to Trappe Station."[13] Simpson, according to the *Sun*, attempted to struggle and remained conscious during the assault. Her assailant released her, and she ran away. After that, the paper said, "her memory seems to be a blank."[14]

Initial newspaper articles reported the time of Simpson's assault as early as 4:00 p.m.[15] However, the exact time of the event kept changing: later newspaper accounts of her testimony at trial reported the assault as taking place between 4:30 and 5:00—one and a half hours after Simpson had left school.[16] Still later in the legal process, the time of the rape would be changed even more, to as late as 5:30 p.m.[17] This ever-shifting timeline for the assault would later have dire consequences for the man accused of the rape.

Other information about the details of the crime also changed, according to later newspaper articles and victim accounts. The *Sun* and *Evening Sun* initially reported that Bertha's assailant passed her while going in the *same* direction and then hid his horse and buggy *ahead* of her in the woods while he waited for her to pass. A later article stated that the assailant passed Bertha while traveling in the *opposite* direction, turned around, caught up with her, ordered her into the buggy, and then pulled off the road to assault her.[18]

Details of what happened after the rape were also inconsistent. In an article published two days after the assault, the *Sun* stated that: "After some time the girl regained her senses and got upon the country road, where she was met by Harriet Freeman, a negress, who took her in her carriage to her home, where she told her story."[19] During the trial, Simpson's testimony, as reported by the *Sun*, was that she went to the nearby home of Harriet Freeman "and asked to be taken home."[20]

Once Simpson arrived at her grandparents' home, a local physician, Dr. Joseph Ross, was called. Ross examined Simpson, treated her, and confirmed that she had been criminally assaulted.[21] In spite of the rape being medically confirmed, the crime wasn't reported to the Talbot County Sheriff until 9:00 Tuesday night—several hours after the attack. Sheriff James L. Stitchberry immediately drove to Trappe to interview Bertha Simpson but had no success. Her grandparents, the Diffenderfers, did not allow the sheriff to conduct an interview with the girl due to her "nervous condition." With little useful information to begin his investigation, the sheriff returned to Easton with plans to talk to Simpson the next morning. He returned to the Diffenderfers' home at 7:30 on Wednesday morning to interview Simpson about her assault.[22] This delay in getting the victim's account of the assault undoubtedly hampered the search for the assailant.

Reports in the *Baltimore Evening Sun* indicate that local citizens heard about the crime even before Sheriff Stitchberry. Many of the local White people promptly armed themselves, formed a posse, and began their own "investigation." Near the site of the assault, the posse found prints of a horse with one unshod hoof. The group followed the prints to the local blacksmith's shop, that of Edward Mullikin. Mullikin told the posse that he had recently shod a horse for Isaiah Fountain, a local Black man.[23] That information, along with the news that Fountain had left town the morning after the crime, was enough to convince the posse that Fountain was the rapist of Bertha Simpson.

By Wednesday evening, the citizens of the Trappe area were clamoring for official news about the rape investigation. A group of "25 or 30 residents" traveled to Easton to visit the sheriff and state's attorney to learn about the progress being made to locate Isaiah Fountain. The group pressured the two officials "to see that the deed should be avenged without delay."[24] In the eyes of many of the Whites from Trappe, the crime was all but solved. Their conclusion was that Isaiah Fountain was the rapist. Fountain just had to be found, arrested, and returned to Talbot County to pay for his crime.

Endnotes

1 "Negro Fiend Not Found," *Easton Star-Democrat*, April 5, 1919, 1.

2 Wikipedia, s.v. "Trappe, Maryland," last modified October 20, 2002, https://en.wikipedia.org/wiki/Trappe%2C_Maryland.

3 Trappe High School no longer exists, but the site is now the location of Trappe Park.

4 1910 Federal Census, Trappe, Talbot, Maryland; Roll: T624_568;. Page: 1B; Enumeration District 0098; FHL microfilm: 1374581. Ancestry.com. (Accessed July 27, 2020.)

5 "Negro Attacks 14-Year-Old Girl," *Washington Times*, April 3, 1919, 12. Newspapers.com. The *Washington Times* spelled Bertha Simpson's grandparents' name "Diefenderfer," while other sources (including court of appeals records) use the spelling, "Diffenderfer." For the sake of consistency, the author uses the spelling "Diffenderfer."

6 The author was unable to definitively find the site of Bertha Simpson's residence, but based on extrapolating directions and descriptions from various sources, it was likely located near the intersection of White Marsh Road and Sanderstown Road, approximately two miles north of Trappe and one mile north of the site of her assault.

7 "Negro Again on Trial for Assault," *Baltimore Sun*, May 6, 1920, 12. Newspapers.com.

8 "Dr. Charles F. Davidson, of Easton, Declares. . .," *Baltimore Sun*, April 30, 1919, 10. Newspapers.com.

9 "Fountain Has Small Chance for Justice," *Baltimore Afro-American*, April 25, 1919, 4. ProQuest.com.

10 "Negro Fiend Not Found," 1.

11 "The Sun Investigates," *Easton Star-Democrat*, May 17, 1919, 11.

12 "Accused Negro Gets Away," *Baltimore Sun*, April 22, 1919, 9. Newspapers.com.

13 "Negro Assaults Girl," *Baltimore Sun*, April 3, 1919, 3: "Negro Assaults 13-Year-Old Girl," *Wilmington Evening Journal*, April 3, 1919, 1. Newspapers.com. The road is now called White Marsh Road, and the assault probably occurred near the intersection of White Marsh Road and Lovers Lane, where White Marsh

Elementary School is now located. Also, the reported time of the assault—initially 4:00 p.m.—would be changed several times by the victim and the court to later times, seemingly to cast doubt on the defendant's confirmed alibi of not being near the crime scene at the time of the crime.

14 "Accused Negro Gets Away," 9.

15 "Negro Assaults 13-Year-Old Girl," *Evening Journal*, April 3, 1919, 5. Newspapers.com. "Negro Assaults Girl," 3.

16 "Fountain Verdict Near," *Baltimore Sun*, May 8, 1920, 7. Newspapers.com.

17 "Court Gives Reasons," *Easton Star-Democrat*, May 22, 1920, 3.

18 "Fountain in Cell Here," *Baltimore Evening Sun*, April 9, 1919, 16. Newspapers.com.

19 "Negro Assaults Girl," 3.

20 "Accused Negro Gets Away," 9.

21 "Negro Assaults Girl," 3.

22 Isaiah Fountain v. State, April Term 1919 No. 39 [MSA S1733-530, 1/65/04/100]. Ct of Appeals: Statement of Sheriff Stitchberry of Talbot County, filed June 5, 1919, at 19.

23 "Posse Loses Negro Assailant's Trail," Baltimore Evening Sun, April 3, 1919, 2. Newspapers.com.

24 "Posse Loses Negro Assailant's Trail," 2.

CHAPTER 3

The Investigation

Go get Fountain.

—CHARLES J. BUTLER

Gathering the Facts (Tuesday, April 1, 1919 to Wednesday, April 2, 1919)

Regardless of the information produced by the informal and unauthorized "investigation" conducted by the citizens of the Trappe area, Sheriff Stitchberry was determined to conduct his own official investigation. Stitchberry's investigation to find Bertha Simpson's assailant began in earnest on Wednesday morning when he returned to interview Simpson. Here is his account, according to his affidavit filed with the Maryland Court of Appeals:

> I returned in the morning at 7:30 to Bertha Simpson's home, and all she could tell me was that it was a large black man with a black horse and good-looking carriage. I immediately started looking for a black horse and carriage. I found three in the Trappe district. She positively refused to identify Fountain's horse and carriage.[1]

Acting on Bertha Simpson's description of the horse and buggy used by her assailant, Sheriff Stitchberry began searching the area for a match. The sheriff found three black horses with three "good-looking" carriages. Stitchberry recalled that he then took Simpson to the scene of her assault and examined the area for clues. He noticed buggy tire imprints in the dirt, as well as horseshoe imprints. He also noticed that the horse's left hind shoe was missing. Stitchberry followed the tracks to see where they would lead. Unlike the earlier reports of the tracks leading the local posse to the nearby blacksmith's shop, Sheriff Stitchberry's tracking efforts led him to the property of a Black man named Andrew Mills, who wasn't home. When Mills returned, the sheriff asked Simpson if she recognized him, and she replied: "No, I never saw this man before." Stitchberry then got Mills's horse, put the tack (that is, harness, reins, bridle, etc.) on it, and positioned the animal next to his car. He turned the horse around so that Simpson could see a rear view of the horse and tack. The sheriff then asked if she could identify the horse. She immediately answered, "Yes, that is the horse because it had a long curly tail." Stitchberry asked her again if she was positive about the horse. She said: "I certainly am, that is the horse." A carriage was sitting in the shed owned by Mr. Mills. Ephraim Diffenderfer, Simpson's uncle, who had accompanied her, asked his niece if she recognized the carriage. Simpson answered that she did, because she remembered it as being "good looking, just like that." She also recognized the reins and harness because they were "nearly new," just like the reins and harness she'd noticed the previous day.[2]

Sheriff Stitchberry then took Simpson to Isaiah Fountain's stable. Fountain was not present during this visit, since he had already left town to find his wife in New Jersey. The sheriff noted that Fountain's horse was also missing a rear shoe. Stitchberry then harnessed Fountain's horse, led it to the car, and turned it around so that Simpson could get a rear view of the animal. According to Stitchberry, "she positively refused to identify the horse, said it was not the horse because it didn't have a curly tail." Simpson added, "The horse I rode behind was a black horse and had a long curly tail." The girl also could not pick Fountain's buggy as the one she rode in. She stated: "No, the buggy I was in was a good-looking carriage." The sheriff said in his sworn statement that the reins of Fountain's buggy "were old and good-for-nothing" and added, "Fountain's buggy would not bring $15.00. It was an old wreck." Sheriff Stitchberry added that he did not notice any irregularities or marks on the tire of the buggy owned by Isaiah Fountain.[3]

After inspecting the horses owned by Andrew Mills and Isaiah Fountain, the sheriff returned Bertha Simpson to her grandparents' home. He then continued to the property of the third Black man who owned a black horse and carriage. This horse also had a missing left hind shoe. The man was named Bailey. Stitchberry also found that all three horses had been shod by Edward Mullikin, the Trappe blacksmith.[4]

According to Sheriff Stitchberry's sworn account, Simpson had emphatically *not* identified Fountain's horse, buggy, or harness as those used during her assault. The horse and buggy tracks from the Simpson crime scene led to Andrew Mills's property, not to Isaiah Fountain's. Most significantly, the sheriff's affidavit stated that Andrew Mills had loaned his horse and buggy—the ones identified by Bertha Simpson—to another man, Eugene Wells. Wells, who was also Black, had used the horse and buggy from "1:00 p.m. Tuesday, April 1st until 6:00 a.m. Wednesday, April 2nd."[5] According to the information contained in Sheriff Stitchberry's statement, Eugene Wells was using the horse and buggy identified by Bertha Simpson during the time she had been raped. It appears that the most likely suspect for the rape of Bertha Simpson should have been Eugene Wells—not Isaiah Fountain.

Disputed Facts

Almost two weeks passed after Sheriff Stitchberry made his sworn statement about Bertha Simpson's positive identifications of a horse, buggy, and harness that did *not* belong to Isaiah Fountain. Simpson and her two uncles then disputed the sheriff's account. Simpson stated that she did say that Andrew Mills's horse looked like the one used during the crime, but she denied saying anything about the horse having a curly tail or about the carriage and reins looking like they were almost new. She also denied that the sheriff had shown her Isaiah Fountain's carriage. She then said that Eugene Wells was not the man who had assaulted her.[6]

Bertha Simpson's uncles, Ephraim Diffenderfer and Harvey Mushaw, submitted sworn statements that supported the girl's account. They both agreed that Simpson had said that Andrew Mills's horse looked familiar, but that she did not say anything about the horse having a curly tail.[7]

On Wednesday, April 2, 1919, Stitchberry reported his investigation results to the Talbot County State's Attorney, Charles Butler.[8] Sheriff Stitchberry likely had concluded that Fountain's horse and buggy had not been at the crime scene and, therefore, Fountain was not involved in Bertha Simpson's assault.

Conclusions and Outrage

Regardless of Sheriff Stitchberry's opinion that Isaiah Fountain was not the rapist of Bertha Simpson, popular sentiment that Fountain was indeed the culprit overwhelmed the official investigation. When the news circulated in the Trappe district that Simpson had been taken to the homes of three local Black men to identify a buggy and a horse with a missing shoe, it seemed apparent that the assailant had to be one of those three. Then it became known that one of the men—Isaiah Fountain—had left town early on Wednesday, April 2, the morning after the crime. Because of Fountain's departure and the apparent match of horseshoe and buggy tire prints, Fountain became the popular suspect. News of the crime and the suspicions about his involvement began to spread. It didn't take long before White people in the Trappe district were talking about lynching Fountain, once he was apprehended. Search parties were soon formed and some feared that "he [would] never be brought to trial but lynched on the spot."[9]

Local and regional newspapers began to report that Fountain was the suspected assailant. Within two days, newspaper articles announced that Fountain had been named by Simpson as her attacker and that the horse and buggy used in the crime were his. By late Wednesday, April 2, the sheriff met with Charles Butler, the Talbot County state's attorney, to share his information about the investigation. At that point, Sherriff Stitchberry knew that Simpson had positively identified Andrew Mills's horse and buggy as those used by her rapist. He undoubtably reported to Butler that Mills had loaned the horse and buggy to another Black man, Eugene Wells, from the afternoon of the crime until the next morning. A Court of Appeals document later stated: "no investigation was made of the whereabouts of the driver of the black horse with long curly tail, good-looking buggy and comparatively new harness and reins, which had been borrowed by a colored boy named Gene Wells at noon of the day of the assault, and not returned till 6 o'clock the next morning."[10] Also, the sheriff did not yet have any eye-witness identification of the rapist—only a general description from the victim and the suppositions about Isaiah Fountain, based on his leaving town the morning after the crime.

Although Sheriff Stitchberry was the county official charged with investigating the crime, State's Attorney Charles Butler was the official in charge of deciding what evidence and testimony was useful for the prosecution of the crime and whom to charge for it. Apparently, Butler ignored the sheriff's information that Eugene Wells had been the man who was using the horse and buggy that had been identified by the victim. Butler also ignored Stitchberry's report that Wells had used the horse and buggy during the time period that the crime was committed.

State's Attorney Butler ignored Sheriff Stitchberry's findings and decided that Isaiah Fountain should be arrested for raping Bertha Simpson. Butler and Fountain had had a run-in two years earlier when Fountain was released from jail for allegedly driving an unshod horse. Whether this past friction was a factor in his naming Fountain as the rape suspect is unknown. Nevertheless, Butler was quoted by the

Afro-American as saying that Fountain would "receive a just and fair trial."[11]

Sheriff Stitchberry was later asked why Eugene Wells, the man who had been using the horse and buggy described by the victim, had not been arrested for Simpson's rape. The sheriff replied that the "popular" suspect was Isaiah Fountain because he had left town the day after the assault. State's Attorney Butler allegedly ordered Sheriff Stitchberry to "Go get Fountain."[12] The official manhunt for Isaiah Fountain had begun.

Endnotes

1 Isaiah Fountain v. State, April Term 1919 No. 39 [MSA S1733-530, 1/65/04/100]. Ct of Appeals: Statement of Sheriff Stitchberry of Talbot County, filed June 5, 1919, at 19.

2 Isaiah Fountain v. State, Statement of Sheriff Stitchberry of Talbot County, filed June 5, 1919, at 19–20.

3 *Id.* at 19–20.

4 *Id.* at 20.

5 *Id.* at 22.

6 Isaiah Fountain v. State, April Term 1919 No. 39 [MSA S1733-530, 1/65/04/100]. Ct of Appeals: Deposition of Bertha Simpson, Regarding the Statement and Affidavit of James L. Stitchberry, filed June 18, 1919, at 23.

7 Isaiah Fountain v. State, April Term 1919 No. 39 [MSA S1733-530, 1/65/04/100]. Ct of Appeals: Deposition of Ephraim Diffenderfer, filed June 18, 1919, at 24. Isaiah Fountain v. State, April Term 1919 No. 39 [MSA S1733-530, 1/65/04/100]. Ct of Appeals: Deposition of Harvey Mushaw, filed June 18, 1919, at 25.

8 Isaiah Fountain v. State, Statement of Sheriff Stitchberry of Talbot County, filed June 5, 1919, at 21.

9 "Negro Assaults 13-Year-Old Girl," *Evening Journal*, April 3, 1919, 5. Newspapers.com.

10 Isaiah Fountain v. State, April Term 1919 No. 39 [MSA S1733-530, 1/65/04/100]. Ct of Appeals: "Stipulation for Appeal," Isaiah Fountain v. State of Maryland, in the Court of Appeals of Maryland, No. 23, April Term, 1919, Appellant's Supplemental Brief on Evidence Only, at 52.

11 "Farmers Crowd Courthouse," *Baltimore Afro-American*, April 18, 1919, A1. ProQuest.com.

12 "New Evidence Clears Fountain," *Baltimore Afro-American*, June 6, 1919, A1. ProQuest.com.

CHAPTER 4

Manhunt, Arrest, and Indictment

It must, however, be admitted that every one here is firmly convinced of the negro's guilt and all are open in their statements that they want him sentenced to death.

—*BALTIMORE SUN*

Manhunt (Wednesday, April 2, 1919 to April 11, 1919)

In the eyes of the citizens of Talbot County and State's Attorney Butler, Isaiah Fountain was a convenient suspect for the rape of Bertha Simpson. He fit the bill: his horse and buggy had supposedly been identified by Bertha; he left town the day after the crime; and he was a Black man. The *Baltimore Sun* reported: "The citizens of Trappe and vicinity are greatly incensed over the brutal outrage."[1] The local newspaper, the *Easton Star-Democrat*, reported: "Intense feeling is shown in Trappe district over the outrage and this is not confined to the locality where the assault was committed, but in the county generally"[2]

Eastern Shore towns, as well as those on the western side of the Chesapeake Bay, were notified to be on the lookout for Isaiah Fountain. When it became known that he had relatives in the Philadelphia area, jurisdictions in Pennsylvania and New Jersey were also alerted. Posses and search parties were quickly formed. The *Wilmington Evening Journal* reported the search efforts and the generally held sentiments:

> The officers have telephoned and telegraphed all over the country a description of him, and it is expected he will soon be caught. It is reported a large party of men in and around St. Michaels, armed with shotguns, rifles and pistols are scouring the country for him. If caught, it is feared he will never be brought to trial, but lynched on the spot.[3]

The local search parties had no success, and their failure to capture Fountain only increased frustrations. The longer Isaiah Fountain remained free, the more the rage of the county residents grew.

Fountain's Arrest (Monday, April 7, 1919)

After spending Sunday, April 6, with his brother John in West Chester, Pennsylvania, the next day, Isaiah Fountain decided to visit his brother at work. On Monday, April 7, as Fountain was heading to his brother's workplace,[4] he was stopped by West Chester Police Chief John Entriken and was arrested. According to Entriken, Fountain identified himself as William Hubbard, but since he matched the fugitive's description, the chief arrested him.[5] Chief Entriken then notified Sheriff Stitchberry in Easton of Fountain's arrest.

Talbot County State's Attorney Charles Butler quickly contacted Maryland Governor Emerson Harrington and secured extradition papers to return Fountain to Talbot County.[6] On Wednesday, April 9, 1919, Sheriff Stitchberry left Easton for West Chester to take custody of Fountain.[7] The plan was to quickly transport him back to Talbot County so that he could be indicted and tried for the rape of Bertha Simpson.

Talbot countians were impatient for Fountain's return. Hearing that Sheriff Stitchberry had left for West Chester, the citizens were expecting his direct return with his prisoner. That evening, crowds gathered around the Easton railroad station and the county jail. The *Baltimore Sun* reported that Fountain was expected to arrive on the evening train, but that he wasn't on it when it pulled into the Easton station.[8]

The mood of the local crowds made it clear that Fountain's life would be in jeopardy if he returned to Talbot County. Because of the threats of lynching, on Friday, April 11, 1919, Stitchberry took Fountain to Baltimore, where he was held in the central police station until a trial date could be set.[9] The *Easton Star-Democrat* downplayed the lynching threats and any idea that Fountain's life was in danger. The paper also blamed reports of the lynching threats on "the city press".[10]

The *Star-Democrat* reported:

> The prisoner is in the custody of Sheriff Stitchberry, but has not yet been brought to Easton. This was not an especial caution, but in the usual procedure in such cases. There is indignation all over the county, but the tales of threatened lynching which have been sent broadcast to the city press are without an[y] foundation whatever. The

prisoner was placed in the Baltimore jail by Sheriff Stitchberry by the demand of Governor Harrington.[11]

Contrary to the *Star-Democrat*'s report, the feelings of
outrage kept growing in the county as the people sought "justice." Now that Fountain had been captured, the pressure was
on Talbot County officials to bring him home to face this
justice—the sooner, the better.

Indictment (Saturday, April 12, 1919)

Even before an indictment was issued for Isaiah Fountain, the
Baltimore Afro-American expressed doubts about his ability to
get a fair trial in Talbot County. The paper wrote that Fountain "very likely … will go before a prejudiced white jury, no
colored man on it, and in less than ten minutes, said jury will
agree to break his neck," and continued: "Everyone can see
how nearly like a lynching our trials are."[12] The *Afro-American*'s comments about Isaiah Fountain's trial proved to be
very perceptive.

The wheels of the Talbot County legal system began to
turn—perhaps faster than they should have. Judge William
H. Adkins was the chief judge of the Talbot County Circuit
Court. He surely knew that he had to act quickly to satisfy
the public's growing clamor for swift justice for Bertha Simpson. Adkins decided to have the case heard by the Talbot
County Grand Jury. In an unusual move, he re-summoned
the *previous* grand jury, which had been empaneled for the
November 1918 term.[13] Normally, the Fountain case would
have been heard by the upcoming session of the grand jury
that was scheduled to convene in just thirty-seven days, on

May 19, 1919.[14] Apparently, Judge Adkins reacted to public pressure and decided that the outraged citizens of Talbot County could not wait that long to have Isaiah Fountain indicted.

According to the grand jury presentment document, on Saturday, April 12, 1919, the recalled grand jury heard testimony from Bertha Simpson; her grandmother, Mrs. Henry Diffenderfer; Dr. Joseph Ross; Sheriff James Stitchberry; and H. E. Mullikin (the horseshoer from Trappe).[15] Despite having no surviving transcripts of the grand jury testimony, one newspaper reported that Simpson identified Fountain as her attacker from an array of seven or eight photographs.[16] This report was later disputed by Sheriff Stitchberry and Fountain's attorneys. After hearing the testimony presented by the state's attorney, the grand jury quickly indicted Fountain. Talbot County State's Attorney, Charles J. Butler, then issued a True Bill listing the charges, which stated that Fountain, "not having the fear of God before his eyes but being moved and seduced by the instigation of the devil. . . unlawfully, violently and feloniously did make an assault and her the said BERTHA SIMPSON then and there violently and against her will, feloniously did ravish and carnally know."[17]

The timing of Fountain's indictment and the legitimacy of Simpson's identification of him were later questioned by Sheriff Stitchberry. In a sworn statement, Stitchberry later related that State's Attorney Butler had invited him to his home one evening "around the middle of April"—that is, *after* the grand jury had indicted Fountain. Butler wanted to set up a meeting for Simpson to identify her assailant from several photos that Butler had obtained from the Baltimore Police Department. Also present that evening were

Mr. Diffenderfer and Mr. Mushaw, Bertha Simpson's two uncles, who also were shown the photographs. The identification meeting was set for 9:00 a.m. the next morning. Sheriff Stitchberry and the two uncles appeared at Butler's house as arranged, along with Simpson and Mrs. Diffenderfer, her grandmother. Stitchberry recollected: "He [Butler] took Mrs. Diffenderfer and Bertha Simpson upstairs into his library, the rest of us were downstairs in the front room and were not present at the identification."[18] Sheriff Stitchberry later expressed concerns about the validity of Simpson's identification of Fountain at this meeting.[19] Based on the sheriff's information, Fountain's lawyer, Eugene O'Dunne, later alleged that Simpson's uncles, having been shown the photos the previous night, had coached their niece to aid her in identifying Fountain's photograph the following morning. O'Dunne also argued that the rush to prosecute Fountain was so great that the grand jury indicted him a few days *before* the victim had actually identified him from the photos. O'Dunne charged that because of "all the feeling in the county," no one wanted Bertha Simpson to make any mistake in identifying Isaiah Fountain as her assailant.[20]

Once again, speed seemed to be of the essence. The *Star-Democrat* reported that "the case was set for trial for Wednesday [April 16], but owing to insufficient time, and at the request of the defense, the case was postponed for Monday morning next [April 21]."[21] Fountain's lawyers had just nine days to prepare a defense to save his life.

Court records establish that on Friday night, April 18, Defense Attorney Eugene O'Dunne met with Judge Adkins. Arguing that Fountain would have difficulty getting a fair trial in Talbot County and that his safety was in jeopardy,

O'Dunne requested that the trial be moved to Baltimore City. Adkins refused and said that if the trial were removed, it would not be sent out of the circuit[22]—in other words, Fountain's trial would be held in a nearby Eastern Shore county. Apparently, this conversation with the judge convinced O'Dunne that a formal motion for a change of venue to Baltimore City would be futile, so he accepted that the trial would be held in Talbot County.

The *Easton Star-Democrat* scoffed at the suggestion that Fountain's life was in danger in Talbot County. The paper promised that "Fountain will have a speedy and fair trial and Talbot County has full confidence in its authorities to see that full and speedy justice is meted out without recourse to the lynch law."[23]

Fountain Returns to Talbot
(Saturday, April 19, 1919)

With the trial set to begin in just two days, Fountain was returned to Easton on Saturday, April 19. His journey back to Easton was done in secret, in hopes of avoiding angry crowds that might demand his lynching, and he was guarded by Sheriff Stitchberry and ten Baltimore City police officers. Despite the secrecy, and expecting that Fountain would be arriving by train, over a thousand men and women gathered at Easton's train station.[24] The *Baltimore Sun* provided a detailed description of the prisoner's furtive journey back to Talbot County:

> Following a trip by boat, train and a wild dash in an automobile, Isaiah Fountain, colored, who is accused of

criminally assaulting Bertha Simpson, the 13-year-old daughter of Mr. and Mrs. Robert Simpson, near her home in Trappe on April 1 last, was landed in the jail in Easton at 9:20 o'clock last night, according to a dispatch from a staff correspondent at THE SUN.

At Claiborne, the negro, with his strong guard, boarded a train, that moved quickly to [Kirkham]. According to the carefully laid plans of Sheriff Stitchberry, the negro was taken from the train at Kirkham and with three policemen, under the command of Sergeant Parr [and] the Sheriff, was loaded into a waiting automobile and a dash was made for the jail, which was reached fully 10 minutes before the train bearing the other policemen arrived at Easton.

A large crowd had gathered at the front entrance of the jail, but the negro was taken into the institution by a rear door. He had been locked in his cell for nearly 15 minutes before any of the citizen watchers were aware of the fact.

Fountain was arrested in West Chester, Pa., and he was brought here 10 days ago by Sheriff Stitchberry. Citizens of Talbot county formed a posse after the discovery of the crime and open threats of lynching were made. Governor Harrington talked with a number of the citizens and he assured them that Fountain would be accorded a swift trial. The negro, it is understood, will be defended by Col. James Mullikin, of Easton, and Eugene O'Dunne, of this city. [25]

Fountain spent Saturday night in his cell in the imposing Talbot County Jail, built in 1878,[26] awaiting his trial for rape. He would spend the next day, Easter Sunday, preparing himself for the trial, which was to begin on Easter Monday.

Easter Sunday Crowds (Sunday, April 20, 1919)

Most of the citizens of Talbot County celebrated Easter Sunday anticipating the start of Isaiah Fountain's trial. Already bustling with out-of-town holiday visitors, the streets of Easton began to swell further with other arrivals—those hoping to attend the rape trial. It had been only twenty days since the crime took place. The population was outraged, not only by the event but also by Fountain's perceived "escape" to New Jersey. Few had any doubt about his guilt.

In this era, when there was even the suspicion of guilt of a Black man—and especially when the crime involved the rape of a White girl or woman—the prospect of lynching was very real. Even the possibility of it was enough to draw crowds of people from far and near. In the Jim Crow era, it wasn't unusual for crowds of thousands to attend a lynching or even a legal execution by hanging. Local author James Dawson wrote about the 1870 hanging of Frederick Lawrence in Easton. Lawrence, a Black man, had been convicted of murdering his wife and was sentenced to hang. An estimated five thousand people crowded into Easton to see his hanging.[27]

According to newspaper reports, crowds began to gather in Easton on Easter Sunday for Isaiah Fountain's trial. The *Afro-American* reported: "News that the prisoner had arrived at Easton jail, on Saturday, brought thousands of farmers to town on Sunday and on Monday." The paper also wrote about "disorderly and mob-like demonstrations around the courthouse" and "the lynching spirit . . . thought to be prevalent only in the far South."[28]

The *Baltimore Sun* also reported the large Easter Sunday crowds. The paper wrote that "Talbot County is at fever heat, awaiting the trial tomorrow of Isaiah Fountain, colored." The paper added: "Hundreds of persons from the lower end of the Eastern Shore peninsula arrived in Easton this afternoon for the trial, and it is expected that practically every resident of Talbot county will come to this city tomorrow morning." It continued:

> There is an intense feeling here against the negro, but Sheriff James Stitchberry has been assured by the leading citizens of Trappe and Easton that nothing will be done to harm him or to prevent the trial from taking place. It must, however, be admitted that *every one here is firmly convinced of the negro's guilt and all are open in their statements that they want him sentenced to death.*[29] [Emphasis added.]

The *Easton Star-Democrat* did not agree with the Baltimore newspaper reports. It wrote: "There is indignation all over the county, but the tales of threatened lynching which have been sent broadcast [*sic*] to the city press are without [any] foundation whatever."[30]

Surely, Fountain was aware of the angry crowds gathered outside the Talbot County Jail. According to the *Sun*, Sheriff Stitchberry said that Fountain was in a "rather jolly mood," in spite of showing fear during his journey to Easton. Fountain spent most of Easter Sunday preparing his defense with his attorneys, Colonel James Mullikin of Easton and Eugene O'Dunne of Baltimore. The *Sun* wrote that Fountain repeatedly declared that he was not guilty of raping Bertha Simpson and that "if he is hung the men who sentence him will have to answer to their Maker on the Judgment Day."[31] Isaiah Fountain's own judgment day was just hours away.

Endnotes

1 "Negro Assaults Girl," *Baltimore Sun*, April 3, 1919, 3. Newspapers. com.

2 "Negro Fiend Not Found," *Star-Democrat*, April 5, 1919, 1.

3 "Negro Assaults 13-Year-Old Girl," *Evening Journal*, April 3, 1919, 5. Newspapers.com.

4 "Death Decree for Fountain," *Baltimore Sun*, April 25, 1919, 3. Newspapers.com.

5 "Negro Assailant of White Girl to Hang," *Wilmington Evening Journal*, April 25, 1919, 24. Newspapers.com.

6 "Grand Jury to Meet Wednesday," *Easton Star-Democrat*, April 12, 1919, 1.

7 "Accused Negro Caught," *Baltimore Sun*, April 9, 1919, 2. Newspapers.com.

8 "Accused Negro Caught," 2.

9 "In and About Town," *Baltimore Sun*, April 11, 1919, 7. Newspapers. com.

10 The *Easton Star-Democrat* waged an ongoing battle of words against the *Baltimore Sun* and the *Baltimore Afro-American*. The *Star-Democrat* felt that "the city press" was biased in favor of Fountain and was constantly trying to make Talbot countians appear backward and prejudiced. On the other hand, the *Star-Democrat* seemed to overlook local faults and biases and portray the county in the best possible light.

11 "Court on Monday Next," *Easton Star-Democrat*, April 19, 1919, 2.

12 "Crimes in Easton and Annapolis," *Baltimore Afro-American*, April 11, 1919, A4. ProQuest.com.

13 Isaiah Fountain v. State, April Term 1919 No. 39 [MSA S1733-530, 1/65/04/100]. Ct of Appeals: Petition and Order of Court for Extension of Time, filed May 27, 1919, at 16.

14 Isaiah Fountain v. State, April Term 1919 No. 39 [MSA S1733-530, 1/65/04/100]. Ct of Appeals: Appeal from the Sentence of Death, at 2.

15 Isaiah Fountain v. State, April Term 1919 No. 39 [MSA S1733-530, 1/65/04/100]. Ct of Appeals: Presentment, filed April 12th, 1919, at 1.

16 "Child Identifies Her Assailant," *Evening Journal*, April 14, 1919, 11. Newspapers.com.

17 Isaiah Fountain v. State, April Term 1919 No. 39 [MSA S1733-530, 1/65/04/100]. Ct of Appeals: Indictment, filed April 12th, 1919, at 2.

18 Isaiah Fountain v. State, April Term 1919 No. 39 [MSA S1733-530, 1/65/04/100]. Ct of Appeals: Statement of Sheriff Stitchberry of Talbot County, filed June 5, 1919, at 22.

19 "New Evidence Clears Fountain," *Baltimore Afro-American*, June 6, 1919, A1. ProQuest.com.

20 "Stipulation for Appeal," Isaiah Fountain v. State of Maryland, in the Court of Appeals of Maryland, No. 23, April Term, 1919, Appellant's Supplemental Brief on Evidence Only, at 43.

21 "Court on Monday Next," 2.

22 Isaiah Fountain v. State, April Term 1919 No. 39 [MSA S1733-530, 1/65/04/100]. Ct of Appeals: *Judge's Certificate*, at 12. The Second Judicial Circuit consisted of Caroline, Cecil, Kent, Queen Anne's and Talbot Counties.

23 "Court on Monday Next," 2.

24 "To Try Fountain Today," *Baltimore Sun*, April 21, 1919, 5. Newspapers.com.

25 "Safe in Easton Jail," *Baltimore Sun*, April 20, 1919, 16. Newspapers.com. The Baltimore, Chesapeake & Atlantic train from the Claiborne ferry landing to Easton crossed St. Michaels Road/ MD Route 33 near Travelers Rest Road; this is the location of the Kirkham train station where Fountain was transferred from the train to an automobile.

26 "Talbot County Jail (Former Site)," Maryland Office of Tourism website, accessed July 22, 2021, https://www.visitmaryland.org/ listing/attraction/talbot-county-jail-former-site.

27 James Dawson, "Easton's Potter's Field," *Tidewater Times* (January 2012): 52.

28 "Fountain Has Small Chance for Justice," *Baltimore Afro-American*, April 25, 1919, A1. ProQuest.com.

29 "To Try Fountain Today," 5.

30 "Court on Monday Next," 2.

31 "To Try Fountain Today," 5.

CHAPTER 5

The Trial

They wanted quick action. In their opinion, Fountain was guilty and they looked upon the formalities of a trial as a useless bit of procedure. They wanted the life of the negro, and made no secret of their intentions.

—BALTIMORE EVENING SUN

Trial Day Crowds (Monday, April 21, 1919)

The crowds that formed in Easton on Easter Sunday had not dispersed by Easter Monday, the day of Fountain's trial. The streets around the Talbot County courthouse and jail were jammed with people eager to attend the trial or, at least, be nearby to receive firsthand news of it.

The *Star-Democrat* and the Baltimore newspapers continued to differ in their descriptions of events relating to the Fountain case. The Easton newspaper usually minimized the size and emotional level of the crowds; it reported that the crowds showed signs of "unusual activity" and that various groups of men were "discussing the case," and described the assembly as "boisterous" and "eager."[1] To read the *Star-Democrat's* reporting, one would think that the crowds had assembled to attend a political rally or a band concert.

The *Baltimore Afro-American* portrayed the Easton crowds differently. It wrote of "disorderly and mob-like demonstrations around the courthouse," and that the neighborhood had "a touch of the lynching spirit." The paper also noted that the crowd was "watching for a favorable opportunity to storm the jail." The *Afro-American* reporter described armed men in the crowd carrying ropes and firearms.[2]

A *Baltimore Sun* article gave this description: "Long before daylight the crowds began to gather around the courthouse and jail, clamoring for admission to the courtroom." The article continued, "there have been repeated threats of lynching . . . the town folk have talked of taking the law into their own hands." The paper reported that the crowds around the courthouse thinned overnight but began to reassemble before daylight. Uniformed Baltimore City policemen guarded the courthouse all night and kept the crowd away from the building. The *Sun* added: "Knowing the feeling that exists among the white people of the county the police were prepared for any eventuality." The police were looking forward to Monday morning, "as they felt better able to handle the situation in daylight."[3]

The people around the courthouse, the *Evening Sun* reported, were "enraged," "maddened," and driven to "fury" at the sight of Fountain being taken the seventy-five yards to there from the jail. The mob shouted threats and advanced menacingly, but the policemen and deputies guarding Fountain managed to keep him safe. Once in the courthouse, Fountain was under the protection of the judges.[4]

Isaiah Fountain's trial was scheduled to start at 9:30 a.m., and the crowd was anxious to get seats in the courtroom. People rushed into the courthouse and headed to the main courtroom on the second floor, where the trial was to take place. There was no way that an influx of so many people could be admitted. The ground floor corridor was soon jammed, as was the stairway leading to the second floor. It became obvious that the courtroom could not accommodate everyone. The *Star-Democrat* described the scene:

> As early as 7 o'clock in the morning Washington Street was the scene of various groups of men discussing the case, and at 8 o'clock the walk from the gate of the court house to the front door was filled with those eager to gain admission to the court room.
>
> The doors of the court house were locked, and policemen from Baltimore, sent here with the prisoner, stood on guard to see that only those with business before the court were admitted. When the session began the room was crowded, with a larger one outside clamoring for admission. Eventually when the door was opened to admit witnesses and jurors the officers were unable to keep the crowd in check and the throng pushed and jammed the doors until they were inside the court house.
>
> Once inside, the next thing was to get into the court room. The stairway was filled with humanity from top to bottom, and the crowd on the landing was so large that many strong men were soon exhausted from the press. The door leading into the court room was closed and guarded by Baltimore police. The crowd became so boisterous outside that the court ordered the stairway cleared.[5]

Another newspaper reported that "spectators stood on chairs and backs of benches, and even in the windows, and clear up to the judge's rail."[6] According to the *Sun*, "only several hundred could be accommodated in the courtroom"; it later mentioned that the courtroom was occupied by over four hundred people.[7] This was certainly a far larger number than would be allowed in the same room today.[8]

When the crowd outside the courtroom had been cleared, the trial began. It was 9:30 a.m., Monday, April 21, 1919. In keeping with the custom of the day, a tribunal of judges officiated, with the chief judge of the Talbot County Circuit Court, William H. Adkins, presiding. Adkins was assisted on the bench by Associate Judges Lewin W. Wickes and Philemon B. Hopper.[9] However, Judge Hopper was then excused from the panel due to sickness.[10]

Fountain requested a trial by a jury of his "peers." In this case, his "peers" would be all White men, since Black men (and women) were not allowed to serve on juries in Talbot County during the Jim Crow era. The court's first order of business was to select the jury. Seventy-five "talismen" [sic], or potential jurors, had been assembled, and by 11:45 a.m., twelve White Talbot County men were selected as jurors.[11]

Opening Arguments

According to the *Star-Democrat*, prior to the opening arguments, the witnesses in the case were ordered to leave the courtroom and wait in a nearby office until it was their turn to testify. Talbot County State's Attorney Charles Butler was the prosecutor, and his opening argument described the State's case against Fountain. Butler said that Fountain had raped Bertha Simpson less than three weeks earlier, and his guilt would be proved by the State's witnesses. Butler began his case by showing the jury a chalkboard diagram of the roads between Easton and Trappe, to familiarize them with the various locations involved in the crime.[12]

The *Sun* reported that Butler emphasized that Fountain's leaving Talbot County to go to New Jersey the morning following the crime was an indicator of his probable guilt. Butler also suggested that during the time Fountain was looking for his wife in Easton, he "knew he was liable to be arrested at any time and charged with the crime and *was planning his defense when he asked the [Easton] chief of police to accompany him to Philadelphia.*"[13] [Emphasis added.] If the *Sun's* account was accurate, Butler's logic was flawed, since it implied that Fountain had prepared an alibi for a crime that had not yet been committed.

The opening argument for the defense came next. Defending Fountain was local lawyer Colonel James C. Mullikin of Easton, who was the dean of the Talbot County Bar and a Union Army veteran of the Battle of Gettysburg. Mullikin was initially appointed as Fountain's sole defense counsel, but he was later joined by Eugene O'Dunne, a prominent lawyer from Baltimore, who was a former assistant state's attorney and professor of criminal law at the University of Maryland Law School.[14] Eugene O'Dunne quickly became the lead lawyer for Fountain's defense.

The *Star-Democrat* reported that O'Dunne addressed the jury, insisting that it was not the defense team's purpose to deny that any crime was committed. Rather, he said, the State had "gotten hold of the wrong man." He went on to explain that Fountain's departure the day after the crime was not an attempt to flee the area, but to find his wife and bring her home. Attorney O'Dunne assured the jury that Isaiah Fountain was not guilty and that testimony would prove it.[15] Part of that testimony would be that on the afternoon of the crime, Fountain had implored Easton Police Chief William Stoops to go to Philadelphia to find his wife and bring her home.[16]

Another newspaper stated that O'Dunne, during his opening statement, downplayed the victim's identification of Fountain by means of a photograph. He maintained that such identifications were often faulty and "never positive." He also cast doubt on Bertha Simpson's identification of Fountain because of her hesitation before identifying him as her attacker.[17]

The Prosecution's Case

State's Attorney Butler was sure he had a solid case against Isaiah Fountain. On the day of the trial, the *Baltimore Sun* said that Butler would introduce fifteen witnesses to testify against Fountain, in addition to the victim, Bertha Simpson. Butler said that he had "not the slightest doubt about the conviction of the negro."[18]

A large part of Butler's case depended on the testimony of the victim, Bertha Simpson. Simpson's testimony took up a large part of the afternoon. Because of the nature of the crime (and, most likely, to avoid undue stress and embarrassment for the victim), Judge Adkins decided that her testimony should be presented not in the main courtroom but in the adjacent grand jury room. Although the spectators in the main courtroom were not permitted to hear Simpson's testimony, the judge did permit the prisoner, lawyers, jury, and newspapermen[19] to be present. Once all were assembled, Simpson was wheeled into the grand jury room in an "invalid chair" (that is, a wheelchair). She was accompanied by two physicians, Dr. Joseph Ross (who had treated her after the assault) and Dr. C. F. Davidson.[20] Simpson then testified about the events of Tuesday, April 1, 1919, the day of her rape. The *Easton Star-Democrat* described her testimony:

> With head resting on pillows, Miss Simpson told in a straightforward manner every step of the road she had traversed after leaving the High School in Trappe until she was assaulted, and her testimony was in no way shaken. When asked to identify the accused as the man who committed the heinous crime she unhesitantly declared that he was the man. Photographs of several colored men were then shown her and she picked out the picture of the accused as the man who assaulted her. The test was also made shortly after the crime had been committed in the office of the States attorney, and with the same result.
>
> Miss Simpson had been under the doctor's care since last Friday, most of the time being confined to her bed. She is threatened with appendicitis. Her physical condition was pitiful and while her voice was weak and [barely] audible at times across the room, yet her testimony was given without any hesitation whatever. She said most emphatically that the accused was the man who did the deed, and was positive she could identify him in spite of the absence of a mustache worn at the time.[21]

Simpson recounted the details of her attack on Tuesday, April 1, 1919, with the particulars of the timing remaining unclear. From the first newspaper accounts of her assault until the end of Fountain's legal process, the newspaper, victim, and trial accounts of the time the crime was committed changed drastically. Although the newspaper accounts of her testimony in court don't specifically mention that she testified about the time the attack occurred, several newspaper articles and court documents stated that the attack happened as early as 4:00 p.m., then 4:30 p.m., and then 5:00 p.m. However, Court of Appeal records show that Simpson testified during the trial *that the attack took place ". . . between 4.30 to 5 p.m.*, Tuesday, April 1st (testimony, pp. 5 and 6)."[22] [Emphasis added.] Later reports even had the attack time moved to as late as 5:15 p.m. and 5:30 p.m.—a difference of up to an hour and a half.[23] As previously noted, this shifting time differential conflicted with Fountain's alibi and played a crucial role in determining his fate. The more the time shifted, the more his alibi seemed to be eroded.

The *Sun* reported that Simpson was asked to identify Isaiah Fountain in person while in the grand jury room but had some difficulty doing so. The accused was seated about eighteen feet from the victim and was asked to stand to be identified. She was not able to identify him from that distance, so Fountain was instructed to move closer. He moved to about ten feet from the victim, and she still was unable to identify him. He then moved to a point about five feet away. The girl still seemed unsure and looked at him for about two minutes. Finally, she said: "That is him. I have no doubt whatever." Simpson also testified that Fountain had a mustache when he attacked her. State's Attorney Butler added that he had information that Fountain had shaved off his mustache two days before leaving the Baltimore City Jail to come to Easton.[24]

At the conclusion of Bertha Simpson's testimony, Judge Adkins called a recess until 7:00 p.m. The *Afro-American* reported that no spectators were allowed into the courtroom for the night session of the trial. This news further angered members of the crowd, some of whom had traveled long distances to attend. Many were upset that Fountain would have a chance to "present an alibi." The size of the crowd outside the courthouse grew to "an army." The paper reported that Judge Adkins ordered that the courtroom doors be locked and only witnesses admitted. Apparently, Judge Adkins was concerned that "his little crowd of police could not hold back the mob from the court room."[25]

The *Evening Sun* noted that the crowd outside the courthouse was receiving regular updates about the trial from messengers traveling to and from the courtroom. The crowd became agitated at the slowness of the proceedings and wanted "quick action." They apparently felt that "Fountain was guilty and looked upon the formalities of a trial as a useless bit of procedure. They wanted the life of the negro, and made no secret of their intentions."[26]

When the evening court session began, State's Attorney Butler called his other witnesses. The *Sun* reported that the State wanted to prove that Fountain had been driving a horse with a missing shoe and that his buggy had a broken tire with a distinctive defect. Marks from the horse and buggy were found in the dirt near the crime scene. Butler called blacksmith Edward Mullikin from Trappe, who testified that he had put a shoe on the left hind foot of Fountain's horse. As part of the testimony, a wheel from Fountain's buggy with a damaged tire was exhibited in court.[27] Curiously, just two days after the assault, the same paper had reported that

Mullikin had replaced the missing shoe on Fountain's horse the *afternoon* of the crime.[28] Without the trial transcript, it's impossible to know if this information was raised at the trial. If the newspaper account was accurate, it seems to cast doubt on Mr. Mullikin's testimony: How could Fountain possibly have had the missing horseshoe replaced at the same time as his wife had driven the horse and buggy to Easton and hidden them in a shed? Also, in his statement that was submitted to the Court of Appeals, Sheriff Stitchberry swore that he had examined Fountain's horse *the day after the crime.* Stitchberry stated: "I stopped into Isaiah Fountain's and went to the stable and saw that his horse also had [the] left hind shoe off."[29] It seems very unlikely that the horseshoe on Fountain's horse could have been replaced by Mullikin on Tuesday afternoon, yet be missing the next morning, as reported by the sheriff.

Prosecutor Butler then put Tillman Slaughter on the stand. Slaughter, a Black man from Trappe, testified that around the time of the attack, he had been hauling a load of hay from Trappe to Easton. Slaughter said that he had seen Isaiah Fountain driving his horse and buggy about one and a quarter miles from the scene of Simpson's assault. Butler said that "other negroes" reported that they had also seen Fountain about the same time in that area.[30]

Dr. Joseph Ross, one of the physicians who had accompanied the victim to court, was also a prosecution witness. Ross testified that he had been called to Simpson's grandparents' house to treat her following her assault on April 1. Ross testified that Simpson had been raped.[31]

Theodore "Swanaker" [Schwaninger], a White resident of the Trappe district, testified that he came upon Fountain as he was walking to Easton. He stopped and offered Fountain a ride to town, and they arrived in Easton "about 3 o'clock."[32]

William Spence, a cashier at the Talbot Bank in Easton, was a witness for the prosecution earlier in the day. He testified that Fountain's wife had withdrawn $10.00 from Isaiah Fountain's bank account. Spence also testified that Fountain had arrived at the bank at 3:25 p.m., well after its 3:00 p.m. closing. Fountain then withdrew an additional $17.00 before he left the bank.[33] Although he testified for the State, Spence's testimony seemed to be more beneficial for Fountain's defense. Spence's account of when Fountain arrived at the bank strengthened his alibi of being in Easton at about the same time the crime was committed.

According to later court documents, several other prosecution witnesses testified, including Bertha Simpson's father, Robert T. Simpson.[34] Unfortunately, no court transcripts or newspaper accounts documented the testimony given by these witnesses. Because the testimonies were not noted, we must assume that they weren't very important to the prosecution's case, or otherwise newsworthy.

Sheriff Stitchberry, as the main investigator of Bertha Simpson's rape, would be expected to be an important prosecution witness. However, Butler did not call the sheriff to testify. Possibly, Butler didn't consider the sheriff's testimony critical to the prosecution's case—or perhaps he thought that testimony might have been more helpful for Fountain's defense. Later statements by Sheriff Stitchberry and Attorney O'Dunne indicate that it was the latter.

It must have been difficult for Isaiah Fountain to listen to the testimony of the various prosecution witnesses and remain composed. Newspaper accounts differed about his attitude and demeanor during the prosecution's presentation of its case. The *Star-Democrat* described Fountain as being relaxed and unworried:

> During the taking of testimony, no matter how damaging it was to the prisoner, he appeared to be at perfect ease. Nothing seemed to ruffle him in the least. He displayed a keen interest in everything that was said or done, and especially when it was adverse to his case. Several times he stepped forward to get a better glimpse of his photograph when it was offered as evidence.
>
> When his counsel were cross-examining a witness he would prompt them to ask questions and correct them in their statements when they forgot the name of persons or places. A sarcastic smile was seen on his face most of the time, and this played an important part in the identification. Miss Simpson said she would recognize that smile anywhere. His general appearance would give one the impression that nothing worried him, and he was in any other predicament than an indictment for a crime the penalty for which is death. [35]

At the other extreme, the *Baltimore Sun* reported that Fountain did not appear comfortable. The paper wrote that he "appeared very nervous and exhibited some fear of the crowd which packed the room." Emphasizing Fountain's distress, the *Sun* added that, during the State's presentation, "everything went against the negro." After Simpson's identification of Fountain, there was talk of lynching him among the members of the angry mob gathered outside the courthouse. The paper reported that Fountain appeared to appreciate the protection that was provided by his courtroom guard, a Baltimore City police officer.[36]

The prosecution witnesses testified into the spring night. Finally, at 10:00 p.m., Judge Adkins adjourned the trial until 9:30 a.m., Tuesday, April 22, 1919.[37] State's Attorney Butler still had one more witness to present. Fountain's defense team would then get to tell Fountain's side of the story.

The jury was to be sequestered in a nearby Easton hotel and was to be taken there by court bailiffs. However, the jurors received instructions to remain in the jury box while Sheriff Stitchberry, his deputies, and ten Baltimore City policemen prepared to return Isaiah Fountain to the adjacent county jail for the night.[38]

Endnotes

1 "Fountain Found Guilty," *Easton Star-Democrat*, April 26, 1919, 1.

2 "Fountain Has Small Chance for Justice," *Baltimore Afro-American*, April 25, 1919, A1. ProQuest.com.

3 "Accused Negro Gets Away," *Baltimore Sun*, April 22, 1919, 9. Newspapers.com.

4 "Mobs with Ropes Race with Sheriff to Capture Negro," *Baltimore Evening Sun*, April 22, 1919, 2. Newspapers.com.

5 "Fountain Found Guilty," 1.

6 "Fountain Has Small Chance for Justice," 4.

7 "Accused Negro Gets Away," 9. "Death Decree for Fountain," *Baltimore Sun*, April 25, 1919, 3.

8 James Daffin, in an email to the author on January 19, 2021, said, "It is very difficult to imagine a crowd of over 400 people occupying the main courtroom of the Talbot County Courthouse today! The normal capacity is about 150 people." Daffin was a former bailiff at the Talbot County Courthouse.

9 Joseph Moore, in an email to the author on September 24, 2019, said: "Indeed, it was common back in the time to have more than one judge on a case, particularly a capital case such as murder. . . but it was a practice more in tradition than rule, as I believe, back in the day. I am not sure when the practice went 'out of vogue,' but even today, there are three judges' chairs on the Circuit Court bench in Worcester County [Maryland] as well as many others, in the older courtrooms, around the state".

10 "Accused Negro Gets Away," 9.

11 "Fountain Found Guilty," 1. "Talismen" is obviously used by the *Star-Democrat* to describe the prospective jurors. However the proper word is "talesmen."

12 "Fountain Found Guilty," 1.

13 "To Try Fountain Today," *Baltimore Sun*, April 21, 1919, 5. Newspapers.com.

14 "Accused Negro Gets Away," 9. "Mullikin" is a common family name in the Trappe district of Talbot County. There's no indication

that Fountain's lawyer, Colonel James C. Mullikin, was closely, or otherwise, related to H. E. Mullikin, a witness for the prosecution.

15 "Fountain Found Guilty," 1.

16 "To Try Fountain Today," 5.

17 "Fountain Has Small Chance for Justice," 4.

18 "To Try Fountain Today," 5.

19 It seems strange today that the rape victim's testimony was given without courtroom spectators being present but allowing newspaper reporters to hear and report her testimony.

20 "Fountain Found Guilty," 1. "Accused Negro Gets Away," 9.

21 "Fountain Found Guilty," 1.

22 Isaiah Fountain v. State, April Term 1919 No. 39 [MSA S1733-530, 1/65/04/100]. Ct of Appeals: Appellant's Supplemental Brief on Evidence Only, April 23, 1919, at 48.

23 Isaiah Fountain v. State, Appellant's Supplemental Brief on Evidence Only, at 48, 50, 51. "Negro Assailant of White Girl to Hang," *Wilmington Evening Journal*, April 25, 1919, 24. Newspapers.com. "Death Decree for Fountain," 3. "Fountain's Case to Be Appealed," A1. "Fountain Verdict Near," 7. "Court Gives Reasons."

24 "Accused Negro Gets Away," 9.

25 "Fountain Has Small Chance for Justice," 4.

26 "Mobs with Ropes Race with Sheriff to Capture Negro," 2.

27 "Accused Negro Gets Away," 9.

28 "Negro Assaults Girl," *Baltimore Sun*, April 3, 1919, 3. Newspapers. com.

29 Isaiah Fountain v. State, April Term 1919 No. 39 [MSA S1733-530, 1/65/04/100]. Ct of Appeals: Statement of Sheriff Stitchberry of Talbot County, filed June 5, 1919, at 19.

30 "Accused Negro Gets Away," 9.

31 "Accused Negro Gets Away," 9.

32 "Negro Assailant of White Girl to Hang," 3 and 24. "Swanaker" is undoubtably misspelled and meant to be "Schwaninger," the name of a local family and road.

33 "Negro Assailant of White Girl to Hang," 3.

34 Isaiah Fountain v. State, April Term 1919 No. 39 [MSA S1733-530, 1/65/04/100]. Ct of Appeals: Abstract from the Minutes of Court, at 17.

35 "Fountain Found Guilty," 1.

36 "Accused Negro Gets Away," 9.

37 Isaiah Fountain v. State, Abstract from the Minutes of Court, at 17.

38 Isaiah Fountain v. State, April Term 1919 No. 39 [MSA S1733-530, 1/65/04/100] Ct of Appeals: Motion to Stay Further Proceedings, April 24, 1919, at 5.

CHAPTER 6

The Mob and the Escape

It was through this mass of enraged humanity that the Sheriff and the Baltimore police led the negro on the way to the jail.

—BALTIMORE SUN

The Lynch Mob

The crowds around the Talbot County Courthouse kept their vigil throughout Easter Monday and into the night while Isaiah Fountain's trial continued. They were upset about the details of the victim's testimony wherein she named Isaiah Fountain as her attacker. They were also angry about not being allowed in the courtroom for the night session. Word about the proceedings spread, and the crowd grew larger and more agitated. The *Sun* wrote that although the people outside were upset, they "made no threats until after the adjournment."[1] By the time court adjourned for the night, the agitated crowd of White Talbot County citizens in front of the Talbot County Courthouse had turned into a mob.

At the door of the courthouse, Isaiah Fountain, guarded by Sheriff Stitchberry, his deputies, and Baltimore City police officers, faced the assembled mob. The *Baltimore Sun* described the hostile situation:

> It was estimated that 2,000 persons were packed in the Courthouse yard following the clearing of the courtroom and it was through this mass of enraged humanity that the Sheriff and the Baltimore police led the negro on the way to the jail, which is 75 yards in the rear of the Courthouse. The negro was not hand-cuffed, a precaution that many thought the Sheriff and police should have taken.[2]

Fountain and his outnumbered protectors made their way through the furious crowd toward the sheriff's house, which was attached to the jail.[3] The mob closed in on the group as they tried to clear a path to the front porch of the house. The *Afro-American* newspaper wrote of Fountain: "He was plainly affected by the constant effort made throughout the day to get hold of him, and the small chance of his few defenders to save his life." The description continued, "cries of 'get the Nigger,' 'lynch the brute,' 'let's take him,' were heard on all sides, as a grand rush was made for the police and the frightened prisoner."[4]

Court of Appeal documents also described the mob's actions:

> . . . as he [Fountain] passed through the crowd, it became apparent that members in the crowd had come there for the purpose of interrupting an orderly procedure of the administration of justice; that some were armed with various weapons, others with ropes and with the avowed purpose of taking him out of the custody of the Sheriff

and lynching him; that threats against his life were made by members of the crowd, and personal violence on him was actually perpetrated, and that the cries of "Lynch him" were then and there made.[5]

An article from the *Baltimore News* was given in later Court of Appeals documents as evidence of the mob's fury. It further described the scene outside the courthouse, recounting the valiant attempts of two Baltimore City police officers who "fought off a number of men who sought to get their hands on Fountain. One man who threw his arm around the negro, was felled by a smashing blow." The *News* account continued:

> If the patrolmen had not pulled their revolvers the attempt on the negro's life would have been successful. They pointed their weapons at the ringleaders while they hustled Fountain into the jail. When the attack on the police was made there were cries of "Lynch him!", "Go in and get him!", "Let us have him!", "Don't let him get away!" and "Lynch the _____!"[6]

The *Sun*'s correspondent reported that Fountain and his guards had almost reached the front porch of the sheriff's house when the crowd surged against them shouting, "Get him!" At least one man had several yards of rope with him, and another got close enough to "put his hands on the negro." Once the party reached the porch, "the sheriff hustled the negro up the steps." While the ten Baltimore City policemen held back the mob, Sheriff Stitchberry's wife opened the door and the prisoner was rushed inside the sheriff's house.[7]

In describing the mob's actions outside the courthouse, the local *Easton Star-Democrat*'s account was, again, restrained. The paper said one man had "taken hold of the prisoner's arm," while someone else called out, "Grab him." The crowd was described as "gathering" on the jail steps.[8] While other newspapers each used several paragraphs and more colorful descriptions to describe the scene, the *Star-Democrat's* entire account was blandly reported in just four sentences.

Run or Die

During his jostled journey from the courthouse to the jail, Isaiah must have been weighing his odds of surviving the night. Certainly, his handful of protectors were no match for the thousands of people who were clamoring for his life.

A Baltimore newspaper described the armed mob as a "blood-thirsty, shrieking mass of humanity." It said that they shouted, "Give him to us! We'll make quick work of the d____ nigger!" After making it through the gauntlet of mob fury, Fountain was described as "trembling with fright and begging to be protected."[9] Fountain must have been asking himself: "Should I run or stay and die?"

Reaching the front porch of the sheriff's house, Sheriff Stitchberry quickly shoved Fountain through the front door but remained outside to deal with the mob. Even inside the walls of the sheriff's house, Fountain was still in danger from the mob. It could have easily overwhelmed the sheriff, his deputies, and the Baltimore policemen and stormed the jail. He weighed his options and acted swiftly to save his life.

The *Baltimore News* reporter wrote that once the prisoner was inside the house, the sheriff's wife, Annie, took charge of him. Mrs. Stitchberry, fearing that the armed mob would begin shooting through the windows, stayed low and crawled to the safety of the jail office. She ordered Fountain also to "drop to the floor and crawl." Fountain did so but crossed the office to an open window and started to crawl through it. Mrs. Stitchberry tried to grab at his leg to stop him but was "unable to hold him because of the frenzied strength he put into play in his endeavor to get away." According to the *Baltimore News*, "Mrs. Stitchberry said that if she had had her revolver she would have emptied it into the body of the negro as he went out." From the window, Fountain crawled over the roof of a shed and jumped into the jail yard. He ran across the yard to a pile of lumber against the wall, climbed it, jumped over the wall, and made good his escape.[10] Fountain's decisiveness had likely saved his life—for the moment.

According to the *Baltimore Afro-American*, Sheriff Stitchberry, his deputies, and the Baltimore City police officers were still holding back the angry mob when Mrs. Stitchberry told the sheriff of Fountain's getaway. He and some of the other lawmen quickly went to the rear of the jail yard and tried to determine where Fountain had gone. Having failed to establish his route, they returned to the front of the jail and Stitchberry announced to the mob that Fountain had escaped. The mob was dubious. The paper reported: "The hysterical crowd, believing the sheriff's story of the escape was simply a ruse, cussed at the sheriff and refused to move from the spot for three hours, while Fountain made good his escape."[11]

The *Sun's* account of Fountain's escape was somewhat different. Its version said that the sheriff and deputies had left the crowd in front of the sheriff's house and pursued Fountain. The mob hesitated to follow and thought the sheriff "was trying a ruse on them." The paper reported that Mrs. Stitchberry made the announcement to the angry mob that Fountain had escaped and was being pursued by the sheriff. The two-thousand-strong crowd then took off in pursuit of Fountain, while the sheriff attempted to keep ahead of the same mob, "which was bent on a lynching." The crowd chasing Fountain then began to suspect that he hadn't really escaped and was still in the jail, so they returned there, began stoning the building, and started to break down the door. At this point, Mrs. Stitchberry came out and invited a committee of five to look through the house and the jail. The committee completed their search and reported to the mob that Fountain was not in the buildings. The crowd still wasn't satisfied and demanded that a second group inspect the premises. By this time, the sheriff had returned from his unsuccessful pursuit of the prisoner and appealed to the mob to help him search for Fountain. The mob finally agreed— if the sheriff would turn Fountain over to them when he was captured. Stitchberry immediately refused and bravely responded: "No. I will protect the negro with my life."[12]

The *Sun*'s account continued: "In spite, however, of the Sheriff's refusal to deliver up the negro, the crowd's blood lust prevailed and in a short time officers and posses of men took up the trail again. Every nook and corner is being scoured and it will be a miracle if the fugitive is not caught within a few hours."[13]

The *Evening Sun* empathized with Isaiah Fountain and described the life-or-death choice that he had faced that night. The paper reported:

Facing death at the end of the hangman's rope in the jail yard, should he be convicted, and on the other hand fearing he would meet a worse fate at the hands of the mob of people whose shouts and threats he could hear while sitting in the courtroom, Fountain is believed to have planned to make a getaway at the first opportunity. . . He was being tossed upon two horns of a dilemma and probably thought he was going to meet death either way, and so he made up his mind to make a break. This is the firm belief of those who watched the trial closely.[14]

Although Sheriff Stitchberry had vowed to protect Fountain with his life, Mrs. Stitchberry had different thoughts about the prisoner's safety, according to the *Sun*. Angered by Fountain's escape while under her watch, she told friends that she hoped that Fountain would never be returned to custody. She added that she would be glad if the mob searching for him "tore him to pieces." Annie Stitchberry was not alone with her vengeful thoughts: the *Sun* reported that "the temper of the whole countryside is bitter against the negro, although the first excitement has given way to determination that he shall not escape."[15]

"Automobile parties" of heavily armed men were organized and drove to different areas of Talbot County to search for Fountain. The searchers opened drawbridges so that the fugitive could not cross various rivers and scoured abandoned farm buildings, railroad cars, and canning factories—any place that could shelter him. A general search was made of the "colored section" of the town to ensure that local negroes weren't hiding Fountain.[16] The manhunt was underway.

Endnotes

1 "Accused Negro Gets Away," *Baltimore Sun*, April 22, 1919, 1. Newspapers.com.

2 "Accused Negro Gets Away," 1.

3 At the time it was common for the sheriff and his family to live in quarters close or attached to the jail. The sheriff's wife usually cooked the prisoners' meals. The Talbot County sheriff's house and jail are still in use, but they have been remodeled and repurposed as the Talbot County State's Attorney's Office.

4 "Fountain Has Small Chance for Justice," *Baltimore Afro-American*, April 25, 1919, A1 and 4. ProQuest.com.

5 Isaiah Fountain v. State, April Term 1919 No. 39 [MSA S1733-530, 1/65/04/100] Ct of Appeals: Motion to Stay Further Proceedings, April 24, 1919, at 5–6.

6 Isaiah Fountain v. State, April Term 1919 No. 39 [MSA S1733-530, 1/65/04/100] Ct of Appeals: Defendant's Motion to Stay Further Proceedings (clipping from The Baltimore News and incorporated as part hereof), April 24, 1919, at 10.

7 "Accused Negro Gets Away," 1.

8 "Fountain Found Guilty," *Easton Star-Democrat*, April 26, 1919, 1.

9 "Mobs with Ropes Race with Sheriff to Capture Negro," *Baltimore Evening Sun*, April 22, 1919, 2. Newspapers.com.

10 Isaiah Fountain v. State, Defendant's Motion to Stay Further Proceedings (clipping from The Baltimore News and incorporated as part hereof), April 24, 1919, at 10.

11 "Fountain Has Small Chance for Justice," 4.

12 "Accused Negro Gets Away," 1 and 9.

13 "Accused Negro Gets Away," 9.

14 "Mobs with Ropes Race with Sheriff to Capture Negro," 2.

15 "All Talbot in Man Hunt," *Baltimore Sun*, April 23, 1919, 8. Newspapers.com.

16 Isaiah Fountain v. State, Defendant's Motion to Stay Further Proceedings (clipping from The Baltimore News and incorporated as part hereof), April 24, 1919, at 11.

CHAPTER 7

Judge Adkins, the Reward, and the Blame

This is the greatest calamity in the history of Talbot County. . . The Court will not place the blame at this time but wants to say that the escape of Isaiah Fountain has brought a blush of shame to the Commonwealth.

—JUDGE WILLIAM H. ADKINS

Judge Adkins's Reward (Tuesday, April 22, 1919)

The next morning, Wednesday, April 22, 1919, the *Sun* reported that "Talbot County today is an armed camp. Nearly every man capable of firing a gun is searching for Isaiah Fountain . . . who escaped last night from Sheriff Stitchberry and an infuriated mob of 1,000 bent on lynching him." The paper added that a crowd of "at least 500 persons" remained in front of the courthouse, talking "about nothing else but the biggest sensation that Talbot County has ever had."[1]

At 9:30 a.m. Judge Adkins called the court to order. The jury had spent the night sequestered in the courtroom[2] because the presence of the mob in the courthouse yard had prevented its members from being taken to their hotel the previous evening. From their vantage point in the second-story courtroom, the jury members had had an unobstructed view of the mob's attempt to lynch Isaiah Fountain just twelve hours earlier.

In addition to the jury, the attorneys and "several hundred" spectators were packed into the courtroom. Court documents noted that Chief Judge Adkins opened the morning session by commenting about the "disgraceful proceedings" of the violent mob outside the courthouse the night before. He noted that the various threats of violence against the prisoner had provoked him to make his escape, and then offered a $5,000 reward (almost $85,000 in 2022 dollars[3]) for Fountain's capture, specifying that he be returned "unharmed" to the custody of the sheriff.[4] Judge Adkins's offer of a reward for the capture of the defendant during the court session—*in the presence of the jury*—was an unheard-of response to such an escape. The *Evening Sun* called it "the most extraordinary measure that has ever been undertaken by any Court in this State, so far as can be learned."[5]

Judge Adkins then instructed Sheriff Stitchberry "in open court" to ask for volunteers from the courtroom spectators to be sworn in as deputy sheriffs. The record states that "several hundred persons volunteered and were sworn in as deputy sheriffs, including Mr. O'Dunne, the prisoner's counsel."[6] The *Baltimore Sun* reported that "Eugene O'Dunne was the first to step forward." The paper also reported that Sheriff Stitchberry swore in as deputies a total of "700 or more men who were in and about the court."[7] It's likely that at least some of the men sworn as deputies that morning to capture and return Isaiah Fountain safely had been in the mob seeking to lynch him the previous night.

Judge Adkins was shocked and embarrassed by the actions of the previous night's mob and their attempts to lynch the prisoner. He instructed the newly sworn deputies "to protect this prisoner even to the point of death so that the honor of this county may be vindicated," and added, "This is the greatest calamity in the history of Talbot County." Adkins spoke of the shame Fountain's escape brought to Maryland, but deferred assigning any specific blame for the fiasco.[8]

Several newspapers also noted that, in addition to being sworn in as a deputy sheriff, Fountain's attorney Eugene O'Dunne also put up $250 of his own money to add to the reward offered by Judge Adkins for Fountain's capture.[9] (With O'Dunne's money added to the $5,000 reward offered by Judge Adkins, the total came to $5,250, worth almost $88,725 in 2022 dollars.)[10] Defense Counsel O'Dunne addressed the court to say that he would give any assistance necessary to bring Fountain back to custody. He said that Fountain's escape was as much a calamity to him as to the citizens of Talbot County.[11] Judge Adkins then suspended the trial until the defendant's capture. He ordered that the jury be sequestered in a hotel in another part of town until the trial could be reconvened.[12]

The Blame

Sheriff Stitchberry was very popular in Talbot County. Such a notorious prisoner escaping on his watch, however, generated a lot of local criticism, especially from the opposing party. Although he was leading the search efforts for Isaiah Fountain, Stitchberry was severely criticized, mainly for not taking steps to handcuff or shackle his prisoner when they left the courtroom to return him to the jail for the night.[13]

A newspaper in Wilmington, Delaware, reported that the high esteem the local people had for Stitchberry had now turned into condemnation for his part in Fountain's escape. It said the sheriff's family had warned Stitchberry that the prisoner "would bear close watching." However, the sheriff "appeared to have confidence in the Negro and said he did not believe that Fountain would make a break for freedom." Most people were astonished that the sheriff had not handcuffed the prisoner and felt that his escape would have been impossible if only he had been shackled.[14] The *Baltimore Sun*'s criticism of the sheriff was harsh: it condemned the sheriff for "losing his head" in the excitement of the mob and not putting Fountain in handcuffs.[15]

The *Sun* interviewed Marshall Carter, a Baltimore police official, about Fountain's escape:

> I am utterly dumbfounded at the apparent neglect in handling the negro from the time that he was taken from the courtroom. Why was he not handcuffed and why was he not guarded by a corps of deputy sheriffs, even after he got inside the sheriff's home, is more than I can comprehend. . . The amazing thing is that the negro outwitted the Talbot County authorities and got out of the house where the city police had aided in getting him there safely.[16]

On the other hand, the *Sun* was quick to absolve the Baltimore City police officers who had been helping to guard

Fountain. In fact, the paper was effusive in praising them for their efforts and said that they "did their best."[17]

Undoubtably, Talbot countians were upset with Sheriff Stitchberry for his negligence in Fountain's escape. However, the local *Easton Star-Democrat* printed no hint of criticism. The paper reported matter-of-factly, "During his [Stitchberry's] absence the prisoner jumped through a small open window and made his escape over the fence at the rear of the jail."[18]

Perhaps the opinion that mattered the most to Sheriff Stitchberry was that of Judge Adkins, who announced in court: "The Court will not place the blame at this time but wants to say that the escape of Isaiah Fountain has brought a blush of shame to the Commonwealth."[19] Adkins's not-too-subtle, on-the-record, criticism of the escape must have affected the sheriff even more than the jabs from the out-of-town newspapers. Surely, Stitchberry wanted to redeem himself in the eyes of the judge and the citizens of Talbot County. After all, his position was an elected one, dependent on the voters' approval. He wanted not only to capture Fountain because it was his duty, but also to satisfy his constituents. Also, Stitchberry needed to return Fountain safely to custody before he could be lynched by other pursuers. This urgency was only confirmed by the local outrage against him, as reported by the *Evening Sun*:

> The hunt has taken on the aspect of a race—a contest between the forces of the Sheriff and his hundreds of special deputies, who seek to return the negro to the court, and the hundreds more of men and boys making up the posse that plans to Lynch Fountain as soon as it lays hands upon him.

Though the Sheriff has more than 700 special deputies, those who seek to Lynch the negro outnumber his forces, and the chances of capturing the accused man favor the would-be lynchers.[20]

The odds seemed stacked against Fountain's safe return to custody. Even Maryland Governor Emerson Harrington said he had "every reason" to believe that Fountain would suffer violence if he fell into the hands of "enraged citizens."[21] Perhaps the sworn efforts of the sheriff to protect Fountain, coupled with Judge Adkins's reward offer, would tilt the odds in Fountain's favor.

Endnotes

1 "All Talbot in Man Hunt," *Baltimore Sun*, April 23, 1919, 8. Newspapers.com.

2 Isaiah Fountain v. State, April Term 1919 No. 39 [MSA S1733-530, 1/65/04/100] Ct of Appeals: Defendant's Motion to Stay Further Proceedings, April 24, 1919, at 6.

3 Inflation Calculator, Saving.org Resources and Calculators, accessed July 25, 2021, https://www.saving.org/inflation/. Due to inflation, $1.00 in 1919 equals $16.90 in 2022.

4 Isaiah Fountain v. State, April Term 1919 No. 39 [MSA S1733-530, 1/65/04/100] Ct of Appeals: Judge's Certificate, April 24, 1919, at 13.

5 "Mobs with Ropes Race with Sheriff to Capture Negro," *Baltimore Evening Sun*, April 22, 1919, 1. Newspapers.com.

6 Isaiah Fountain v. State, Judge's Certificate, April 24, 1919, at 13.

7 "All Talbot in Man Hunt," 8.

8 "All Talbot in Man Hunt," 8.

9 "All Talbot in Man Hunt," 8. "Troops Guard Accused Negro," *Baltimore Sun*, April 24, 1919, 3. Newspapers.com. "Negro Fugitive Ran Down," *Evening Journal*, April 23, 1919, 1. Newspapers.com. Isaiah Fountain v. State, April Term 1919 No. 39 [MSA S1733-530, 1/65/04/100] Ct of Appeals: Defendant's Motion to Stay Further Proceedings (clipping from the *Baltimore News* and incorporated as part hereof), April 24, 1919, at 11. The *Baltimore Sun*, on April 23, 1919, erroneously reported O'Dunne's portion of the offered reward as $500; the amount was later correctly reported as $250 in an April 23, 1919 article.

10 Inflation Calculator at Saving.org website.

11 "Mobs with Ropes Race with Sheriff to Capture Negro," 1.

12 *Id.* at 13-14.

13 "Negro Fugitive Ran Down," *Wilmington Evening Journal*, April 23, 1919, 1 and 11. Newspapers.com.

14 "Negro Fugitive Ran Down," 11.

15 "All Talbot in Man Hunt," 8.

16 "All Talbot in Man Hunt," 8.

17 "All Talbot in Man Hunt," 8.

18 "Fountain Found Guilty," *Easton Star-Democrat*, April 26, 1919, 1. Judge Adkins's use of the word "Commonwealth" is curious, since Maryland is officially designated a state, not a commonwealth.

19 "All Talbot in Man Hunt," 8.

20 "Mobs with Ropes Race with Sheriff to Capture Negro," 1.

21 "Governor Ready, He Says, to Back Up County Authorities," *Baltimore Evening Sun*, April 22, 1919, 2. Newspapers.com.

CHAPTER 8

The Manhunt

The Sheriff, fully aware of the attitude of the enraged countians, knows there will be trouble in store for him the minute Fountain is captured. He is prepared for anything that may happen and tonight reiterated that he would protect the prisoner and hold him for court, even though he jeopardized his own life in the attempt.

—BALTIMORE SUN

The Pressure (Monday, April 21, 1919 to Wednesday, April 23, 1919)

The pressure was on. Sheriff Stitchberry had to find Fountain before he could be lynched by other pursuers. At the same time, Fountain's intent was to evade the lynchers long enough to escape altogether or at least be captured by those who would not lynch him.

Fountain's escape was no longer just a Talbot County matter. Governor Harrington was troubled by the escape and wanted every effort made to capture "the negro." He directed police officials in all nearby cities to be notified to be on the lookout for Isaiah Fountain.[1]

In Talbot County alone, Sheriff Stitchberry now had at his command a battalion-sized group of volunteers sworn in as deputy sheriffs to search for the fugitive. Local, state, and out-of-state newspapers had spread the news of Fountain's alleged crime and his escape. The surrounding counties and the entire Eastern Shore were also invested in finding the escaped prisoner to guarantee that justice was done, and even nearby states were looking for Fountain.

The Search

One newspaper reported that Fountain had received aid from "some Negroes in town" and was thought to be armed. People were warned to be cautious, and many armed themselves. The paper added: "Nearly every man seen in and around Easton today is carrying a pistol or gun."[2] Another paper wrote that there was "determination on the part of a large percentage of the male population to fire first, if the negro is sighted, and ask questions afterward."[3] All this, in spite of Judge Adkins's warning that Fountain should be captured and returned alive. Apparently, some of the searchers were more interested in killing Fountain than returning him alive and getting the judge's $5,000 reward.

Sheriff Stitchberry set up a manhunt command post at his office in the jail and waited for news from the various posses that were scouring Talbot County. He ordered that checkpoints and roadblocks be established on roads, ferries, and bridges throughout the county. Volunteer searchers reported to him from Talbot County, other Eastern Shore counties, and other parts of Maryland.

The *Sun* recounted that several local Black people had been arrested for suspicion of aiding Fountain after he made his escape. One escape theory had Fountain hiding in Easton, even though every Black dwelling had "been searched at least twice during the day." A local Black man, Richard Nixon (also reported as "Dixon"), was arrested. Nixon lived in the Black settlement of Sanderstown in the Trappe district. The Baltimore policemen who arrested him suspected that he had given Fountain a ride out of Easton on the night of his escape from the mob. The police were suspicious of Nixon because his car's engine was still warm in the morning, and he had been seen driving through Easton the night before.[4]

The *Wilmington Evening Journal* reported that another Black man arrested during the search was "Gene" Fountain, identified as the brother of Isaiah Fountain.[5] Eugene Fountain was arrested and held as a State's witness. Amid all the outrage, anger, and hate that the White citizens of Talbot County directed toward Isaiah Fountain and other Black people, the *Evening Journal* related a minor incident of kindness. When Gene Fountain had been arrested in Easton, he had been driving a mare with a very young colt, only two weeks old and still dependent on its mother for milk. After Gene Fountain's arrest, the mare and colt were separated, and the mare was kept in an Easton stable, under orders from State's Attorney Charles Butler. The colt was in danger of starving. Two White men from the neighborhood were concerned about the colt's condition. The men notified Butler of the situation, whereupon he humanely rescinded his order and allowed the mare to be reunited with her hungry colt.[6]

The animosity that Butler and the White populace had for
Isaiah Fountain apparently did not apply to an animal owned
by his brother.

Concerns about the Search

Some concerns were voiced about the motives of the hundreds of deputy sheriffs and other searchers involved in the
effort to find Isaiah Fountain. The *Baltimore Afro-American* wondered how many of these same people had also been
in the Monday night mob that had tried to lynch Fountain
and caused him to flee in the first place. The newspaper
commented:

> A travesty upon American civilization in this year of our
> Lord 1919, is the fact that some of the very mob leaders
> who attempted to Lynch Fountain are reported to have
> been sworn in as deputy sheriffs to catch the escaped
> prisoner.
>
> In the last analysis, which is worse, a criminal guilty of
> rape, or two thousand lawless persons who THINK AND
> ATTEMPT MURDER.[7]

The *Afro-American* did not stop at questioning the
makeup and motives of the many volunteers searching for
Fountain. The paper also wanted official assurance from the
governor that once captured, Fountain would be protected.
The editors of the newspaper sent a telegram to Governor
Harrington stating: "After witnessing the mob-like disturbances in Easton, Maryland, during the trial of Isaiah
Fountain for alleged assault, the AFRO-AMERICAN, in
the name of its 18,500 readers urges you to take the necessary

steps to capture the escaped prisoner and see to it that he has a fair and orderly trial."[8]

The public plea from the *Afro-American* editors apparently influenced the governor. The *Baltimore Sun* wrote:

> Governor Harrington last night issued an appeal to the farmers and other residents of Talbot County to assist in running down Fountain and to refrain from violence when he is caught.
>
> "I sincerely hope and trust," he stated, "that the people of the county will let the law take its course, notwithstanding their great provocation and their desire for speedy justice. The courts can be depended upon to act promptly when the man is brought to trial, and I hope the people will realize this."[9]

The *Baltimore Evening Sun* reported that some Easton residents were content to let the authorities handle the capture of Fountain. Many expressed shock at all the unfavorable publicity the county was receiving, with its residents being portrayed as "bloodthirsty." They believed that the majority of people in Easton had not been involved in the attempted lynching of Fountain and felt that the "mob element" came from other parts of the county. The *Evening Sun* reported that this belief was "not strictly true," and added, "It has been noted that the people of Easton are as interested in the matter as any others, and many of them, it is known, have been active participants in the searching parties that have been scouring the county."[10]

The same newspaper report noted that "nobody in Talbot County, apparently, is working." The men were described as arming themselves with rifles and shotguns and going out to search for Fountain, while the women neglected their household duties to gather and talk about the latest search news. The paper observed: "The capture of the negro is the one absorbing thought and other considerations are definitely put aside."[11]

Fountain Sightings

The various appeals for aid in finding Isaiah Fountain issued by Sheriff Stitchberry, Judge Adkins, and Governor Harrington had the desired effect. Reports were pouring in from across the Eastern Shore and beyond. As Fountain sightings were reported, armed patrols were dispatched to investigate. As many as forty armed automobile patrols were used by the searchers, each automobile manned by five or six men.[12] The governor also dispatched eight "road deputies" to Easton to aid in the search.[13]

In addition to carrying out searches at the homes of local Black people and Fountain's family and friends, the posses responded to many alleged Fountain sightings. He was reported just about everywhere. Calls came from places all over Talbot County and from Preston, Tuckahoe, Ridgely, and Greensboro, in Caroline County. Police investigated Fountain sightings in Baltimore City and the District of Columbia, with searches of the local "negro sections."[14] He was even "sighted" at Union Station in Baltimore, supposedly boarding a train for Philadelphia.[15]

One of these reports, however, proved useful. On Wednesday morning, April 23, 1919, Sheriff Stitchberry received word that Fountain had been seen the previous night in Greensboro, Caroline County. Greensboro is a small town about twenty-two miles northeast of Easton and only about four miles from the Delaware state line. Stitchberry correctly believed that Fountain meant to flee to Delaware.

Fountain's Capture (Wednesday, April 23, 1919)

As with other sightings, when the word came in that Fountain may have been seen in Greensboro, Sheriff Stitchberry immediately dispatched a "squad of deputies" along with ten Baltimore City policemen there to investigate. They found that a man matching Fountain's description had gone to a local drugstore and grocery store in Greensboro the previous evening and had bought some cigarettes and cakes. Mrs. Hobbs, the owner of the grocery store, readily sold the cakes to the man who, she said, forced a smile and "look[ed] pleasant." The next morning, Wednesday, she noticed Fountain's picture in the newspaper and recognized him because of his smile. She promptly notified the authorities.[16]

The *Baltimore Sun* reported that when the sheriff's manhunters from Easton arrived in Greensboro, they received a report of a man making his way through the nearby woods, toward the Delaware border. The search party followed, crossed into Delaware, and found that the suspect was heading north toward Hartly, Delaware, approximately fifteen miles away. The ten Baltimore police officers piled into their cars and headed for Hartly, leaving the squad of Talbot County deputies to follow on their own. The two groups of searchers arrived at a farm near Hartly, quickly reorganized, and interviewed a man who reported seeing a person who fit Fountain's description. They began to search the farm's outbuildings. Two of the Baltimore police officers entered a barn and, suspecting that Fountain was hidden in the hayloft, ordered him to show himself. Fountain crawled out from the hay and surrendered.[17]

The *Sun* reported that when he saw another group of searchers coming toward the barn, he "pleaded with his captors not to let them lynch him." He said he was willing to die but asked to be electrocuted instead of hanged. Fountain was captured at 1:45 p.m., Wednesday afternoon. After being hunted by more than two thousand deputy sheriffs, Baltimore police officers, volunteers, and ordinary citizens, Isaiah Fountain's almost forty hours of desperate freedom had come to an end.[18]

The Suspect's Return

At the time of Fountain's recapture, other groups of armed men were also hunting for him in the area near Hartly. These searchers were more interested in lynching the escapee than returning him for trial in Easton. Fountain's captors realized that he was still in danger of being lynched and quickly loaded their prisoner into one of their automobiles. The caravan of cars then raced to Easton, hoping to arrive before the news of Fountain's capture could reach the town and cause a reappearance of the angry mob.[19] The captors were so intent on getting Fountain back to the safety of the Talbot County Jail that they ignored the fact that since he had been captured in Delaware, he should have been formally extradited back to Maryland.[20] As with most matters involving the Fountain case, speed trumped legal formalities.

The returning convoy of the captors and their prisoner reached speeds of up to forty-five miles per hour, but news of their passenger preceded them, and crowds of farmers and residents appeared along the road as the automobiles sped by. According to the *Sun*, the crowds along the route "shouted threats at the negro" and clamored for the deputies to turn Fountain over to them. The paper wrote that men along the road shouted that they "would be in Easton tonight to get the negro."[21]

The *Sun* wrote that at 2:00 p.m., Sheriff Stitchberry in Easton received the news that Fountain had been captured and was being rushed there "at breakneck speed." The sheriff "hoped to get the prisoner back behind bars before the crowd learned that he had been caught," but the news soon spread, and the people waiting around the jail and courthouse grew "nervous and impatient." With Fountain and his captors still in transit, the mayor, Francis Wrightson, addressed the agitated crowd and "admonished them to keep their heads and not do anything rash."[22] Chief Judge William Adkins, Fountain's lawyer, Eugene O'Dunne, and Mr. W. Mason Shehan, a prominent citizen and former judge, all also addressed the crowd and pleaded for them to remain orderly.[23]

The *Baltimore Sun* reported that while the town leaders were addressing the crowd, the caravan of automobiles bearing Isaiah Fountain arrived at the rear of the jail. The guards held their prisoner in the vehicle until the speakers had finished their speeches and the crowd was cheering. At that point, Fountain was rushed through the jail's rear entrance, his arms shackled and held by two Baltimore police officers, while two deputy sheriffs cleared a path through the crowd. The newspaper reported that Fountain was "clearly showing the fear that was in his heart." He was promptly taken to his cell, and the door was locked behind him. Fountain was quoted by the paper as saying, "For God's sake, don't let them come in. Protect me. I'll kill myself before I'll let the mob get me."[24]

Trouble for Easton

Fountain's fear of being lynched was well founded. Governor Harrington had warned Judge Adkins of potential trouble, saying that he had reliable information that a mob was at that time heading to Easton from Delaware "with the avowed intention of storming the jail and wrecking the structure if necessary in order to lynch or burn Fountain."[25]

Fountain's trial would be reconvened the following morning. Court of Appeals records show that following the speeches to the assembled crowds, Chief Judge Adkins invited "those who had been sworn in as deputy sheriffs and others who desired to be sworn in as deputy sheriffs to report to the court room across the open green; that he had further matters to communicate to them." In the crowded courtroom, Adkins informed the group that he had received information from the governor that an additional three or four thousand people were expected to arrive in Easton by the next day. Judge Adkins and the courtroom crowd discussed whether the already sworn and newly sworn deputies and the ten Baltimore police officers already on the scene would be sufficient to handle the influx. With the crowd's consensus, Adkins decided that the prudent move would be to request that the governor dispatch additional police officers from Baltimore City, as well as troops from the Maryland Militia.[26]

Reinforcements to Easton
(Thursday, April 24, 1919)

At the request of Judge Adkins, Governor Harrington ordered the Maryland State Militia to Easton for the resumption of Isaiah Fountain's trial on Thursday, April 24, 1919, as well as more Baltimore City Police officers.[27] In effect, martial law had been declared for Easton—at least in the area around the courthouse.

Maryland's adjutant general, Henry Warfield, promptly issued "Special Orders No. 5" to the commanding officer of the 2nd Infantry Regiment of the Maryland State Guard in Salisbury, Maryland (approximately fifty miles from Easton). Company I was to assemble and proceed to Easton "via the quickest transportation available." The orders specified that "troops will be uniformed, armed, and equipped, including ammunition for possible riot duty."[28]

Between midnight and dawn of Thursday, April 24, the company of uniformed and armed Maryland Militia arrived at the Talbot County Courthouse to control the expected crowds and to protect Isaiah Fountain. Court records stated that the troops were assigned to guard the approaches to the courthouse and jail. The armed troops had orders to admit to the courthouse grounds only authorized individuals with official business in the court. This included the several hundred special deputies that had been sworn in the previous day. The infantry troops were deployed, with their rifles and fixed bayonets, inside the cast-iron fence that surrounded the courthouse grounds. Twenty-five additional Baltimore Police officers also arrived in Easton during the night "by machine" (that is, automobiles). They supplemented the Baltimore Police officers already on duty in Easton.[29]

A Wilmington, Delaware, newspaper reported that even more security for the trial had been added during the night to prevent a "surprise attack" on the Talbot County Jail. Police patrols were stationed on the roads leading into Easton with orders to turn back all automobiles whose occupants could not give a valid reason for visiting the town. "It was estimated that nearly 1,000 automobiles, mostly with persons curious to learn whether any attempt would be made to lynch Fountain, were turned back by the highway policemen."[30]

Isaiah Fountain, back in his jail cell, was apparently aware of the reports of approaching lynchers and feared what would happen if his protectors were overwhelmed by the mobs. The *Sun* reported that Fountain "spent a very restless night, walking up and down his cell and muttering to himself." The prisoner was so worried and agitated that he unsuccessfully begged one of his guards to give him some poison pills.[31]

As dawn approached, Easton was an armed camp, with a company of armed infantry soldiers and hundreds of deputies and policemen all determined to protect the accused man, Isaiah Fountain. Thousands more people jammed the town to get as close as they could to view the legal spectacle. Some were there to bear witness to the proceedings, some hoped to do harm to Fountain, and some hoped to witness his lynching. The trial was about to reconvene.

Endnotes

1 "Fountain Reported Here," *Baltimore Sun*, April 23, 1919, 8. Newspapers.com.

2 "Negro Fugitive Ran Down Today," *Wilmington Evening Journal*, April 23, 1919, 11.

3 "All Talbot in Man Hunt," *Baltimore Sun*, April 23, 1919, 1 and 8. Newspapers.com.

4 "All Talbot in Man Hunt," 8. "Troops in Easton Protect Fountain," *Wilmington Evening Journal*, April 24, 1919, 7. Newspapers.com. The *Sun* reported the man's last name was Nixon; the *Evening Journal* identified him as Dixon.

5 1910 Federal Census, Trappe, Talbot, Maryland; Roll: T624_568; Page: 1B; Enumeration District 0098; FHL microfilm: 1374581. Ancestry.com. (Accessed July 27, 2020.) Although US census records do not show a Fountain sibling as "Gene" or "Eugene," a younger brother, James E. Fountain, is listed. Possibly the middle initial stands for Eugene.

6 "Troops in Easton Protect Fountain," *Evening Journal*, April 24, 1919, 7. Newspapers.com.

7 Article 2, untitled, *Baltimore Afro-American*, April 25, 1919, 4. ProQuest.com. The article implied that Fountain was guilty when, in fact, his trial was in recess due to his escape.

8 "Telegram Sent to Governor on Monday," *Baltimore Afro-American*, April 25, 1919, A1. ProQuest.com.

9 "Governor Issues Appeal," *Baltimore Sun*, April 23, 1919, 8. Newspapers.com.

10 "Isaiah Fountain Captured in Barn at Hartley, Del.," *Baltimore Evening Sun*, 12. Newspapers.com.

11 "Isaiah Fountain Captured in Barn at Hartley, Del.," 12.

12 "All Talbot in Man Hunt," 1.

13 "Governor Issues Appeal," 8. "Road deputies" were the precursors to the Maryland State Police and reported to the State Road Commissioner. In 1921, the force was given statewide policing authority. In 1935, the force became a separate state department. "Department of State Police—Origin," Maryland State Archives, accessed July 26,

2021. https://msa.maryland.gov/msa/mdmanual/23dsp/html/dspf. html.

14 "City Police on Jump Running Down Clues," *Baltimore Evening Sun*, April 23, 1919, 12. Newspapers.com. "Washington Police on Hunt for Negro," *Baltimore Evening Sun*, April 23, 1919, 12. Newspapers.com.

15 "Fountain Reported Here," 8.

16 "Troops Guard Accused Negro," *Baltimore Sun*, April 24, 1919, 3.

17 "Troops Guard Accused Negro," 3.

18 "Troops Guard Accused Negro," 3.

19 "Troops Guard Accused Negro," 3.

20 "Troops in Easton Protect Fountain," *Evening Journal*, April 24, 1919, 7. Newspapers.com.

21 "Troops Guard Accused Negro," 3.

22 "Troops Guard Accused Negro," 3.

23 Fountain v. State (No. 39) (Court of Appeals of Maryland, Opinion of the Court. July 17, 1919.), *The Atlantic Reporter, Volume 107,* at 555. https://www.google.com/books/edition/The_Atlantic_ Reporter/znb7Nl_5wUC?hl=en&gbpv=1&dq=the+Atlantic+report-er,+volume+107&pg=PR14&printsec=frontcover.

24 "Troops Guard Accused Negro," 3.

25 "Troops Guard Accused Negro," 3.

26 Fountain v. State of Maryland, Court of Appeals of Maryland, Opinion of the Court, filed July 17, 1919, at 555.

27 The term "State Militia" was used to refer to what is now called the Maryland National Guard, which now has army and air force components. The Baltimore City police force was founded as a state agency by the Maryland legislature in 1853 and, to this day, the Baltimore City Police Department is still under state authority. Ordering the Baltimore police to Easton was within the governor's authority.

28 Isaiah Fountain v. State, April Term 1919 No. 39 [MSA S1733-530, 1/65/04/100]. Ct of Appeals, Copy of Order of Adjutant General, April 23, 1919, at 29–30.

29 Isaiah Fountain v. State, April Term 1919 No. 39 [MSA S1733-530, 1/65/04/100]. Ct of Appeals, Certificate of the Court, June 18, 1919, at 28.

30 "Troops in Easton Protect Fountain," *Evening Journal*, April 24, 1919, 7. Newspapers.com.

31 "Death Decree for Fountain," *Baltimore Sun*, April 25, 1919, 3. Newspapers.com.

CHAPTER 9

The Trial Continues

*Of the trial itself, opinion is general that Fountain,
whether innocent or guilty, did not have a ghost of
a show. Had the jury failed to bring in a sentence of
guilty, judge, jury and officers would have suffered
violence from the mob that threatened
the prisoner at every turn.*

—BALTIMORE AFRO-AMERICAN

Securing the Courthouse

On the morning of Thursday, April 24, 1919, a much more
orderly scene around the Talbot County Courthouse was
reported by the various newspapers covering the trial. Many
of the thousands of people who had gathered overnight had
left by dawn. However, despite the efforts to keep the crowds
away from the area, the climax of Isaiah Fountain's trial still
drew over a thousand people. The crowd, tense but mostly
orderly, pressed against the iron fence that lined the perimeter of the courthouse grounds. Uniformed troops armed with

fixed bayonets stood just feet apart along the inside of the fence. The many deputy sheriffs also assembled there wore red ribbons for identification.[1]

Isaiah Fountain's trial was set to reconvene at 9:30 a.m., but first the defendant had to take his place in the courtroom. The *Baltimore Evening Sun* reported that Fountain was taken from the jail "promptly at 9:00 o'clock." When he appeared at the jail door, there was a stirring in the crowd. The guards hurried him along to the security of the brick courthouse. The strong display of armed troops and deputies had the desired effect, reported the newspaper, and "no one had the temerity to attempt interference."[2]

Next, the members of the jury had to take their places in the jury box. Since the interruption of the trial on Monday night, the jury had been sequestered in a hotel in another part of Easton. As they approached the courthouse grounds, under escort of court bailiffs, the jury members had to pass the line of bayonet-wielding state militia troops and armed deputies.[3] The impressive display of armed security must have surprised the newly emerged jurors.

With all the actors in place inside the main courtroom on the second floor, the trial was set to resume. A strong sense of order and security was evident with over 400 deputized citizens and regular law enforcement officers packed into the chamber, seriously straining the capacity of the courtroom and leaving little room for spectators.[4]

Court Reconvenes (Thursday, April 24, 1919)

Chief Judge Adkins, assisted by Associate Judge Wickes, called the court to order at 9:30 a.m. and addressed the jury.

Adkins began by thanking the jury members and commending them for their "loyalty and patience" while they had been locked up in their hotel rooms for the past two days. He then spoke to the jury about the defendant's escape and the events of the previous Tuesday, when he had offered a reward for Fountain's capture.[5]

It had been just two days since Judge Adkins announced the escape of Isaiah Fountain in open court with the jury present. By now, Adkins realized that he had created a huge problem by making such a statement in open court, likely prejudicing the jury to think that only a guilty man would try to escape. He had "rung a bell" and now wished to "un-ring" it. Judge Adkins asked the jury to "forget about it" in the following statement:

> Before resuming the trial, the Court wants to say to you that it is proper that you should know a little more definitely why the trial was interrupted so you can come back as if it was not interrupted. The Court simply said to you when you were excused for the time being 'that the prisoner had escaped.' Now, that might have misled you, led you to a false impression when the Court said that the prisoner escaped. What we meant to say was that he escaped from violence; he believed he escaped from people who intended to do violence to him. That was the impression. Therefore, it would be improper for you in hearing this case to infer from that any evidence of guilt. You must decide the question of innocence or guilt on the testimony and not from any inference from the fact that he got away. We think it fair to say that any reasonable man would say the reason he got away was he was afraid of the crowd which tried to take him. . . We want you to

go back to the trial as if there was no interruption. *The case will be resumed with the understanding that you are to absolutely forget that there has been any interruption.*[6] [Emphasis added.]

Judge Adkins also attempted to absolve the citizens of Talbot County of any responsibility for trying to lynch Isaiah Fountain. He stated: "Our belief is that the crowd were not Maryland people, but people who came from another state."[7]

Eugene O'Dunne, the lead defense counsel, immediately objected to Judge Adkins's statement and declared that the sitting jury certainly had been prejudiced against Fountain by the judge's remarks. In addition, he argued, the jury itself had been threatened by the mob's attempt to lynch Fountain. It was the lynch mob, said O'Dunne, that prompted the prisoner to escape and so delayed the trial. The judge's offer of a reward—made in the presence of the jury—O'Dunne argued, was also prejudicial. O'Dunne felt that the jury *had* been prejudiced, in spite of Adkins's astonishing instruction that the judge expected the jury to conveniently forget that the trial had been interrupted and that Fountain had escaped.[8] O'Dunne concluded, "Therefore, because of the interruption of the proceedings by the operating of mob violence in the precincts of the Court, the prisoner desires to reserve an exception to the proceedings." Judge Adkins overruled O'Dunne's objection, and O'Dunne promptly reserved the right to appeal the judge's ruling.[9]

The State's Case Continues

After a two-day hiatus, the trial resumed with State's Attorney Charles Butler calling his final prosecution witness, Chief of Police John Entriken, from West Chester, Pennsylvania. Chief Entriken had arrested Fountain there on Monday, April 7. Entriken testified he had received information from Talbot County that Fountain might be headed to his area. He headed to the house of John Fountain, Isaiah's brother, about eight miles away. After waiting all night, the chief saw a wagon approaching carrying Fountain and two women. He stopped the wagon and asked Fountain to identify himself. The chief said that Fountain fit the description of the fugitive but gave another name when he was questioned. Entriken then placed Fountain under arrest and notified Sheriff Stitchberry. After a cross-examination by Defense Lawyer O'Dunne, the chief of police was excused. State's Attorney Butler then rested the prosecution's case against Isaiah Fountain.[10]

Fountain Testifies

The defense for Fountain was simple: someone had raped Bertha Simpson, but it wasn't Isaiah Fountain because he was in Easton at the time of the crime. The defense team immediately called Isaiah Fountain himself to the witness stand. A newspaper reporter observed that the stand where Fountain would testify was close to a partially opened window. Before Fountain got to it, an alert Baltimore City police officer positioned himself between the witness stand and the open window. Obviously, the officer wanted to discourage the prisoner from another escape attempt.[11] With over four hundred police and deputies in the room, it's hard to believe that the prisoner could even move about, much less escape.

Eugene O'Dunne began his questioning of Isaiah Fountain at 10:50 a.m. As described by the *Evening Sun*, Fountain testified that on Monday morning, March 31, and Tuesday morning, April 1 (the day of the crime), his wife had been in the Trappe area driving his horse with the missing rear shoe and the buggy with the defective tire. The unique horseshoe and tire tracks that had been traced to him, he said, were created by her recent travels in the area with the same horse and buggy. Fountain went on to say that when his wife hadn't returned from her trip to the bank, he became worried and decided to go to Easton to look for her. He left his Williamsburg farm at 2:00 p.m. and began the four-mile walk to Easton.[12]

On the way to Easton, Fountain first met Morris Bannon, a local Black man, and he asked Bannon if he had seen his wife. Fountain said he was concerned for her safety because the horse she was driving was "skittish." Farther on, Fountain encountered Theodore Schwaninger, a White neighbor, who stopped and offered him a ride to Easton. They arrived in Easton "about 3 o'clock." Fountain's account had earlier been corroborated by Mr. Schwaninger, a witness for the State.[13]

On arriving in Easton, Fountain said, he went to the Talbot Bank at 3:25 p.m. At the bank, he discovered that his wife had withdrawn money from his account and, instead of returning with the money to pay for a baby pig that Isaiah had bought the previous day, had used the money to visit her family in Camden, New Jersey.[14] After withdrawing money from his account, Fountain left the bank to look for his horse and buggy. He searched without success and then went to the Talbot County Courthouse to see the assistant county treasurer, Charles Baker.[15]

Next Fountain visited the Easton police chief, William Stoops, to inquire if the chief could go to Camden to bring Fountain's wife back to Maryland. In addition to Chief Stoops, Fountain said he had spoken with several other people in Easton that afternoon. He finally found his horse and buggy parked in a shed and left town around 4:00 p.m. Fountain went home and remained there until 7:00 p.m. and later visited with some neighbors to get information about his wife.[16]

Fountain was asked about his horse having a missing shoe. The prisoner replied that he didn't know anything about the shoe being missing from the animal because he didn't use the horse very much and didn't pay much attention to its feet. Fountain added that he had driven the horse and buggy home from Easton over a stone road and didn't notice the missing shoe because of the noise the buggy made on the rough stone surface.[17]

Fountain continued his testimony describing his journey to Camden, New Jersey the next morning (Wednesday, April 2) to confront his wife, who agreed to return home in a week. Next, he traveled by trolley to West Chester, Pennsylvania, to see his brother John. Fountain spent Sunday, April 6 with his brother and planned to visit him at work the next day. Before he had a chance to visit his brother at his workplace, Fountain was arrested by the West Chester chief of police on Monday, April 7.[18]

Attorney O'Dunne asked Fountain if he had been on the road near where Bertha Simpson had been assaulted.

Fountain said he had not been on that road for over a week before the assault. He also testified that he had told people he was going to Philadelphia but had not given the true reason for his trip because he didn't want his neighbors to gossip about his marital problems. Fountain also testified that he knew Simpson's grandfather, Mr. Diffenderfer, "but didn't know he had any children."[19]

Near the conclusion of Isaiah Fountain's testimony, Attorney O'Dunne asked the defendant directly if he had assaulted Bertha Simpson. Fountain replied emphatically: "No. The Lord knows I never seen the girl to know who she is in my life. I was not up the road where she says I was, and I never laid my hands on her."[20]

Other Defense Witnesses

The *Evening Sun* reported that the testimony of several witnesses—both for the State and the defense—supported Fountain's account of events, including his alibi of being in Easton at the time the crime was committed. Fountain's testimony that his wife had been driving his horse and buggy in the Trappe area was supported by Mrs. Howard Barnes. She testified that Fountain's wife "had washed" (done the laundry) at her home near Trappe the day before the assault. Mrs. Barnes also testified that Mrs. Fountain was planning to leave her husband to go to Camden, New Jersey because of "his treatment of her." She added that Isaiah Fountain had visited her at about 7:00 p.m. Tuesday evening, in "a nasty mood," looking for his wife.[21]

Mrs. Clara Streets, "a white woman of eminent respectability," lived a mile from Fountain's house and testified that she also had talked with Fountain on Tuesday evening. O'Dunne expressed amazement that a person who had supposedly just violently raped a young girl could so easily converse with two women just hours later. O'Dunne argued, "We invoke the Court's knowledge of human nature as to whether his action and conversation, as related by [Mrs. Street], are consistent with those of a man who has just raped a white girl, in the immediate neighborhood, a little earlier in the evening."[22]

The *Wilmington Evening Journal* reported that Mr. O'Dunne called Charles Baker to the stand. Baker—described as "a prominent citizen"—was the assistant treasurer for Talbot County. He testified that Isaiah Fountain had visited his office at 4:00 p.m. on the afternoon of the assault and they had conversed for "at least 15 minutes." The newspaper added: "This is regarded as significant, inasmuch as the crime is supposed to have been committed *between 3.45 and 4.45 p.m.*"[23] [Emphasis added.] Court records support the newspaper's information and indicate that "it was after 4.30 when [Fountain] left Baker's office."[24]

The next witness to see Fountain in Easton that afternoon was Easton Chief of Police Stoops. According to the Court of Appeal records about Chief Stoops's testimony, "*it would make it 5 o'clock or a little after, before he* [Fountain] *left* the jail or Chief of Police's office in Easton." [Emphasis added.] O'Dunne also spoke about the poor condition of Isaiah Fountain's farm horse and old buggy, saying that it would have taken Fountain nearly an hour to travel from Easton to the crime scene. Exasperated, he exclaimed to the court: "In Easton till after 5 p.m., yet assaulting a girl 7 miles from there between 4.30 and 5!!"[25]

In addition to the defense witnesses who supported Fountain's alibi, two witnesses for the prosecution had earlier given testimony that seemed to be more beneficial to the defense than to the prosecution. Their testimonies also supported Fountain's alibi that he was in Easton at the time of the attack on Bertha Simpson.

Theodore Schwaninger had testified that he had given Fountain a ride into town and arrived there at about 3:00 p.m. The other witness was William Spence, a cashier at the Talbot Bank in Easton. He testified that Fountain had withdrawn $17 from his account after his wife had earlier withdrawn $10 to go to New Jersey. Spence also said that Fountain had arrived at the bank after its 3:00 p.m. closing time—around 3:25 p.m.[26]

Fountain must have felt optimistic that his lawyers had been able to elicit solid testimony to support his alibi. Even more impressive was that the corroborating testimony came from several very respectable *White* citizens and two government officials, including Easton's chief of police. Isaiah Fountain and his defense team must have been satisfied when they rested their case.

Closing Arguments

There is no surviving record of State's Attorney Butler's closing argument, but it was reported that he spoke for seventeen minutes and told the jury that Isaiah Fountain should be found guilty and sentenced to death. Defense Attorney O'Dunne addressed the jury for about an hour with his summation. The *Baltimore Sun* summarized O'Dunne's closing argument:[27]

He made a remarkable plea on behalf of the prisoner. He said there was not the slightest doubt of the fact that the girl had been assaulted, and painted an interesting word-picture of the child, her beauty and her innocence. He argued, however, that so far as Fountain was concerned, it was a case of mistaken identity. "He is not the man," O'Dunne said.

He explained that, while the child had testified that she did not know Fountain, it was highly probable that she had seen him at one time or another on the road, and when she was confronted with him in the Courtroom on Monday she had immediately recalled the face and associated it with that of the man who had committed the crime.

He maintained that Fountain had made out a complete alibi, proving that he had been in Eason at 4.15 o'clock on the afternoon of the assault and declaring that it was impossible for him to have reached the neighborhood by 5 o'clock, when the crime was said to have been perpetrated.

Furthermore, said he, Fountain and every negro in Talbot County knew the penalty for criminal assault, and in the face of that fact it was not likely that he would have gone about in his neighborhood immediately following the crime and told a number of people that he was going to leave there the next morning.[28]

Another newspaper reported that Isaiah Fountain's defense testimony supported his alibi that he had been in Easton until 4:30 p.m. It went on to say that "officers admit that he would not have stayed in town that long if he had planned the crime several days ahead and knew that the girl left school at 3:30."[29] Remember, initial reports of the attack on Bertha Simpson listed the time of the attack as 4:00 p.m.[30] As the trial went on, the timing of the attack was shifted to between 4:30 and 5:00 p.m.[31] Even using the latest reported times for the attack, it would have been almost impossible for Fountain to leave Easton at 4:15 or 4:30 p.m., drive his farm horse and decrepit buggy the nine miles to the site of the attack (a journey of almost an hour), lie in wait for the schoolgirl, and then attack her. Using the most liberal estimates of time and distance, Fountain would have had to do all this within forty-five minutes.

Both sides had now presented their witnesses and made their best arguments for and against Isaiah Fountain. Judge Adkins charged the twelve jury members to decide the defendant's guilt or innocence.

The Verdict and the Sentence

The twelve White men of the jury left the courtroom at 4:56 p.m. to deliberate in the adjoining jury room. As they filed out, Judge Adkins warned those remaining in the courtroom that he would tolerate no demonstrations of any kind when the verdict was announced. He ordered the officers present to arrest anyone who defied his order. Just nine minutes later, at 5:05 p.m., the jury returned with the verdict. Everyone in the courtroom was anxious about the verdict, but none more so than Isaiah Fountain. As he stood and faced the jury, the moment of reckoning had arrived. The audience in the courtroom tried to watch both Fountain and the jury at the same time, while Chief Judge Adkins asked the jury foreman for the verdict. The jury foreman and the other eleven jury members responded as one, shouting "Guilty!" An observer in the room reported that the courtroom fell silent. He added, "Fountain wore the same nervous grin which characterized him, a grin of abject terror."[32]

Fountain remained silent, a blank look on his face, while his counsel, Eugene O'Dunne, rose from his seat and addressed the two judges. O'Dunne told the judges that the defense was ready for the sentencing of the defendant. Chief Judge Adkins and Associate Judge Wickes met in chambers for about ten minutes before returning at 5:15 p.m. with Fountain's sentence.[33] Judge Adkins pronounced the sentence: "Is[a]iah Fountain, you have been found guilty of the crime of which you are charged. You are sentenced to be hung by the neck until you are dead on a day to be set by the governor, and may God have mercy on your soul."[34] Once Fountain had recovered from the stunning news, he asked his attorney if he could have some snuff.[35]

The *Baltimore Sun* reported that two Baltimore City police officers quickly moved toward Fountain to return him to the jail and protect him from the crowd. Fountain said to the officers: "Boss, I is innocent. I am a married man. Just to think that they accused a married man of such a thing." The police officers handcuffed Fountain and cleared a path from the courtroom to the jail. The path was lined by policemen, deputies, and members of the state militia. Although a large crowd was assembled outside the courthouse awaiting news of the verdict, there was no violent demonstration, only a few cheers and the honking of some car horns. The policemen and deputies surrounded Fountain and rushed him to the jail, almost completely screening him from the crowd. He was back in his cell within twenty-five minutes of the end of the trial's closing arguments. The *Baltimore Sun* described the scene: "There was a mob outside the [court]house today—a mob that was kept at the proper distance, but which, instead of murmuring and threatening as did the mob Monday night, kept an almost unbroken silence."[36]

Finally, the crowds that had been in Easton since Easter weekend began to disperse. The *Sun* reported that the area in front of the Talbot County Courthouse was "back to normal" by 8:00 p.m. and that Easton had "dropped back to the even tenor of its way after four days of wild excitement."[37]

Securing the Prisoner

Easton may have returned to normal, but with a newly convicted rapist in his jail, Sheriff Stitchberry still faced problems. Although the angry crowds had left, finally satisfied with Fountain's conviction and death sentence, the sheriff knew that the public's attitude could change at any time. The governor still had to set the date for Fountain's execution, and if it was unnecessarily delayed, the public's desire for swift justice would be thwarted. Public sentiment could again turn ugly and produce violent mobs bent on lynching Fountain. Stitchberry knew he couldn't keep the current level of security at the county jail to protect Fountain if a determined mob launched another assault. The Maryland Militia troops were preparing to return to Salisbury, the special deputies would go back to their farms and businesses, and the Baltimore Police contingent would return to their duties in the city. A secret plan had already been laid to move the condemned man to Baltimore for safekeeping.

Stitchberry planned to transport Fountain to the boat dock at Easton Point, from where a steamer would take him to Baltimore. Easton Point was located about one and a half miles west of the jail, on the Tred Avon River. The Chesapeake Bay steamer *Talbot* was to dock at Easton Point and leave for Baltimore at 9:30 p.m. Only the sheriff and members of the Baltimore City Police contingent knew about the plan to move Fountain. Word got out, however, and people began to gather at Easton Point. When the sheriff learned about the assembled crowd there, he realized he would need to change his plan.[38]

The weather came to Sheriff Stitchberry's aid. High winds started blowing at Easton Point and increased to gale force by nightfall. Steamboat officials contacted Stitchberry and told him the *Talbot* would be landing at Oxford instead of Easton Point. Shortly after 8:00 p.m., the sheriff and Baltimore police assembled several automobiles and "autotrucks." The open trucks were driven to the jail without headlights and were met by an automobile parked just outside. Sheriff Stitchberry and Fountain, who was handcuffed to a Baltimore City policeman, quickly left the jail and got into the car. All the vehicles then sped to Oxford with their headlights extinguished, "making from 40 to 45 miles per hour." At Oxford, Fountain and his escorts immediately boarded the overnight steamer for Baltimore.[39]

In his diary entry on April 25, 1919, Charles Willis, a farmer from the Trappe district, recorded his observations: "The negro was taken to Balto. by about 28 city police, who had earlier appeared upon the scene to preserve order—as there were severe signs of Fountain being lynched—& he surely barely escaped."[40]

Fountain Speaks

The steamboat *Talbot* left Oxford, steamed south on the Tred Avon River, then headed west on the Choptank River before reaching the Chesapeake Bay. It then turned north to Baltimore. A *Baltimore Evening Sun* reporter who had been sworn in as a special deputy was aboard the *Talbot* during the trip. He reported that Isaiah Fountain had been placed in "stateroom No. 1." This was a rare "privilege" for Fountain, for Black people would have normally been denied such first-class accommodations under the Jim Crow laws of the time. The handcuffed Fountain spent the overnight voyage answering questions about his escape posed by Sheriff Stitchberry, the Baltimore City officers, and reporters. Fountain repeatedly denied raping Bertha Simpson and said, "Them folks down there lied on me and told things that were not true." He went on, "I got to die for something I did not do. I am going to take my medicine." Fountain continued, "I did not do it gentlemen. I will stick to that until the end. They got the wrong man."[41]

Fountain then spoke about his escape and why he ran from the lynch mob:

> Fountain declared time and time again. . . that he did not run away because he feared the outcome of his trial. 'Mr. Stitchberry is my good friend,' he said. 'He has always helped me and I know he will protect me all through this thing. I was not running to get away from him. I knew the crowd was after me. They was going to kill me and I was trying to get away.'
>
> '. . . I was running and I was putting out as fast as I could. I wanted to get as far away from Easton and them white

people as I could.' Fountain then said that until the jury brought in the verdict yesterday afternoon he always felt that he would be acquitted.[42]

The condemned Fountain then described the fear he experienced as the lynch mob had closed in on him, hollering, "Get him! Lynch him!" He said, "I knew I would be a dead nigger if they got me." Isaiah said that after escaping from the mob through the open window in the sheriff's house, he had run down the street behind the jail (West Street) and through "a big crowd of people" who apparently did not recognize him. After running through an alley and several other streets, he came across a Black man in a carriage. He told the man who he was and that "he wanted to get away." The other man told him to get into the carriage, and they traveled until they were near Ridgely, about seventeen miles from Easton. Fountain then walked the main road for five more miles until he reached Greensboro and then headed for Delaware where, he said, "I went to a farm where colored folks lived." He hid in the hayloft in the barn until the police patrol recaptured him.[43]

Fountain recounted his impressions of the high-speed race to get him back to Easton and the mobs of people gathered along the way:

> You remember there were crowds gathered on the roads in every town we passed through on the way back. They must have heard we was coming. Every time I saw a crowd I thought my time had come.
>
> I expected to be lynched at any moment. They shouted at me all the time. One of the policemen wanted to stop the machine to telephone, but Mr. Ledmus, the white fellow

driving, said he would not stop for anything until we reached the jail in Easton. Gentlemen, if he had stopped those men would have got me and I would be dead now. Well, they got me back and here I am.[44]

The *Talbot* and her condemned prisoner arrived at the Light Street Pier in Baltimore Harbor at 6:00 a.m. Friday, April 25, 1919. Fountain was quickly taken from the steamer to the imposing, stone castle-like Baltimore City Jail, less than a mile from the harbor. Isaiah Fountain would remain at the jail until his fate was decided by others.[45]

Endnotes

1 "Fountain Denies Guilt and Tries to Prove an Alibi," *Baltimore Evening Sun*, April 24, 1919, 2. Newspapers.com.

2 "Fountain Denies Guilt and Tries to Prove an Alibi," 2.

3 Fountain v. State (No. 39) (Court of Appeals of Maryland, Opinion of the Court. July 17, 1919*.), The Atlantic Reporter, Volume 107,* at 555. https://www.google.com/books/edition/The_Atlantic_Reporter/Kznb7Nl_5wUC?hl=en&gbpv=1&dq=the+Atlantic+reporter,+volume+107&pg=PR14&printsec=frontcover.

4 "Death Decree for Fountain," *Baltimore Sun*, April 25, 1919, 3. Newspapers.com.

5 "Death Decree for Fountain," 3. On April 23, the *Baltimore Evening Sun* expressed sympathy for the jury and wrote that the jury members were "the real victims of the Fountain escape," because of being "locked up and cut off from communications with the outside world." At the time the article was published, the jury had been sequestered for less than two days.

6 Isaiah Fountain v. State, April Term 1919 No. 39 [MSA S1733-530, 1/65/04/100]. Ct of Appeals, Defendant's Bill of Exception, filed June 19, 1919, at 33–34.

7 *Id.* at 33.

8 *Id.* at 34.

9 *Id.* at 34.

10 "Death Decree for Fountain," 3.

11 "Fountain Denies Guilt and Tries to Prove an Alibi," 2.

12 "Fountain Denies Guilt and Tries to Prove an Alibi," 2.

13 "Negro Assailant of White Girl to Hang," *Wilmington Evening Journal*, April 25, 1919, 3 and 24.

14 "Fountain Denies Guilt and Tries to Prove an Alibi," 2.

15 "Negro Assailant of White Girl to Hang," 3.

16 "Fountain Denies Guilt and Tries to Prove an Alibi," 2.

17 "Fountain Denies Guilt and Tries to Prove an Alibi," 2.

18 "Death Decree for Fountain," 3.

19 "Negro Assailant of White Girl to Hang," 24.

20 "Death Decree for Fountain," 3.

21 "Fountain Denies Guilt and Tries to Prove an Alibi," 2.

22 Isaiah Fountain v. State, April Term 1919 No. 39 [MSA S1733-530, 1/65/04/100]. Ct of Appeals: "Stipulation for Appeal," Isaiah Fountain v. State of Maryland, in the Court of Appeals of Maryland, No. 23, April Term, 1919, Appellant's Supplemental Brief on Evidence Only, at 51–52.

23 "Negro Assailant of White Girl to Hang," 3.

24 Isaiah Fountain v. State, Supplemental Brief on Evidence Only, April 23, 1919, at 50.

25 *Id.* at 50–51. O'Dunne mentioned that the distance from Easton to the crime scene was "7 miles." Perhaps there was a shortcut in 1919; traveling today's roads, the distance would be more like 8 to 9 miles, according to Google Maps.

26 "Fountain Denies Guilt and Tries to Prove an Alibi," 2. "Negro Assailant of White Girl to Hang," 24.

27 "Death Decree for Fountain," 3.

28 "Death Decree for Fountain," 3.

29 "Fountain's Case to Be Appealed," *Baltimore Afro-American*, May 2, 1919, A1. ProQuest.com.

30 "Negro Assaults 13-Year-Old Girl," *Evening Journal*, April 3, 1919, 5. Newspapers.com. "Negro Assaults Girl," 3.

31 "Negro Assailant of White Girl to Hang," *Wilmington Evening Journal*, April 25, 1919, 3. "Fountain Verdict Near," *Baltimore Sun*, May 8, 1920, 7. Newspapers.com.

32 "Death Decree for Fountain," 1.

33 "Death Decree for Fountain," 1.

34 "Fountain Found Guilty," *Easton Star-Democrat*, April 26, 1919, 1.

35 "Death Decree for Fountain," 1.

36 "Death Decree for Fountain," 1.

37 "Death Decree for Fountain," 1.

38 "Fountain Brought to City for Safety," *Baltimore Evening Sun*, April 25, 1919, 32. Newspapers.com.

39 "Fountain Brought to City for Safety," 32–23.

40 James Dawson, *100 Years of Change on the Eastern Shore: Extracts from the Willis Family Journals 1847–1951* (2015), 331.

41 "Condemned Negro Tells about His Dash for Liberty," *Baltimore Evening Sun*, April 25, 1919, 23. Newspapers.com.

42 "Condemned Negro Tells about His Dash for Liberty," 23.

43 "Condemned Negro Tells about His Dash for Liberty," 23.

44 "Condemned Negro Tells about His Dash for Liberty," 23.

45 "Fountain Brought Here," *Baltimore Sun*, April 26, 1919, 16. Newspapers.com.

CHAPTER 10

Media Wars

Of all the things to be resented, next to the crime itself,
the absolute contempt for the truth, the utter barefaced
lies published by the press of Baltimore city,
is most to be condemned.

—*EASTON STAR-DEMOCRAT*

The 1919 Media

Once Isaiah Fountain had been moved to the Baltimore
City Jail for safekeeping, he was physically out of the public
spotlight. His name and his legal battle, though, continued
to generate controversy. Fountain's defense lawyers had to
decide about appealing the outcome of his trial, while other
peripheral but related issues continued to make news.

Keep in mind that 1919 was decades removed from
television broadcasts, twenty-four-hour news channels, Facebook, Twitter, Instagram, YouTube, selfies, and other media
outlets that we now take for granted. Telephones were used,
but they were far from common. Newspapers were the social

media of the day, and the populace relied on them for news and opinion. During the more than two and a half years that the Fountain case was in the news, the main newspaper sources that I relied on for this book generated over 350 news articles, editorials, and other reports about the case. Hundreds more articles were written by other newspapers on the Eastern Shore, throughout Maryland, and in other states. The daily, and weekly papers were the public's only official source of news.

Stories directly and indirectly related to the Fountain case were trumpeted by the Baltimore newspapers and the Eastern Shore local papers. There had always been differences between the city newspapers and the Eastern Shore publications in the way the case was reported. During and after Fountain's trial these differences became even more distinct and divisive. The Baltimore papers were usually critical of the way the trial was conducted, the rush to judgment to convict Fountain, and the Eastern Shore attitudes about lynching. The local, weekly *Easton Star-Democrat* usually railed against the way the city papers wrote about the town, its citizens, and the actors in the local justice system. Private citizens made their feelings and opinions known by writing letters to the editors. If words were bullets, the readers of the time would have found their newspapers too heavy to lift.

The Opening Salvo

The first salvo of the media wars came from the *Easton Star-Democrat* after the conclusion of Isaiah Fountain's Easton trial. Clearly upset about the coverage of the events surrounding Fountain's trial and attempted lynching, the

Star-Democrat featured an angry editorial that attacked the reporting of the Baltimore newspapers.

The editorial began by citing the *Baltimore American*, *Baltimore Sun*, and *Baltimore News*, ". . . whose uncensored attempts at sensation at the expense of the truth were not only unfair but disgusting." According to the *Star-Democrat*, the articles were written by "the mob of raw cub reporters" sent to Easton by the Baltimore papers. Those papers, said the editorial, printed ". . . screaming headlines picturing our county as in the hands of an uncontrolled mob armed to the teeth and with blood in their hearts demanding and attempting the death of the prisoner without trial."[1]

The *Star Democrat* continued: "Nothing could be further from the truth. . . at no time was Isaiah Fountain in danger at the hands of the people of Talbot County. At no time has there been an armed mob about the court-house. At no time could one hear threats of lynching the negro." The writer then opined that Fountain didn't escape because of threats from an angry mob, but simply because he wasn't handcuffed and took advantage of the opportunity to escape "like any other prisoner accused of a capital crime."[2]

In defending Talbot County and its citizens, the editorial writer stated: "They have nothing to live down but the memory of a horrible crime, and the only scandal upon us is one that has been created by the lying reports of newspaper writers, whose chief object seems to have been the furnishing of sensation at the expense of our county." The editorial concluded by demanding that the Baltimore newspapers print retractions for ". . . the injustice they have done Talbot County and her citizens."[3]

Despite the editorial writer's assertions that Fountain had not been in danger and that there were no armed mobs or threats of lynching, another *Star-Democrat* article, in the *same edition* of the paper, told a different story. Contradicting the editorial, the article euphemistically described "the disturbances of Monday night, during which the prisoner escaped." Nor did the articles report that the judge spoke of the large crowd that tried in vain to lynch Fountain.[4]

The April 26, 1919 edition of the *Star-Democrat* featured a dozen articles (including the editorial) about Fountain's trial. For some reason, none of the *Star-Democrat* articles mentioned that Judge Adkins addressed the jury when the trial was resumed and was quoted in court documents as saying that Fountain ". . . escaped from violence." Nor did the articles report that the judge spoke of the large crowd that tried in vain to lynch Fountain.[5]

Despite the complaints about the reporting by the Baltimore media, the *Star-Democrat's* own coverage of the Fountain's attempted lynching was one-sided, uncoordinated, and sketchy. The Easton newspaper's first salvo of the Fountain case media wars was all gunpowder and no shot.

Barefaced Lies

Two days after Fountain's trial, the *Easton Star-Democrat* wrote of "the glances of grim satisfaction on the faces" of the people who watched the condemned man as he was taken from the courthouse to the jail. The paper continued, of the trial: "It has been the occasion of much that has been deeply deplore[d]. It has been exaggerated by the city press, embellished with sensational details that never happened, and insult on insult piled on a community known throughout the State as one of the most law abiding."[6]

The article ended with a damning statement that the paper set in bold type: **"Of all the things to be resented, next to the crime itself, the absolute contempt for the truth, the utter barefaced lies published by the press of Baltimore city, is most to be condemned."**[7] Later *Star-Democrat* articles mentioned "the malicious reports in Baltimore papers of the trial in Easton,"[8] "Baltimore Papers Lying,"[9] and "the lying accounts of the trial in the *Baltimore Sun* and other papers."[10] The war of words with the city newspapers continued.

Trial by Jury—or by Mob

Just two days after Isaiah Fountain's conviction, Eugene O'Dunne issued a statement. In it he said that there was clear bias at the trial and that the jury's verdict was not based upon the evidence but "according to the will of the mob." O'Dunne gave specifics:

> When a jury drawn locally from a rural community finds itself surrounded, in its consideration of a case, by some 2,000 of its neighbors, seething with indignation and clamoring for the life of an accused; when the jury sits in an atmosphere surcharged with hatred, race prejudice, desire for revenge; when the courtroom is packed to suffocation, and the clamoring populace on the outside, unable to get admission, is kept advised of the progress of the fake drama being enacted, under the guise of law, through the formal operation of the machinery of government, can the jury be said to be unmoved and unaffected by anything but the sworn testimony adduced in court?

As they walk around the jury rooms during recess hours, as they make their way through the crowds on Courthouse Plaza, and are led in a body through the streets to where their meals are served, and as they return to the Courthouse and pass through a line of State uniformed militiamen, with fixed bayonets, holding the crowd from the Courthouse doors, can they be said to be uninfluenced and unaffected by anything except the testimony received in open court from the witnesses under oath?[11]

"Is such a trial by jury, or is it a trial by the mob?" O'Dunne asked. He implied that the jury members were intimidated by the mob and wondered if they had "dared render a verdict which would have still further infuriated an angry populace, if such were possible?" Attorney O'Dunne then suggested that if his motion for a mistrial had been accepted by Judge Adkins, his client would have been lynched "then and there" by the angry mob. Further, O'Dunne said that if Fountain had been convicted and *not* received the death penalty, he would have been immediately lynched. The only way for Fountain to have left Talbot County alive, O'Dunne said, "was to go through the form of a conviction and sentence of death."[12]

O'Dunne's statement touched all the bases. He had censured the jury members, the trial judge, the mob, and the citizens of Talbot County. He had surely fired a powerful and explosive broadside on behalf of his client.

Calls for an Appeal

It didn't take long for even more anger to be generated in Talbot County. The *Baltimore Sun* published an editorial titled "Let Justice Be Done," arguing the need to appeal the conviction of Isaiah Fountain. The editorial agreed that if a community felt that justice couldn't be obtained in the courts, or if a guilty person escaped punishment because of legal technicalities, then it would be understandable if, right or wrong, "they [took] the matter into their own hands." The editorial then stated that Isaiah Fountain didn't have a fair trial and should be given a second chance:

> If the negro is not guilty, it would be equally regrettable and utterly shameful that he should be done to death simply because a crime has been committed that calls for a victim. It must be confessed that he did not have a fair trial, within the meaning of the law, at Easton. That was made impossible by the very natural aroused feeling of the people of the vicinity. If the verdict of the jury there represented essential justice, if there were no doubt of the guilt of the accused man, it might be possible to overlook the manner of the trial. But it seems there is serious doubts as to the guilt of the negro, in the minds of many who have read the full reports published of the trial and some who attended it. In their minds the alibi presented by his counsel was a convincing one.

> In view of these facts, it is desirable that the application for a new trial should be heard without prejudice and in an atmosphere far removed from that which enveloped the courtroom at Easton. Justice must be done, but justice means vindication for the innocent as well as swift punishment for the guilty.[13]

That same day, the *Sun* reported that a group of Baltimore businessmen had started a movement to take Fountain's case to the Maryland Court of Appeals. A spokesman for the group said that Fountain's race and guilty verdict were not the issues. He went on: "The point is that if one man can be sentenced to death under conditions which strongly suggest that the Court was intimidated by besieging mobs demanding conviction, the same fate may befall another."[14]

The same article reported that Sheriff James Stitchberry had received a "black hand letter" (that is, a letter threatening bodily harm) at his home in Easton. The letter threatened death to the sheriff, his family, Judge Adkins, the jury members, and the state's attorney, if Fountain were hanged. Stitchberry turned the letter over to the postal authorities for investigation.[15]

In Defense of the Court

The *Easton Star-Democrat* quickly responded to the *Sun*'s push for a new trial for Fountain. The paper complained that an appeal would result in "the ultimate punishment of the negro [being] deferred until sometime next year." It continued: "This condition has resulted entirely because of the lying accounts of the trial in the *Baltimore Sun* and other papers, which had created a sympathy for the prisoner which is entirely undeserved." The *Star-Democrat* then quoted Edwin Brown, editor of the *Centreville Record* and state's attorney of adjacent Queen Anne's County. Brown wrote that the newspapers were not the place to try the Fountain case and that "it is not very becoming of the reputable citizens of Baltimore to attempt to cast reflections on the Talbot court from hearsay and from accounts in the papers." Brown went on to defend the Talbot County Circuit Court, saying: "This court is a fearless one; it is not afraid of mobs and is not swayed by public opinion, and their judgment is always based on the evidence and not what the people want. This has been shown in many cases that have been tried before them, and we resent the imputation that is now being placed on them, and know that it is unjust, uncalled-for, and not fair."[16]

Brown's defense of the Talbot County Circuit Court must have earned him points as a state's attorney and prosecutor. Judge Adkins, whose actions Brown so boldly defended, was the chief judge of the Second Judicial Circuit that happened to include Queen Anne's County where Brown was the state's attorney.

Judicial Fairness

While the *Star-Democrat* expressed concern about the perceived unfairness being shown to the Talbot County Circuit Court, Baltimore's *Afro-American* newspaper was more concerned about the unfair treatment that the Jim Crow judicial system was according Isaiah Fountain and other Black people. The *Afro* reported that Lee Calding, a White man in Anne Arundel County, Maryland, had been arrested for sexually assaulting a thirteen-year-old "colored girl." Unlike Fountain, Calding was released on bail and the county grand jury chose not to indict him. He was released because "the colored child did not report the case until one week after it happened." Asking its readers to compare the Calding case with Isaiah Fountain's, the paper wrote, "a fool could see how much chance Calding would have for his life in Annapolis if he had been colored and the child would have been white."[17]

Talbot Gives Its Side

In response to the *Easton Star-Democrat*'s charges that the *Baltimore Sun* lied about how the town had reacted during the trial of Isaiah Fountain, the *Sun* sent a staff correspondent to get Talbot County's side of the story. The *Sun* wrote about its intentions:

> The people of Talbot County feeling that they have been unjustly reflected upon by the accounts in *The Sun* and other Baltimore papers, and that the attitude of its people had been misrepresented in regard to the Fountain trial. *The Sun*, at the request of a number of residents of the county, sent a staff correspondent to Easton to enable them to present their side of the situation.[18]

The visiting *Sun* reporter then reviewed the trial and the other events that had been reported. The *Sun* reported: "A negro brute had debauched a gentle young girl in so horrible a way that death . . . would seem almost a God's mercy to her." The reporter agreed that the community had a right to be upset by such a brutal crime but said that "all the foremost men of the county worked together to prevent lynching, and were supported by the substantial men from every section of the county." The reporter talked with various local people, who all agreed that most of the trouble was caused "by visitors from other places." Easton Mayor Francis Wrightson was interviewed and said that Fountain had received a fair trial. Wrightson added that most residents wanted the law "to take its course." Wrightson agreed that "there were some young fellows and larger boys, who talked a great deal," who might be influenced by others and he further noted: "We

feared that this sort of a case would bring to the town reck-
less men from neighboring counties and Delaware—there
are some everywhere—and that a bold spirit might organize
a lynching gang. There was always the danger that such
men might bring in whiskey, too." According to Wrightson:
"Under all the circumstances [Easton's citizens] exercised
great restraint."[19]

Although the *Sun* printed comments from local officials
that defended the local judiciary, leadership, and citizens, the
paper concluded that how the facts about the case are interpreted depends on whom one talks to. The paper wrote:

> Men who came to Talbot County while the case was in
> court here in Easton saw one thing; residents of Talbot
> County saw another thing.
>
> The visitors saw the irresistible demand of a community
> for the life of a man who it believed guilty of the worst of
> crimes, committed in the worst of ways. The home people
> of Talbot saw in the same events the struggle of an old and
> finely schooled community of English blood to proceed
> in the business of punishment according to the law, rather
> than to the natural impulses of every man worthy of the
> name of man.[20]

The *Star–Democrat* was not satisfied with the *Sun's*
attempt to mend journalistic fences and print justifiable
explanations from Talbot County citizens. It reprinted por-
tions of the *Sun's* article but wrote: "The *Sun* admits no
wrongdoing on its part and probably thinks it has done its
full duty."[21] So much for the *Sun's* efforts to present both sides
of the story—the thin-skinned *Star–Democrat* was not yet
ready to accept an olive branch.

O'Dunne's Compensation

Even the fees that Eugene O'Dunne received for his defense of Isaiah Fountain created media controversy. In the *Sun*'s article of April 29, 1919, reporting a movement to have the Fountain case appealed, one sentence started the controversy. It read: "It is understood that [O'Dunne] defended Fountain without compensation."[22] The statement was inaccurate, and the *Easton Star-Democrat*, as well as many readers of the *Sun*, reacted vigorously. The *Star-Democrat* responded with an article that again accused the *Sun* of lying, saying: "The Baltimore papers are lauding the disinterestedness of Attorney Eugene O'Dunne, counsel for Isaiah Fountain, in that he was counsel without any remuneration. If Mr. O'Dunne has contradicted any of these statements it has not been observed." The Easton paper then described a bill of sale that was recorded by the Talbot County Clerk of Court and signed by Isaiah Fountain for "value received." To pay O'Dunne his attorney's fees, Fountain had signed over to O'Dunne farm equipment, animals, and crops "valued easily at $600 or more." The paper also reported that O'Dunne received a "counsel fee" of $100 from Talbot County.[23]

More letters were then sent to the *Baltimore Sun*'s editor, criticizing the paper's reporting as well as Eugene O'Dunne's pay for Isaiah Fountain's defense. O'Dunne defended his professional compensation with his own letter to the paper. He stated that he didn't take on the Fountain defense through "humanitarian impulses," but "in the practice of my profession, and for which I expected to be fairly and fully compensated." He said that having Fountain's assets signed over to him was suggested by his co-counsel, Colonel James

Mullikin, and that he had never stated that he was handling Fountain's defense on a pro bono basis.[24]

Letters to the Editors

Of course, the many letters to the editors of the various newspapers often added fuel to the flames of the media war. Some asserted that Isaiah Fountain was guilty and deserved the harshest punishment available. Some felt that the Talbot County trial and the related events were totally justified. Some applauded Attorney O'Dunne's statements about the conduct of the trial, while others condemned him for casting aspersions on the court and the citizens of Talbot County. One letter would often incite others, keeping the sparks of controversy about the Fountain case glowing. The mere idea of appealing Fountain's conviction inspired still more spirited opinions and editorial attacks. The media war continued.

Endnotes

1 Editorial, *Easton Star-Democrat*, April 26, 1919, 5.

2 Editorial, 5.

3 Editorial, 5.

4 "The Negro's Return." *Easton Star-Democrat*, April 26, 1919, 6.

5 Isaiah Fountain v. State, April Term 1919 No. 39 [MSA S1733-530, 1/65/04/100]. Ct of Appeals, Defendant's Bill of Exception, filed June 19, 1919, at 33–34.

6 "Fountain Found Guilty," *Easton Star-Democrat*, April 26, 1919, 1.

7 "Fountain Found Guilty," 1.

8 "Want Fountain Retried," *Easton Star-Democrat*, May 3, 1919, 1.

9 "O'Dunne's Pay," *Easton Star-Democrat*, May 3, 1919, 2.

10 "Want a New Trial," *Easton Star-Democrat*, May 10, 1919, 2.

11 "Fountain's Counsel Issues Statement," *Baltimore Evening Sun*, April 26, 1919, 16. Newspapers.com.

12 "Fountain's Counsel Issues Statement," 16.

13 "Let Justice Be Done," *Baltimore Sun*, April 29, 1919, 4. Newspapers.com.

14 "Would Try Fountain Again," *Baltimore Sun*, April 29, 1919, 13. Newspapers.com.

15 "Would Try Fountain Again," 13.

16 "Want a New Trial," 2.

17 "Alleged White Rapist Goes Free," *Baltimore Afro-American*, May 2, 1919, A1. ProQuest.com.

18 "Talbot Gives Its Side," *Baltimore Sun*, May 11, 1919, 6. Newspapers.com.

19 "Talbot Gives Its Side," 6.

20 "Talbot Gives Its Side," 6.

21 "The Sun Investigates," *Easton Star-Democrat*, May 17, 1919, 11.

22 "Would Try Fountain Again," 13.

23 "O'Dunne's Pay," 2.

24 "Mr. O'Dunne Replies to Letters," *Baltimore Sun*, May 8, 1919, 10. Newspapers.com.

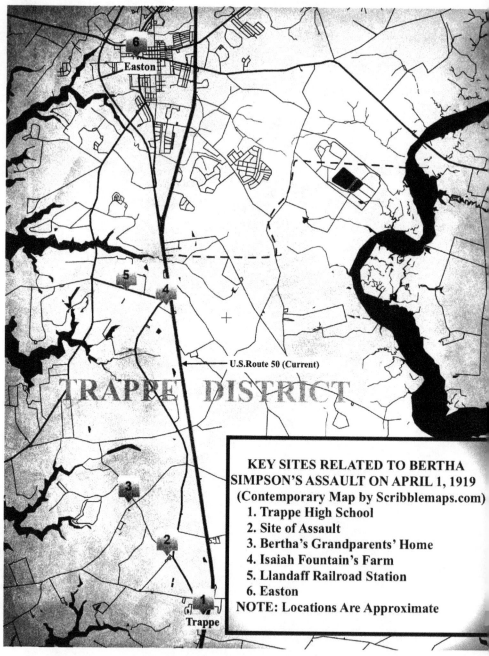

KEY SITES RELATED TO BERTHA
SIMPSON'S ASSAULT ON APRIL 1, 1919
(Contemporary Map by Scribblemaps.com)
1. Trappe High School
2. Site of Assault
3. Bertha's Grandparents' Home
4. Isaiah Fountain's Farm
5. Llandaff Railroad Station
6. Easton
NOTE: Locations Are Approximate

This contemporary map shows the relationship of the various sites
associated with the assault of Bertha Simpson on April 1, 1919.
(Adapted from Google/Scribblemaps.com)

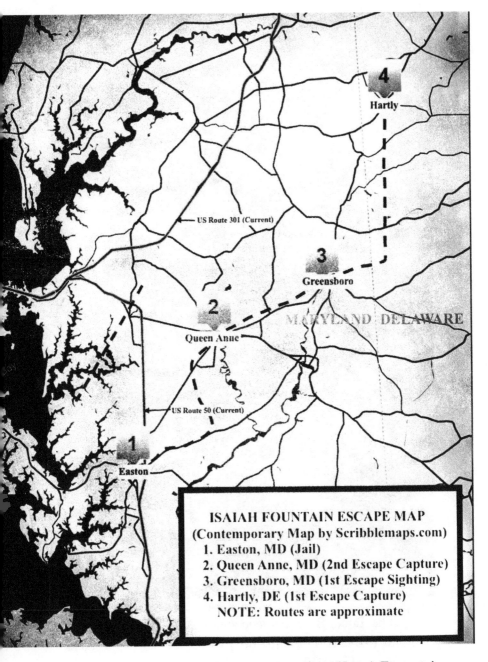

US Route 301 (Current)

4
Hartly

3
Greensboro

2
Queen Anne

MARYLAND DELAWARE

US Route 50 (Current)

1
Easton

ISAIAH FOUNTAIN ESCAPE MAP
(Contemporary Map by Scribblemaps.com)
1. Easton, MD (Jail)
2. Queen Anne, MD (2nd Escape Capture)
3. Greensboro, MD (1st Escape Sighting)
4. Hartly, DE (1st Escape Capture)
NOTE: Routes are approximate

This contemporary map shows the approximate routes of Isaiah Fountain's two escapes from custody in Easton. (Adapted from Google/Scribblemaps. com)

The Talbot Boys Confederate monument was completed in 1916 during the period of "Lost Cause" fervor. After years of protests to remove it, the monument was moved to another location on March 14, 2022 after a vote by the Talbot County Council. (J. Koper)

Joseph B. Seth (1845-1927) came from a slave-holding family in Talbot County and was a believer in the "Lost Cause" myth. He was also a major organizer of the movement to erect the Talbot Boys Confederate monument in front of the Talbot County Courthouse in Easton. (Talbot Historical Society)

The Trappe High School where Bertha Simpson was a student was located on Main Street in Trappe, Maryland. The site is now occupied by the Veterans' Memorial Park. (UnicornBookshop.com)

Negro Fiend Not Found.

The negro fiend who assaulted the little 11-year-old daughter of Mr and Mrs. Robert Simpson. near Trappe, on Tuesday afternoon, had not been apprehended at 3 o'clock yesterday afternoon. The State's attorney and sheriff have been diligent since the case was first reported to them, and they will not let up until the man is arrested While Talbot is loath to think of lynch law in this county, yet it must be admitted that there has been much probabilities of this. Several clues as to the man's whereabouts are being followed by the officers and there is little doubt but that he will be found in a very short time. Intense feeling is shown in Trappe district over the outrage and this is not confined to the locality where the assault was committed. but in the county generally.

The Easton *Star-Democrat* news article from April 5, 1919, reported the assault of Bertha Simpson. (Maryland Room, Talbot County Free Library/ *Star-Democrat*)

A front view mugshot photo of Isaiah Fountain was taken when he was booked at the Baltimore City Jail following his arrest in West Chester, Pennsylvania and before his return to Easton for trial. (*Baltimore Sun*/Newspapers.com)

TALBOT COUNTY COURT HOUSE AND JAIL, EASTON, MD.

HAND-COLORED

The Talbot County Courthouse in Easton, MD is shown with the sheriff's house and jail located to its right side and rear. The photo was taken prior to the erection of the Talbot Boys Confederate monument in 1916. (Talbot Historical Society)

A contemporary photograph of the Talbot County Courthouse shows the Talbot Boys Confederate monument (left) and the Frederick Douglass monument (right). (J. Koper)

Talbot County Circuit Court Chief Judge William H. Adkins (1862-1950). Adkins presided at Isaiah Fountain's trial in Easton and offered a $5,000 reward for the capture of Fountain after his escape from a lynch mob. The verdict of the trial was later appealed and a new trial was granted. (*Baltimore Sun/* Newspapers.com)

Eugene O'Dunne (1875-1959) was Isaiah Fountain's chief defense lawyer. O'Dunne was a prominent Baltimore lawyer, a former assistant state's attorney, and professor of criminal law at the University of Baltimore. (Maryland State Archives)

This 1930 photo shows the Talbot County sheriff's house and jail (located to the right rear). The jail yard was located to the left of the front porch. (Maryland Room, Talbot County Free Library)

This contemporary photo shows the rear of the Talbot County Courthouse from the porch of the old sheriff's house. The jurors from Isaiah Fountain's trial were still in the second-story courtroom as Fountain was being taken to the sheriff's house. From the courtroom's multi-paned casement windows, they had a bird's eye view of the mob that tried to lynch Fountain. (J. Koper)

The former Talbot County sheriff's house and jail is now the office of the Talbot County state's attorney. The view is from the rear of the courthouse. (J. Koper)

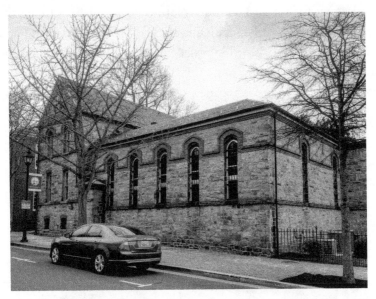

The photo shows the north side and rear of the former Talbot County sheriff's house and jail, built in 1878. For Isaiah Fountain's execution a gallows was custom-built inside the jail in the corridor just behind the five arched windows. The building is now used as the Talbot County's state's attorney's office (J. Koper)

Price Of $5,000 On His Head

ISAIAH FOUNTAIN.
Profile and Full Face View.
The pictures above show two photo-graphs of Isaiah Fountain, who is being hunted by posses all over the Eastern Shore. Judge Adkins, of the Easton Court, has put a price of $5,000 on his head if captured and surrendered to the Court alive.

A mug shot and reward advertisement appeared in various newspapers during the massive dragnet for Isaiah Fountain. Note that the caption states that Fountain must be "surrendered to the court alive" in order for the person who captures him to qualify for the reward. (*Baltimore Sun*/Newspapers.com)

The photo shows the window through which Isaiah Fountain crawled to escape the lynch mob. Once through the window, he jumped from the shed roof into the jail yard below. (*Baltimore Evening Sun*/Newspapers.com)

The photo shows the front and side of the Talbot County sheriff's house and the location of the window that Isaiah Fountain crawled through (arrow) to escape the lynch mob. (*Baltimore Evening Sun*/Newspapers.com)

This view of the Talbot County jail yard shows where Isaiah Fountain used a pile of lumber to climb over the fence to escape from the mob trying to lynch him. (*Baltimore Evening Sun*/Newspapers.com)

The photo shows the rear and side of the Talbot County jail from West Street. An "X" marks the spot where Isaiah Fountain crawled over the wooden jail yard fence to escape south on West Street. (*Baltimore Evening Sun*/Newspapers.com)

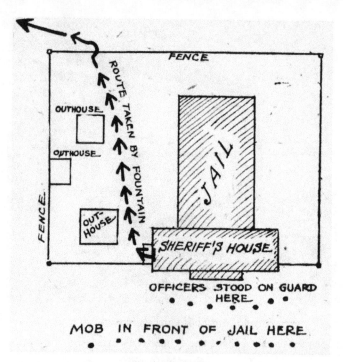

The sketch shows the route Isaiah Fountain took to escape the lynch mob. While the lynch mob was gathered in front of the sheriff's house, Fountain crawled through an open window, ran through the adjacent jail yard, climbed the wooden fence, and ran south on West Street. (*Baltimore Evening Sun*/Newspapers.com)

Sheriff Stitchberry's wife, Annie, tried to protect Isaiah Fountain from the lynch mob gathered outside the jail. Annie cautioned Fountain to keep low in case shots were fired, but Fountain crawled through an open window and escaped through the adjacent jail yard. Fountain's escape while in her custody so angered Annie that she later said she would be glad if the lynch mob "tore him to pieces." (*Baltimore Evening Sun*/Newspapers.com)

A large crowd of outraged citizens gathered on the courthouse lawn in front of the jail to see Isaiah Fountain after his capture in Hartly, Delaware. Several local leaders spoke to the crowd before Fountain arrived at the jail. The leaders pleaded with the crowd to remain calm and let justice take its course. The view is from the front of the Talbot County sheriff's house and jail looking toward Washington Street and the north side of the courthouse. (*Baltimore Evening Sun*/Newspapers.com)

After his capture in Delaware, a shackled and frightened Isaiah Fountain is led through the excited crowd to the safety of the Talbot County jail by a Baltimore City Police officer. (*Baltimore Evening Sun*/Newspapers.com)

This editorial cartoon compares the Easton lynch mob's threats to lynch Isaiah Fountain with the opposition and anger various countries had against secret treaties following World War I. (*Baltimore Evening Sun*/Newspapers.com)

This aerial view of the Talbot County Courthouse square shows the relationship of the courthouse and jail. In all likelihood, Fountain would have been taken from the right side door of the courthouse to the front door of the sheriff's house, with the lynch mob assembled in front of, and to the right side of, the courthouse. (H. Robbins Hollyday Collection, Talbot Historical Society)

The bay steamer *Talbot* was the vessel that transported Isaiah Fountain from Oxford to Baltimore following his first trial. During the overnight trip Fountain stayed in a stateroom with his guards. Normally, during the Jim Crow era, Blacks would not have been permitted in staterooms on the bay steamers, but assigned to lesser segregated accommodations. (Oxford Museum Photo Archives)

CONVICTED NEGRO WHO ESCAPED FROM JAIL.

This "snapshot" of Isaiah Fountain was made in the Court Room at Towson when he was facing the Court for his second trial. Upon the granting of a new trial the case was removed from Talbott to Baltimore county.

The Towson *Jeffersonian* newspaper printed a courtroom sketch of Isaiah Fountain that was drawn during his second trial in Towson. (Maryland State Archives)

Easton Chief of Police William R. Stoops was one of three prominent White witnesses who confirmed Isaiah Fountain's alibi about being in Easton at about the time of the crime. Despite their prominence in the community, the witnesses' objective testimonies in both trials were ignored. (Maryland Room, Talbot County Free Library)

The imposing Baltimore County Courthouse in Towson was the site for Isaiah Fountain's second trial. (Enoch Pratt Free Library, Maryland State Library Resource Center)

Baltimore County Circuit Court Judge T. Scott Offutt (1872-1943) was the presiding judge at Isaiah Fountain's second trial in Towson. Judge Offutt issued the statement of the tribunal's reasons for convicting and condemning Fountain. In the statement, Offutt admitted that the judges modified the timeline of the crime so that it was possible for Fountain to travel to the crime scene to be able to commit the rape. At the same time, the judges ignored the testimonies of three very credible White witnesses who corroborated Fountain's alibi of being in Easton at about the same time the crime was being committed. (*Distinguished Men of Baltimore and Maryland.* 1914, Baltimore: Baltimore American)

FOUNTAIN'S MOTHER ROUGHLY HANDLED — MEANWHILE MOB STOLE HER CHICKENS

This editorial cartoon appeared in the *Baltimore Afro-American* newspaper illustrating the rough treatment suffered by Isaiah Fountain's mother, Fannie, during Isaiah's second escape dragnet. (*Baltimore Afro-American*/Ancestry.com)

July 23 Friday at 3:15 this morning a niger I. Fountain was hanged in Easton for the crime of assault of a white girl & own in Kappe district. People were very well worked & a niger uprising was feared and some politicians tried to sang the niger but Iuffe would not sland for it.) *July 24 Saturday*

On July 23, 1920, sixteen year old Alice Gale Reddie wrote the above diary entry about the early morning execution of Isaiah Fountain. Alice and her family lived on South Harrison Street, just a few blocks from the Talbot County Jail, where Fountain was hanged. (Alice Gale Reddie Diary, Talbot Historical Society)

This photograph depicts a scene in the 1928 silent movie, *The First Kiss*, starring Gary Cooper and Fay Wray, which was filmed in the same Talbot County courtroom where Isaiah Fountain was tried just a few years earlier. It's difficult to imagine this room packed with over 400 deputies and policemen, plus spectators and court officials, as it was for Fountain's first trial in Easton. (H. Robins Hollyday Collection, Talbot Historical Society)

What Is Civilization?

IF LYNCHING PARTIES DO THIS IN MISSISSIPPI:

AND OFFICERS OF THE LAW DO THIS IN EASTON, MD.:

ISN'T IT AL-RIGHT FOR NEW GUINEA SAVAGES TO DO THIS?

Lawsuits were filed against Talbot County Sheriff Charles Soulsby for acts of cruelty to Isaiah Fountain's mother and other local African Americans. Soulsby was also accused of physically mistreating Fountain prior to his execution. The Baltimore Afro-American cartoon compares the alleged Talbot County cruelty to a lynching in Mississippi and "savages" cooking people alive in New Guinea. (*Baltimore Afro-American*/Ancestry.com)

The grim north corridor of the old Talbot County Jail, with barred windows, overlooks Federal Street. According to newspaper accounts, Isaiah Fountain's execution was conducted in this area of the jail. A custom-built gallows was constructed in the cramped corridor to ensure that Fountain's execution would be private and secure from angry spectators. (H. Robins Hollyday Collection, Talbot Historical Society)

The Oxford High School on North Morris Street in Oxford, Maryland was located on the north side of the Oxford Town Park, where the Oxford United Methodist Church now stands. The high school was attended by a second Talbot County girl, who was allegedly attacked on her way home from school by a local Black man. (Oxford Museum Photo Archives)

CHAPTER 11

Fountain and the Court of Appeals

It must be confessed that he did not have a fair trial,
within the meaning of the law, at Easton.

—BALTIMORE SUN

Fountain's Appeal

While Isaiah Fountain languished in the Baltimore City Jail and the city and Eastern Shore newspapers engaged in their war of words about his case, his lawyers worked on his appeal. Eugene O'Dunne argued that the circumstances surrounding Isaiah's first trial made a fair decision impossible. O'Dunne felt that the lynching attempt, Fountain's escape, Judge Adkins's reward offer, threats of mob violence, and the martial atmosphere surrounding the courthouse had intimidated not only the jury, but also the judges. O'Dunne felt that under these circumstances, Fountain could not get a fair trial.

Fountain's attorneys, O'Dunne and Mullikin, filed their appeal with the Maryland Court of Appeals in Annapolis on May 3, 1919. In the next few weeks, they would file for extensions to further prepare the appeal, have typewritten transcripts of the trial sent to the appeals court, and submit the printed records and briefs for the appeal. Finally, the Maryland Court of Appeals set June 24, 1919, to hear the oral arguments in the case of *Isaiah Fountain v. State*.[1]

Appeal Issues

Fountain's appeal was based on two main issues. First, as soon as Fountain's trial continued after his escape and capture, Lawyer O'Dunne had made a motion to postpone it because the mob violence would have influenced the jury and the court. That motion was immediately denied by Chief Judge Adkins. Second, when the trial resumed, Judge Adkins had asked the jury to "forget" what had happened earlier, saying, "We want you to go back to the trial as if there was no interruption. The case will be resumed with the understanding that you are to absolutely forget that there has been any interruption." O'Dunne had promptly objected and again been overruled by Judge Adkins.[2]

The very first sentence of Eugene O'Dunne's appellant's brief to the Maryland Court of Appeals was shocking. It read: "Paradoxical as it may sound, *the sentence of death was the only thing that saved the prisoner's life.*" [Emphasis added.] O'Dunne also said that "the docket entries in the Fountain case emphasize the fact that too much haste in a criminal case also produces a miscarriage of justice."[3]

One of the documents that the defense sent to the court of appeals contained a timeline listing the dates and various steps of the legal proceedings against Isaiah Fountain. In the item following his recapture, the defense team caustically wrote, "April 24. So-called trial resumed." There is no record of whether O'Dunne and Mullikin's pointed sarcasm was noticed by the appeals court.[4]

In his motion O'Dunne continued his argument by describing to the Appeals judges how the crowd that gathered outside the courthouse during the trial had turned violent and threatened to lynch Isaiah Fountain. It was the fear of death, said O'Dunne, that caused Fountain to escape from the violent two-thousand-strong mob. The defense team described how Judge Adkins—in the presence of the jury—announced that the defendant had escaped and then offered a reward for his capture. They recounted how, when the trial continued, the jury was first exposed to the angry crowds and the presence of hundreds of deputies, policemen, and militia troops with fixed bayonets and then asked by Judge Adkins to forget all that had happened before the trial was interrupted. Adding to their own descriptions, Fountain's lawyers presented various newspaper articles that detailed the trial, the attempt to lynch Fountain, his escape, and other related events.[5]

Lawyers O'Dunne and Mullikin argued that Isaiah Fountain was denied due process in his trial because the orderly proceedings of law were interrupted and influenced by mob violence. They said that the jury had been prejudiced to believe that Fountain was guilty by Judge Adkins's announcement that he had escaped from custody. They also argued that both the jury and the court had been intimidated by the angry and violent crowds surrounding the courthouse. The presence of the mob had so influenced the jury, they maintained, that it was unable to render a free and fair verdict, "solely from the standpoint of the law and the evidence given under oath in open Court."[6]

Evidentiary Consideration
(The Victim's Identification)

Fountain's lawyers also submitted to the court of appeals a supplemental brief that analyzed different phases of testimony and questionable evidence from the trial. They wanted the appeals judges to review the evidence relating to Fountain's identification, his alibi of being in Easton at the time of the crime, and his flight to escape death by lynching.

The first testimony that Fountain's lawyers sought to undermine was Bertha Simpson's identification of Isaiah Fountain as her attacker. The defense questioned the initial photo identification of the assailant. Although Sheriff Stitchberry and two other people were asked to be present, only State's Attorney Butler and Bertha Simpson's grandmother were in fact in the room when the girl identified Fountain from photos. The defense argued that the identification was flawed because Simpson's two uncles had already viewed the same photos the night before and had possibly coached their niece to identify Fountain. Also, the defense argued, Fountain had already been indicted before Simpson even identified a photo of him. The defense lawyers cast doubt on the photo identification also because Bertha had probably seen Fountain in the neighborhood at times before she was raped. His face was familiar to her, so she picked his photo out from others of total strangers. The defense concluded that "We all know photographic identification is inherently weak and unsatisfactory."[7]

Nor were the defense lawyers satisfied with Bertha's identification of Isaiah Fountain in court. First, they said, just a few minutes before she testified in court, her memory was "*refreshed* by the defendant's photograph being shown to her." This coaching was done by a private detective who had been helping her with the identification. Second, when she was asked to identify Fountain during the trial, he was the only Black man in the room. Despite this, she initially could not identify him and said, "I can't see him very good." Only when Fountain was asked to stand within ten feet of her did she eventually select him.[8]

Supplemental Issues (Fountain's Alibi)

The defense attorneys pointed out in their brief that Bertha Simpson had pinpointed the time of her assault as being between 4:30 and 5:00 p.m., after leaving school at 3:30 that afternoon. They said that Isaiah Fountain's movements on that day were described in detail during the defense's opening statement and *before* the victim even testified to the time of the assault. The defense team calculated the distance from Easton to the assault site and argued that it would have been impossible for Fountain to drive his horse and buggy to the crime scene and rape the victim, given her own testimony. Said the defense: "As the testimony developed, it showed that the defendant *was in the town of Easton at the time the girl was assaulted some seven miles from there.*"[9]

Fountain's lawyers went on to mention that several "people of unimpeachable veracity" (that is, a White bank teller and two White government officials) confirmed that Isaiah Fountain was in Easton at the time of the rape. These individuals, they said, "confirm his statement, *and fix the time* of the transactions, with such reasonable certainty, as to make his presence 6 to 7 miles [actually, nine or ten miles] from there, at the time of the assault, *a physical impos-sibility, under the circumstances.*" How, the defense argued, could Fountain have been in Easton until after 5:00 p.m. and yet have assaulted Bertha Simpson between 4:30 and 5:00? Fountain's lawyers declared that the jury completely ignored this unimpeachable testimony and, "in less than five minutes' deliberation, ... returned [a] unanimous verdict in accordance with the public demonstration of the WILL OF THE MOB!" The defense, using capital letters to drive their point home as emphatically as possible, again emphasized that: "THE IMMEDIATE SENTENCE OF DEATH, BEFORE THE CROWD DISPERSED, WAS THE ONLY THING THAT SAVED THE PRISONER'S LIFE!!"[10]

Other Supplemental Issues
(Including Stitchberry and Butler)

Attorneys O'Dunne and Mullikin next argued that the local citizenry and county authorities (that is, the Talbot County State's Attorney) had presumed that Fountain was guilty of Bertha Simpson's rape because he happened to leave the area the morning after the crime. Despite the accused's reasonable explanation that he traveled to New Jersey to find his wife—and had told other people that he planned to do so—the public and authorities had all concluded that he fled the area because he was guilty of the crime.[11]

Another important issue developed after the trial and was included in Fountain's appeal. Six weeks after the trial, Sheriff Stitchberry visited Eugene O'Dunne in his Balti-more office and provided the defense lawyer with an affidavit detailing key information that was not presented by the state's attorney during the trial. The defense lawyers acknowledged that by providing this new information for the appeal, Stitchberry's actions were "intensely unpopular in his county." However, it proved him to be a "man of high character and imperturbable courage."[12]

This new information enabled Fountain's team to ask why Sheriff Stitchberry, the chief investigator of the crime, was not fully questioned about his part in the investigation during the trial by State's Attorney Butler. If he had been questioned, Stitchberry could have testified that Bertha Simpson did not identify Fountain's farm horse and decrepit buggy as being the ones involved in the crime. She had identified the horse as having a long curly tail, which Fountain's horse did not. She also described the horse as being good-looking and having a new harness and reins, not matching Fountain's shabby buggy and tack! Stitchberry could have told the court that just such a good-looking horse and buggy had been driven at the time and place of the crime by a Black man named Eugene Wells. The appeal defense charged that State's Attorney Butler was aware of the suspicions about Wells but had never investigated him or had Simpson try to identify him. O'Dunne stated: "The will of the mob was 'give us FOUNTAIN. We want FOUNTAIN,' and Fountain they got!"[13]

Finally, the defense team alleged that State's Attorney Butler knowingly withheld Sheriff Stitchberry's investigative information that would have aided Isaiah Fountain's case. In this regard, O'Dunne and Mullikin questioned the state's attorney's ethics and impartiality:

Where human life hangs in the balance, if the State, in the face of the sentiment of the County, did not want to develop the testimony in the breast of the Sheriff, would not the law of "*fair and impartial trial*" have made it eminently appropriate, if not MORALLY OBLIGATORY, to have *privately* communicated to the counsel for defense the alleged existence of such testimony[?][14]

O'Dunne and Mullikin wanted it to be clear to the court of appeals that the state's attorney and Sheriff Stitchberry had very different agendas. The difference had been displayed at the trial by the evidence and testimony that Butler presented—and withheld—during Fountain's prosecution.

The State Responds to Fountain's Appeal

Three attorneys represented the State of Maryland in answering Isaiah Fountain's appeal. They were Attorney General Albert Ritchie, Assistant Attorney General Ogle Marbury, and Talbot County State's Attorney Charles Butler.[15] The State's written brief in response to Fountain's appeal was only twelve pages long.

The State of Maryland began its argument by saying that Fountain's jury was not at all affected by "the public excitement caused by the escape" because it was totally unaware of "all knowledge of conditions and circumstances surrounding the escape and the effort to recapture the prisoner and bring him back." The attorneys continued their argument for the State:

It would therefore seem that the jurors who finally convicted Fountain were the only men in the county who had

164

[no] knowledge of the public excitement occasioned by his escape, and they were, therefore, of all the people in Talbot County, the ones who could best deal impartially with the question of his guilt or innocence if the public excitement was so great as to influence the minds of those who came in contact with it.[16]

The state's attorneys continued by saying that Judge Adkins's announcement in the presence of the jury about Isaiah Fountain's escape was not prejudicial. Any prejudice attached to that announcement, the State said, was erased by Judge Adkins's statement to the jury when the trial reconvened after the defendant's capture. The fact that Adkins told the jury to forget about what had happened was sufficient to erase any bias the jury members might have formed against Fountain. The State even went so far as to argue that Judge Adkins's statement was prejudicial *to the State* and not Isaiah Fountain. Referring to Adkins's statement, they said: "It was a statement by the Court to the jury putting the case in the most favorable light possible for the defendant, without requiring him to show the conditions in such a way as to intimidate the jury."[17]

The State insisted that the Fountain jury had no way to know *anything* about Fountain's near lynching, his escape, the angry mobs around the courthouse, or the large number of deputies, police, and militia troops assembled around the courthouse. The State claimed: "The public state of mind did not in any way reach the jury, is not alleged to have reached the jury, and on the contrary is shown by the record to have been kept from the jury by the seclusion of the latter."[18]

The State's lawyers then appeared to hedge their bets by saying that possibly the jury was aware of some "public excitement" after all, and that their impartiality could have changed. The State's argument continued:

> It should be observed in this connection that in a case of the character of this one there is always more or less public excitement. It would be impossible to have a trial of one accused of such a crime without some excitement or prejudice. There is no constitutional right in the accused to have his trial in a place free from all popular feeling. The right is only to a fair and impartial trial by a jury. The jury must be impartial at the time of its selection. It is not claimed in any way that the jury which convicted this appellant was not impartial. On the contrary, the record shows that it was selected without any challenges. The jury, of course, was not expected to continue impartial during the trial. It was there to become partial and to decide in accordance with its opinion.
>
> *If the question before the lower Court was whether any popular prejudice reached the jury, it must be remembered that there is no such allegation. Under such circumstances, it could never be said that there was an abuse of discretion by the trial Court.* [Emphasis in document.][19]

Fountain's defense lawyers and the State's lawyers presented their oral arguments to the judges of the Maryland Court of Appeals in the afternoon of June 24, 1919. Fountain's prosecutor, Talbot County State's Attorney Charles Butler, was listed as one of the attorneys for the State and, by custom, was asked to take part in the oral proceedings. Butler declined to take part, possibly due to being a candidate for re-election.[20] Isaiah Fountain's fate was again in the hands of judges.

The Appeals Court Decides

The six judges of the Maryland Court of Appeals took three weeks to deliberate on Isaiah Fountain's request for a new trial. On July 17, 1919, they issued their judgment. Judge Hammond Urner wrote the ten-page opinion summarizing the court's decision.

Judge Urner wrote that the jury had not decided that Fountain was guilty solely on the evidence presented at the trial but that it was influenced by "popular sentiment" and "the demonstrations made against the accused in the immediate neighborhood of the Court in which the trial was being conducted." The judge continued: "It is difficult to imagine that the jurors could have remained in ignorance of the presence, temper, and conduct of the crowd on the Court House grounds through which they passed repeatedly on their way to and from the session of the Court." The appeals court agreed that Judge Adkins's announcement to the jurors about Fountain's escape, the reward offer, and the deputizing of citizens in the courtroom all contributed to the defendant not having a fair trial. The appeals judges appeared to absolve Judge Adkins somewhat, by stating that he "made earnest efforts to protect the defendant's right to a fair trial," but acknowledged that the existing condition made his efforts impossible.[21]

The appeals court refused to make any judgments about the trial evidence and testimony and whether it supported the defendant's guilty verdict. The court did not consider the sworn statement of Sheriff Stitchberry and the allegation that State's Attorney Butler withheld information that would have been beneficial to the defense. It was up to a jury to decide guilt or innocence, the court noted, based on the evidence and without any outside influences. The conclusion of the Maryland Court of Appeals was that "the prisoner did not have a fair trial and that his motion for a temporary stay of the proceeding should have been granted." The judgment of the Talbot County Circuit Court was reversed, and a new trial for Isaiah Fountain was granted.[22]

Reactions to the Appeals Decision

Not surprisingly, the Easton paper disagreed with the decision, along with many of its readers. The *Star-Democrat* reported that "many [are] regretting the decision of the Court of Appeals." The Easton paper accused the Baltimore papers of falsely reporting "wild excitement" in Talbot County. The *Star-Democrat* went on:

> This is regretted here, as there is no difference of opinion as to Fountain's guilt, but the reports of wild excitement told of in the Baltimore papers, when the news reached here is an absolute lie and in line with the scandalous reports put out by these yellow rags at the time of the trial. It's impossible for these papers to tell the truth about the case and the people here know it.[23]

The Easton paper interviewed State's Attorney Charles Butler, who said: "As prosecuting attorney I do feel that Fountain is guilty. And I really do not think the verdict of the jury was influenced by threats of hanging, etc., as was claimed by some papers."[24]

Another report in the *Star-Democrat* was much more scathing. In the article's headline the "Special Staff

Correspondent" opined that Isaiah Fountain's attorney, Eugene O'Dunne, "Pictures Easton as Filled with People Carrying Rope, Baseball Bats, and Halters, Bent On Lynching the Negro." The correspondent wrote that O'Dunne gave the impression "that Easton was not unlike the towns described in the dime novels featuring the lawlessness and crime said to hold sway in the West." The writer added that O'Dunne faulted State's Attorney Butler because Butler had "put one over on him by placing the sheriff on the stand and not calling him again as he said he would, and thus denying the lawyer for the prisoner the opportunity for cross-examination." The piece also accused O'Dunne of introducing the "lies" of the *Baltimore Sun* as part of his petition to the court of appeals. The "Special Correspondent" praised the State's lawyers for their able arguments against Fountain's case and mentioned some of the cases they had cited. The article concluded that, "With these fine points of the law made very clear it was evident that the lawyer for the prisoner had little or no grounds for an appeal."[25]

Most other newspapers—including the Baltimore papers—reported the appeals court's decision rather matter-of-factly, without any mention of public turmoil or "wild excitement" in Talbot County. In fact, the *Baltimore Sun*—the *Star Democrat's* main journalistic nemesis—reported that "the people of Easton took the court's action calmly." The *Sun's* reporter interviewed Sheriff Stitchberry, who said, "Easton is absolutely unexcited. [...] There is no public feeling of any kind, and no one has said anything about it to me. It is only what everybody expected and there is no reason why there should be any demonstration."[26] One can only wonder why the *Easton Star-Democrat* found the *Baltimore Sun*'s so-called "lies" to be so malicious toward Talbot County.

Another Appeal

Fountain and his lawyers must have been happy about their court of appeals victory giving Fountain a new trial. The lawyers realized, though, that having the second trial again in Talbot County, or anywhere on the Eastern Shore, would surely result in another guilty verdict, due to the prevailing public feeling against their client. Although sentiments about the crime might have cooled somewhat, outrage had grown about other aspects of the situation. Many members of the community felt that the delay caused by Fountain's appeal was impeding justice and was just a legal tactic for Fountain to escape his death sentence. The urge for swift justice had been demonstrated in Talbot County as far back as April, when Fountain was indicted by summoning the "old" grand jury instead of waiting five weeks for the next grand jury term to begin. Now it was July, and Fountain's attorneys knew that their client would not get a fair trial anywhere on the Eastern Shore. They needed a change of venue.

On July 23, 1919, just six days after winning their first appeal, Fountain's lawyers filed a second one. This appeal claimed that Isaiah Fountain could not get a fair and impartial trial in Talbot County or elsewhere on the Eastern Shore. They asked for his new trial to be held in Baltimore City.[27] Eugene O'Dunne argued that the Maryland Court of Appeals had the authority to grant his request for a change of venue.[28]

Appeals Court Judge John R. Pattison delivered the opinion of the court on October 29, 1919. Pattison stated that under the Maryland Constitution, no change of venue could be granted because the law cited by Fountain's lawyers applied only to civil cases, not criminal ones. The court of appeals concluded that "it is without power to grant the prayer of the appellant's petition."[29]

The Fountain Case Goes Back to Talbot

Isaiah Fountain's case landed back in the jurisdiction of the Talbot County Circuit Court. Once again, it was up to the circuit court to decide whether a change of venue should be granted. The court session of Wednesday, November 26, 1919 was reported by the *Star-Democrat*, whose reporter had to walk only half a block to get to the courthouse in Easton. Eugene O'Dunne argued that by having the trial in Talbot County, Fountain would again be denied a fair and impartial jury. He argued that having Fountain's new trial in Baltimore City made sense because he would be more likely to get a panel of jurors who would not be biased by outside influences. O'Dunne added that since Fountain was already incarcerated at the Baltimore City Jail it would also be more convenient, and the governor would not have to supply extra police or military security. O'Dunne also said he would ask for the judge to decide Fountain's fate.[30]

State's Attorney Butler responded to the argument by implying that O'Dunne politely "threatened" the court when he said that he would ask for a trial by judge if the case was heard locally. Butler rejected the idea of moving the trial to Baltimore City. The *Star-Democrat*'s reporter wrote:

"Baltimore City," said Mr. Butler "would not be a proper place to send this case from the very fact that the newspapers printed in that city had erroneously and inaccurately published conditions surrounding the trial, especially in regard to mob violence. Since the decision of the Court of Appeals in granting Fountain a new trial the great majority of citizenship of Baltimore seemed to gain the impression that Fountain was not guilty, and it is impossible that the case of the State could be fairly presented where the atmosphere is permeated with the idea of the innocence of the accused. This impression prevails because of the untruthful accounts published in the Baltimore papers, so untruthful that the indignation of the people here caused one of the Baltimore papers to send an experienced staff man here to investigate and to later publish a partial retraction."[31]

Butler clearly considered the news media and populace of Baltimore to be pro-Fountain and would have preferred the trial to move to just about any other jurisdiction, given his aim of convicting the defendant a second time. He suggested that even though the law gave O'Dunne the right to request a change of venue for his client, it didn't go so far as to allow him to choose the venue. The court session adjourned without a ruling.[32]

In early December, the Talbot County Circuit Court approved Isaiah Fountain's request for a change of venue for his second trial. The new venue was to be in Towson, the county seat of Baltimore County. State's Attorney Butler was not happy with the location since Towson was located only seven miles from Baltimore City. The *Star-Democrat* reported that he could petition the court and ask to have the trial moved to another venue, which would likely be Anne Arundel County.[33] After considering his choices, however, Butler apparently decided to take his chances trying Fountain in the Baltimore County Circuit Court. The trial was scheduled for the first week in January. According to the *Star-Democrat*, Butler was already preparing for the new trial and planned to use evidence that he hadn't used in the first trial.[34]

The wheels of justice had turned rapidly for Fountain's first trial in April, but not so for his second. Isaiah Fountain would have plenty of time to ponder his fate while waiting in his cell behind the grim walls of the Baltimore City Jail.

Endnotes

1 Isaiah Fountain v. State, April Term 1919 No. 39 [MSA S1733-530, 1/65/04/100] Ct of Appeals: Appeal From the Sentence of Death, at 2–3.

2 Isaiah Fountain v. State, April Term 1919 No. 39 [MSA S1733-530, 1/65/04/100]. Ct of Appeals: Defendant's Bill of Exception, filed June 19, 1919, at 32–34.

3 Isaiah Fountain v. State, Appeal from the Sentence of Death, June 24, 1919, at 1.

4 *Id.* at 2.

5 Isaiah Fountain v. State, April Term 1919 No. 39 [MSA S1733-530, 1/65/04/100] Ct of Appeals: Motion to Stay Further Proceedings, filed June 24, 1919, at 3–8.

6 Isaiah Fountain v. State, Motion to Stay Further Proceedings, filed June 24, 1919, at 5–7.

7 Isaiah Fountain v. State, April Term 1919 No. 39 [MSA S1733-530, 1/65/04/100]. Ct of Appeals: "Stipulation for Appeal," Isaiah Fountain v. State of Maryland, in the Court of Appeals of Maryland, No. 23, April Term, 1919, Appellant's Supplemental Brief on Evidence Only, at 43-44.

8 Isaiah Fountain v. State, Appellant's Supplemental Brief on Evidence Only, April 23, 1919, at 43–47.

9 *Id.* at 48. According to Google Maps and driving the possible routes, the mileage from Easton to the approximate crime scene is more like eight to nine miles instead of the seven miles mentioned by the defense.

10 *Id.* at 48–51.

11 *Id.* at 51.

12 *Id.* at 54.

13 *Id.* at 52–54.

14 *Id.* at 54.

15 Isaiah Fountain v. State, April Term 1919 No. 39 [MSA S1733-530, 1/65/04/100]. Ct of Appeals, Brief on Behalf of State of Maryland, Appellee, Conclusion, April Term, 1919. At 12.

16 Isaiah Fountain v. State, April Term 1919 No. 39 [MSA S1733-530, 1/65/04/100]. Ct of Appeals, Brief on Behalf of State of Maryland, Appellee, Statement, April Term, 1919. At 2.

17 Isaiah Fountain v. State, April Term 1919 No. 39 [MSA S1733-530, 1/65/04/100]. Ct of Appeals, Brief on Behalf of State of Maryland, Appellee, Argument, April Term, 1919. at 5.

18 Isaiah Fountain v. State, Brief on Behalf of State of Maryland, Argument, at 10.

19 *Id*. at 10–11.

20 "Fountain's Appeal Heard at Annapolis," *Evening Sun*, June 24, 1919, 24. Newspapers.com.

21 Fountain v. State (No. 39) (Court of Appeals of Maryland, July 17, 1919). *The Atlantic Reporter*, Volume 107, at 556. Google Books, accessed July 21, 2020. https://www.google.com/books/edition/The_Atlantic_Reporter/Kznb7Nl_5wUC?hl=en&gbpv=1&d-q=the+Atlantic+reporter,+volume+107&pg=PR14&printsec=front-cover

22 Fountain v. State. (No. 39), at 557.

23 "New Trial for Fountain," *Easton Star-Democrat*, July 19, 1919, 1.

24 "New Trial for Fountain," 1. The term "yellow" is used to refer to "yellow journalism," a term that was popular to describe sensationalistic reporting.

25 "Fountain Appeal Heard," *Easton Star-Democrat*, June 28, 1919, 2.

26 "To Try Fountain Again," *Baltimore Sun*, July 18, 1919, 18. Newspapers.com.

27 Fountain v. State, 135 Md. 87 (1919), (Court of Appeals of Maryland, Opinion of the Court. October 29, 1919.), *LexRoll (MD)*, last modified November 22, 2017. https://maryland.lexroll.com/fountain-v-state-of-maryland-135-md-87-1919/.

28 "Fountain Retrial in Talbot," *Baltimore Sun*, October 31, 1919, 2. Newspapers.com.

29 Fountain v. State of Maryland, Court of Appeals of Maryland, Opinion of the Court, decided October 29, 1919.

30 "Fountain to Baltimore?" *Star-Democrat*, November 29, 1919, 1.

31 "Fountain to Baltimore?" 1.

32 "Fountain to Baltimore?" 1.

33 "Fountain Trial to Baltimore County," *Easton Star-Democrat,* December 6, 1919, 2.

34 "Fountain Trial in January," *Easton Star-Democrat,* December 13, 1919.

CHAPTER 12

Between the Trials

The counsel for the defense argued for its [the trial's] removal to some other place for fear of another attempt at mob law. . .

—BALTIMORE SUN

Waiting for Trial

After April's initial rush to indict, try, convict, and lynch him, by the 1920 New Year, all Isaiah Fountain could do was wait. While Fountain was confined to the jail in Baltimore City, his lawyers were preparing for his retrial in Towson. The year turned, but the second trial did not begin as scheduled in the first week of January. Several trial dates were scheduled, rescheduled, and then rescheduled again, due to various motions, hearings, delays, and legal maneuverings. The White people of Talbot County began to wonder if Fountain would ever be tried and punished for his alleged crime of rape. In their eyes, the many delays meant only that Isaiah Fountain was avoiding justice and punishment. The opinions of the Black population of Talbot County concerning the Fountain case were rarely reported. During the time of Jim Crow, most Blacks likely were reluctant to share opinions and feelings outside of their families and close friends for fear of retaliation.

Of course, the trial delays were faithfully reported in the Eastern Shore newspapers, as well as in Baltimore and throughout Maryland. The papers provided a steady diet of Fountain-related stories, and the residents of Talbot County took particular notice of any news related to the case.

The Reward

One of the biggest news items to come out of Isaiah Fountain's April trial was the $5,000 reward that was offered by Chief Judge Adkins after Fountain escaped from custody and the lynch mob. An extra $250 was added by Fountain's attorney, Eugene O'Dunne. The sum of $5,250 was a huge amount at the time that would be equivalent to $88,725 in 2022 dollars.[1] Hundreds of deputies, road police, citizens, and Baltimore police officers were involved in searching for Fountain, and his capture involved several people. Who would get the reward money and how would it be divided?

This question arose almost immediately after Isaiah Fountain's conviction at the end of April. Some citizens felt that the sum should be given to the rape victim, Bertha Simpson. Others thought that a court-appointed committee should be formed to decide on the disposition of the money. It was reported that the three Delaware men who discovered Fountain in their barn had hired lawyers to make sure that they would get their fair share.[2] A newspaper article on May

8, 1919, noted that the Talbot County Circuit Court had appointed a committee of three local officials "to investigate the claims of all who think they should receive the $5,250 reward." Appointed to the committee were Easton Mayor Francis Wrightson, State's Attorney Charles Butler, and W. Mason Shehan. At least six men had already laid claim to the reward money.[3]

Within a few weeks, the number claiming the reward for capturing Isaiah Fountain had risen to at least fifteen, according to the *Baltimore Sun*. The claims varied: Some said they had been the first to report Fountain, some said they had been the first to see him in hiding, and others claimed that they had been the first to physically apprehend the escapee.[4] The reward committee evaluated the claim of each man and decided to split the reward between eight of the claimants. Each would receive $623.37 (over $10,500 in 2022 dollars[5]), after deductions for stenography, publishing, and notary expenses. The reward recipients were a diverse lot: two from Easton, one from Marydel, Maryland, two from Hartly, Delaware, and three Baltimore City police officers. The three policemen were required to turn their reward over to the Baltimore Board of Police Commissioners; the *Sun* noted that in some cases the officers would receive only half of the reward money, with the remainder being kept by the police department.[6]

Before the reward money could be distributed, Judge Adkins, who had offered the $5,000 reward, was informed that Talbot County would only pay half of the reward money. The county commissioners ruled that Adkins was personally responsible for the balance.[7] This decision no doubt came as a surprise to Judge Adkins and must have sadly dented his bank account.

The Wrong Fountain

While Isaiah Fountain's appeal was grinding through Maryland's legal system, anti-Fountain sentiment was still boiling in Talbot County. A month after Fountain had been spirited away under cover of darkness to the Baltimore City Jail, word spread throughout Easton and Talbot County that he had died. According to the rumor, Fountain's body was being shipped back to Easton for burial. Some people were suspicious and suspected that "a ruse was being worked" to secretly free Fountain by substituting and burying the corpse of another man.[8] A large crowd gathered at the Easton railroad station on May 24, 1919, to see for themselves if Fountain was really dead. The *Easton Star-Democrat* reported: "Some were glad that it would make execution unnecessary; others regretted that the man should have come to his end so peacefully." Those in the crowd hoping for a dead Isaiah Fountain were disappointed when they discovered that the body was that of *Isaac*, not Isaiah, Fountain. Isaac Fountain, who had died in a Baltimore hospital, was Isaiah's father.[9]

Many Talbot countians were still enraged about Isaiah Fountain's crime and the perceived "unnecessary" delay in carrying out his death sentence. One wonders what the crowd at the railroad station would have done if the coffin on the train *had* contained Isaiah Fountain's body and not his father's.

Ex-Sheriff Stitchberry

Sheriff James Stitchberry had been in office for two years and was up for re-election in November 1919. According to various accounts, Stitchberry was popular and well liked in Talbot County, even though he was a Republican in a heavily Democratic county. Stitchberry had been severely criticized and blamed for the escape of Isaiah Fountain and vilified by some for coming forward with the information that State's Attorney Butler had withheld at Fountain's first trial. In addition, about eleven weeks after the Fountain escape, four more prisoners managed to escape from the Talbot County Jail.[10] It's not known whether his lack of success in keeping prisoners under custody caused Stitchberry to decide not to run for sheriff again or if the Republican Party decided not to nominate him. Whatever the reason, in the November 1919 election, the citizens of Talbot County elected a new sheriff, one Charles M. Soulsby.[11] Soulsby, a former Easton fire chief, would soon need all his fire-fighting skills to quench some incendiary situations relating to the Fountain case.

Talbot's Debt

"The Police Board is hot on the trail of an expense account amounting to nearly $600," wrote the *Baltimore Sun* of the money owed by Talbot County to the Baltimore Police Department. The amount (worth $10,140 today[12]) was billed to Talbot County to cover police expenses incurred in searching for Isaiah Fountain and providing security at his trial. The bill included charges for automobile costs, meals, and hotel expenses while the police officers were in Easton.

The article said that the police department sent at least three notices of payment to Talbot County, including a "kindly remit" letter to State's Attorney Butler. The Police Board received no reply and referred the matter to the Maryland Attorney General. The *Sun* added, "It is possible that the Talbot County officials have overlooked the matter, but if this is true it is likely that the subject will again be brought to their attention."[13]

Despite its earlier praise for the Baltimore Police officers for their aid during the Fountain trial and his escape, the *Easton Star-Democrat* took issue with the "exorbitant charges" that were billed to the county. The paper complained:

> Talbot does not dispute that something is coming to the Baltimore police, for some of them did good work, while others enjoyed themselves exceedingly under the shade of the trees in the court-house yard or indulging in boastful talk in the offices in the court-house. They were also as regular as the clock when the dining-room doors of the hotel swung open, and stayed there as long as the next one—and then some—all at the expense of Talbot County, who promptly paid the bill.[14]

The article claimed that the county was being overcharged by the Baltimore Police for various items listed on the bill. It detailed some of the other expenses associated with the Fountain trial, such as costs for the jurors, witnesses, court officers, expenses for keeping the prisoner at the Baltimore City Jail, appeals costs, and so on. The paper estimated that by the end of the Fountain case, total costs would exceed $6,000 (over $101,000 in 2022 dollars[15]).[16]

Still Waiting for Trial

The date for Isaiah Fountain's second trial kept changing. Initially, it was set for January 12, then January 14, and was then postponed because some witnesses were sick. February 25, 1920, was set as the new trial date.[17] The legal wrangling continued, and the trial date continued to change.

Well before the trial, Eugene O'Dunne indicated that he would request a trial by judge and not a jury trial. At the end of April, the court announced May 4, 1920, as the new trial date. When Fountain's lawyers received the news, they officially waived a jury trial and requested that the case be heard by the chief judge of the Baltimore County Circuit Court and two associate judges. Eugene O'Dunne then filed a motion asking that the State pay the expense for three defense witnesses to travel to Towson from Easton, because Fountain was unable to afford his defense and counsel fees.[18] It is unclear how, or if, O'Dunne and Mullikin were paid for defending Fountain at his second trial.

After months of preparation, delays, and waiting, the judge's gavel for the second Fountain trial would soon come down. Would the excitement, danger, and drama of the first Fountain trial be matched by the second?

Endnotes

1 Inflation Calculator, Saving.org Resources and Calculators, accessed March 30, 2022, https://www.saving.org/inflation/. Due to inflation, $1.00 in 1919 equals $16.90 in 2022.

2 "Many Claim Reward," *Baltimore Sun*, June 17, 1919, 6. Newspapers.com.

3 "State to Probe Reward Claims," *Evening Journal*, May 8, 1919, 16. Newspapers.com.

4 "Many Claim Reward," 6.

5 Inflation Calculator at Saving.org website.

6 "Fountain Fund to Eight," *Baltimore Sun*, June 18, 1919, 10. Newspapers.com.

7 "Judge Must Pay One-Half of Reward," *Wilmington Evening Journal*," June 9, 1919, 10. Newspapers.com. "Fountain Trial Costs," *Easton Star-Democrat*, December 6, 1919, 1.

8 "Agog over Fountain's Corpse," *Baltimore Sun*, June 6, 1919, 26. Newspapers.com.

9 "The Wrong Fountain," *Easton Star-Democrat*, May 31, 1919, 2.

10 "Man Hunt Excites Talbot County Again," *Baltimore Evening Sun*, July 12, 1919, 2. Newspapers.com.

11 "Talbot True to Ritchie," *Baltimore Sun*, November 6, 1919, 6. Newspapers.com.

12 Inflation Calculator at Saving.org website.

13 "Police Try to Collect," *Baltimore Sun*, July 31, 1919, 16. Newspapers.com.

14 "Fountain Trial Costs," 1.

15 Inflation Calculator at Saving.org website.

16 "Fountain Trial Costs," 1.

17 "Fountain Trial Set Again," *Baltimore Sun*, February 13, 1920, 18. Newspapers.com.

18 "Court Asked to Call Witnesses for Negro Accused of Assault," *Baltimore Sun*, April 25, 1920, 10. Newspapers.com.

CHAPTER 13

The Second Trial

Judge, your honor, I haven't anything to say, only my life is in your hands; that I do not know anything about the crime they got me charged with at all.

—ISAIAH FOUNTAIN

Final Preparations

Isaiah Fountain's second trial was finally approaching. On Saturday, May 1, 1920, Fountain was removed from his cell at the grim Baltimore City Jail and taken to the much smaller Baltimore County Jail in Towson. The Towson facility was located approximately seven miles north of Baltimore. Isaiah was escorted by the new Talbot County sheriff, Charles M. Soulsby, as well as the sheriff of Baltimore County and his deputy.[1] Towson, being in central Maryland, was a far safer place for Fountain than the Talbot County Jail would have been. However, the Towson jail had its own history of violence involving Black prisoners. For instance, in 1885 a Black 17-year-old named Howard Cooper, also accused of raping a

White girl, was violently taken from his jail cell by a masked mob and lynched on the jail property. Whether or not Fountain realized it, the practice of lynching existed in Baltimore County also.[2]

On Sunday night, May 2, a contingent of about forty-five witnesses left Easton to testify at the trial,[3] only to find it was delayed once more, by a single day, until Wednesday, May 5, 1920.[4]

Many of the newspaper accounts about Isaiah Fountain's first trial were corroborated by records from the Maryland Court of Appeals. These records were prepared after Fountain appealed the decision of his first trial. However, no transcripts from the second trial remain. The following trial accounts are based on contemporaneous newspaper articles. The newspaper coverage was not as detailed as it had been for Fountain's first trial, since most of the key witnesses were the same, and much of the testimony was repeated.

Trial—Day One (Wednesday, May 5, 1920)

Thirteen months and four days had passed since Bertha Simpson had been raped in Talbot County. The second trial for her accused assailant, Isaiah Fountain, began on Tuesday, May 5, 1920 in Towson, Maryland, the county seat of Baltimore County. Just before the trial started, Fountain was taken from his cell in the sturdy stone Baltimore County Jail. He was transported four blocks north to the imposing Baltimore County Courthouse, with its limestone walls and impressive Doric columns. As expected, Fountain's defense team opted to have their client's fate decided by a panel of three judges instead of a jury. The panel was composed of Chief Judge

T. Scott Offutt and Associate Judges Duncan and McLane. Once again, the case was prosecuted by Talbot County State's Attorney Charles Butler, assisted by Baltimore County State's Attorney H. Courtney Jenifer. Fountain's defense counsels remained the same—Eugene O'Dunne and James Mullikin. The courtroom was crowded with observers, including a large contingent from the Trappe district in Talbot County.[5] The *Easton Star-Democrat* reported that "never in the history of Towson has such a large crowd made an effort to attend a criminal trial, but it is an orderly crowd."[6]

After opening arguments, the first witness was called by State's Attorney Butler. The horseshoer from Trappe, H. E. Mullikin, again testified that imprints of a broken horseshoe and damaged wagon tire were found in the area of Bertha Simpson's assault. As in the first trial, Mullikin testified that the prints matched Isaiah Fountain's horse and buggy.[7]

After the lunch recess, Bertha Simpson was called to the witness stand. Once again, her testimony was given in private, not in open court. Her account was substantially the same as in the first trial.[8] However, the *Baltimore Sun* reported that when she was cross-examined by Eugene O'Dunne, in two instances the testimony she gave "was contradictory to statements that she made at the trial in Easton." The paper added: "During the cross-examination of the child Eugene O'Dunne read her the stenographic report of her previous testimony. When he completed his reading of the testimony the girl simply said she didn't remember having given the testimony." The newspaper report didn't specify the parts of the testimony Bertha failed to remember. It did specify that Bertha, as she had done in the first trial, pointed to Fountain as the man who had attacked her. After Simpson

completed her testimony, Judge Offutt adjourned court until
10:00 a.m. Thursday.[9]

Trial—Day Two (Thursday, May 6, 1920)

A surprise witness was called by the prosecution on the trial's
second day. Kate Webster, the common-law wife of Isaiah
Fountain's brother John, was put on the stand. Webster, the
Wilmington News Journal reported, testified that Fountain,
while at his brother's house a few days after the crime took
place, showed signs of fear and nervousness. Webster stated
that Fountain told her that he had "run over a white girl
and did not know how seriously she had been hurt." The
cross-examination by Fountain's lawyer, O'Dunne, "failed to
shake Webster's testimony."[10]

State's Attorney Butler then called Eugene Wells to the
stand. Wells was the Black man who had borrowed the horse
and buggy that Bertha Simpson had initially identified as
being used by her attacker. Evidence gathered by former
Sheriff Stitchberry showed that Wells was using that horse
and buggy at the time of the assault and was in the same
area. Butler, though, didn't consider Wells to be a suspect for
the rape, and Simpson failed to identify him as her attacker.
Wells testified that he had spent the afternoon and evening
of the day of the assault at the home of a "colored man near
Trappe."[11]

Trial—Day Three (Friday, May 7, 1920)

On the third day of the trial, Eugene O'Dunne called
former Talbot County Sheriff James Stitchberry to the stand.

Although Stitchberry had been the prime investigator of the Simpson rape, his testimony had been withheld by the prosecution at Fountain's first trial. After the trial, the sheriff had provided the defense team with crucial evidence that had not been revealed in court. His sworn statement had already been publicized, so Stitchberry's testimony was highly anticipated. He said that he initially suspected that Fountain was the assailant because of Bertha Simpson's description. She told the sheriff that her assailant had "a peculiar grin," which reminded the sheriff of Isaiah Fountain.[12] The *Evening Sun* reported that Stitchberry then testified that "the Simpson girl had failed to identify the team driven by Fountain, but had designated another team, driven by a negro named Eugene Wells, as the one used by the perpetrator of the assault." The paper reported that during the cross-examination, Butler and Stitchberry "had several sharp verbal encounters during the course of the testimony, indicating considerable feeling between the two." Butler had failed to shake the sheriff's testimony, but he said he would later introduce witnesses to dispute Stitchberry's story.[13] Later, Butler put two of the grand jury members who had indicted Fountain on the stand. They both testified that the sheriff had told the grand jury that the victim had positively identified Fountain's horse and buggy. Six other witnesses produced by Butler related similar testimony.[14]

In an unusual move, Defense Counsel O'Dunne called State's Attorney Butler to the witness stand. Butler admitted that when Simpson identified Fountain, he had been the only Black man in the room and was surrounded by uniformed Baltimore police officers.[15] O'Dunne used Butler's own testimony to raise doubt about his methods to get Bertha Simpson to name Isaiah Fountain as her assailant.

O'Dunne then put his client on the stand in his own defense. Fountain again denied raping Bertha Simpson. He stuck to his original alibi that he was in Easton looking for his horse and buggy and meeting with various people, including the Easton police chief. Fountain testified that he left Easton at 4:30 p.m. and went home "by way of the State road." The *Sun* reported: "Fountain stuck to his original story despite the grueling cross-examination of State's Attorney Charles J. Butler, of Talbot County."[16]

Attorney O'Dunne ended the day by calling as witnesses the Talbot Bank clerk, the assistant county treasurer, and the Easton police chief. These three prominent White citizens again verified Isaiah Fountain's alibi. They all agreed that Fountain was in Easton at nearly the same time that Bertha Simpson was being assaulted.[17] O'Dunne then summarized Fountain's defense for the three judges. He emphasized that Fountain did not flee from any crime: he happened to go to New Jersey to find his wife and had told neighbors about his plans, just as he and they had testified. Finally, O'Dunne impressed upon the judges that it was impossible for Fountain to have committed the rape that the victim had testified had occurred between 4:30 and 5:00 p.m. Fountain simply could not have left Easton "around 4:30 o'clock" and still have traveled the "10 miles" to the scene of the crime and raped the victim. Lawyer O'Dunne rested his case.[18]

Trial—Day Four (Saturday, May 8, 1920)

In 1920, it was unusual to have a trial session on a Saturday, but the three judges hearing Fountain's case no doubt considered that the trial was almost completed and recognized the expense of accommodating the large number of out-of-town witnesses over the weekend. The newspapers speculated too that Saturday would be the final day of the trial.

As reported by the *Evening Sun*, the trial resumed at 10:00 a.m. on Saturday morning, and the attorneys made their final statements. State's Attorney Butler waived making a closing argument but reserved the right to respond to statements made by the defense team.[19]

Eugene O'Dunne briefly addressed the court and admitted that some of the testimony against Isaiah Fountain was damaging. In particular, O'Dunne mentioned Bertha Simpson's description of her assailant as a "man with a peculiar smile." His client, O'Dunne admitted, did smile in a peculiar manner. The *Evening Sun* acknowledged in a headline that Fountain's "Smile May Cost Him Dear."[20]

After the closing arguments, Baltimore County Judges Offutt, McLane, and Duncan retired to chambers to consider the rape charge against Isaiah Fountain, according to the *Baltimore Sun*. The three judges deliberated for over an hour, then returned to the courtroom to deliver their verdict. They declared Fountain guilty and sentenced him to death by hanging. Observers reported that Fountain showed no emotion when the verdict and sentence were read. Before the sentencing, however, he said: "Your honors, my life is in your hands. Before God I know nothing about the crime I am accused of." The *Sun* reported that, "white and colored persons" who filled the courtroom showed no emotion, and there was no demonstration of any kind. Most of the spectators began to file out of the courtroom immediately following the sentencing.[21]

The Judges' Explanation

The *Baltimore Sun* reported that after announcing the verdict, Chief Judge Offutt read a detailed and lengthy explanation of the court's reasoning in reaching its decision. Judge Offutt stated that he and his fellow judges "were guided only by the evidence provided." The *Easton Star-Democrat* later published the complete judges' statement, but the *Sun* printed only a summary of the explanation. The *Sun's* summary reads:

> He [Offutt] said the evidence clearly proved that the girl, when she was 14 years old, was assaulted by a negro in the manner she described. He said she had full opportunity to observe her assailant while riding in the buggy with him at the time of the assault. It was the opinion of the court, he said, that the girl positively identified Fountain as her assailant.
>
> Another important factor, according to Judge Offutt, was that an examination of the ground near the scene of the assault showed the horse driven there wore a broken shoe on its right front foot and that the left hind shoe was missing. An examination of Fountain's horse the morning after the crime showed such conditions.[22]

An analysis of Judge Offutt's complete statement to the court shows that it was much more detailed and somewhat bewildering. Offutt began his statement by admitting that "the Court is human." He continued, "We can only be controlled in our deliberations and judgment, by the evidence actually before us, and by nothing else." Offutt said that the only *direct evidence* in the case was that Bertha Simpson was raped. As to the identity of the assailant, however, he said, "that testimony is [both] direct and *circumstantial.*" [Emphasis added.] The judges placed a lot of weight on the victim's identification of her assailant and her opportunity to see the assailant's face while she was in the buggy with him. They also noted that he "bore a distinguishing and striking characteristic [. . .] a peculiar facial expression, which has been described in the case as 'a grin,' or as 'a funny grin,' or as 'a silly grin,' but a grin." The judges also gave credence to the prosecution's evidence of the buggy tire and horseshoe prints that were found near the crime scene. Offutt then commented that a suspect leaving the state the day following a crime, as Fountain did to go to New Jersey, "is usually accepted as a circumstance tending to show guilt." Concerning the State's testimony, Offutt said: "So far, then, the case of the State would appear to have been made out beyond any reasonable doubt."[23]

Judge Offutt then addressed the testimony and evidence presented by Fountain's defense team. He said that Fountain's lawyers set up two defenses: one of mistaken identity, and one maintaining that Fountain had not been at the scene at the time of the crime. For the first of these, the court accepted the prosecution's evidence and was persuaded that Fountain had been properly identified as the assailant.[24] As to the second, the judges *completely ignored* significant and credible defense evidence for Fountain's alibi from the victim herself and several prominent defense witnesses, and instead created their own timeline of events to support their findings.

The judges made several assumptions about the victim's timeline. They added their own time estimates to Bertha Simpson's version of events, even though she had testified that she left school at 3:30 and had been raped between 4:30 and 5:00 p.m. The judges blatantly ignored her words and added time to the different stops she made after leaving school. For example, in her testimony, Bertha Simpson said it took her only fifteen minutes to walk to her aunt's house.[25] The judges ignored her testimony and concluded it had been longer. They also presumed that Bertha's testimony about the time she spent at her aunt's was not as she stated. Judge Offutt continued:

> Her estimate of the time it took to go there was fifteen minutes. *It may well have been longer.* She stayed there thirty to forty minutes, she thinks. For the reasons that have already been stated *it is manifestly difficult to estimate the time spent in a casual conversation.* It depends upon so many factors, upon the nature of things you discuss and of their interest to the people you are discussing them with, and to their attention to it, and other things.[26] [Emphasis added.]

The testimony of multiple witnesses established that Fountain left Easton "around 4:30 o'clock." Judge Offutt said, however, "The testimony in the case seems to have established, beyond any reasonable doubt, that [Fountain] left Easton somewhere in the neighborhood of 4 o'clock."[27]—earlier by thirty minutes. The court ignored the testimonies of the prominent *White* witnesses who had supported Fountain's alibi of being in Easton right up to 4:30.

In their statement, the judges admitted that they gave "all the latitude which the circumstances of the case seem to warrant in estimating the time taken." So instead of accepting Bertha Simpson's testimony about when the rape occurred, the judges *estimated* the time. Their statement goes on to admit that they judged the timeline "backward from the time the doctor was notified" instead of strictly from the victim's testimony.[28]

Thanks to the extra time that the judges added to Bertha Simpson's stops, Judge Offutt was able to claim that Fountain *did* have enough time to travel from Easton to the crime scene and assault Simpson. After juggling both the time of the assault and the time of Fountain's departure from Easton, they then concluded "that the assault occurred anytime between 5:15 o'clock and 5:30 o'clock; that it is hardly likely it occurred as early as 5 o'clock." Judge Offutt added that, based on the court's calculation and depending on the route taken to the assault site, Fountain left Easton "an hour and fifteen minutes or an hour and a half" before the assault took place. Regarding his alibi, Offutt concluded: "There is nothing, therefore, in that testimony to destroy the inference compelled by the other testimony in the case that the defendant was at the place of the assault at the time it occurred."[29] In other words, the judges concluded that Fountain left Easton in plenty of time to find and assault Bertha Simpson—based on *their* time estimates.

Thus it was the court, not the prosecution, that effectively demolished Fountain's alibi. So much for the judges' assertion that "We can only be controlled in our deliberations and judgment, by the evidence actually before us, and by nothing else."[30]

Judge Offutt ended the proceedings by announcing Isaiah Fountain's sentence: "The judgment of the Court is that you, Isaiah Fountain, be taken to the jail of Talbot County, from whence you came, and thence to the place of execution at such time as the governor of this State shall appoint, and there be hanged by the neck until you be dead, and may God have mercy upon your soul."[31] For the second time, Isaiah Fountain was condemned to hang for a crime he still vehemently denied committing.

Endnotes

1 "Fountain Taken to Towson," *Baltimore Sun*, May 2, 1920, 12. Newspapers.com.

2 "Howard Cooper," Maryland State Archives Biographical Series, MSA SC 3520-13733. Accessed July 18, 2021. https://msa.maryland.gov/megafile/msa/speccol/sc3500/sc3520/013700/013733/html/13733bio.html.

3 "Fountain Trial Tuesday," *Baltimore Sun*, May 1, 1920, 8. Newspapers.com.

4 "Trial of Isaiah Fountain Delayed until Tomorrow," *Baltimore Sun*, May 4, 1920, 9. Newspapers.com.

5 "Fountain Again Put on Trial in Towson," *Baltimore Evening Sun*, May 5, 1920, 32. Newspapers.com.

6 "Fountain Verdict Today," *Easton Star-Democrat*, May 8, 1920, 1.

7 "Negro Again on Trial for Alleged Assault," *Baltimore Sun*, May 6, 1920, 12. Newspapers.com.

8 "Fountain Again Put on Trial in Towson," 32.

9 "Negro Again on Trial for Alleged Assault," 12.

10 "Trial of Isaiah Fountain," *Wilmington News Journal*, May 7, 1920, 15. Newspapers.com.

11 "Tells of Negro's Fears," *Baltimore Sun*, May 7, 1920, 6. Newspapers.com.

12 "Fountain Verdict Near," *Baltimore Sun*, May 8, 1920, 7. Newspapers.com.

13 "Sheriff on the Stand," *Baltimore Evening Sun*, May 7, 1920, 36. Newspapers.com.

14 "Fountain Verdict Near," 7.

15 "Sheriff on the Stand," 36. "Fountain Verdict Near," 7.

16 "Fountain Verdict Near," 7. The "State Road" referred to by Fountain is most likely MD Route 565 (Old Trappe Road) that runs from Easton to Trappe.

17 "Fountain Verdict," *Wilmington News Journal*, May 8, 1920, 1. Newspapers.com.

18 "Fountain Verdict Near," 7. In this account, O'Dunne states that the distance was "10 miles." In an earlier account, he mentioned 7 miles. The discrepancy may be due to the route used to get to the crime scene. Google maps lists either 8 or 9 miles to the crime scene on modern roads, depending on the route used. Even if one uses the shortest distance O'Dunne mentioned (7 miles), it would still have been nearly impossible for Fountain to travel from Easton to the crime scene with his horse and buggy and commit the crime at the stated time(s).

19 "To Learn Fate Today," *Baltimore Evening Sun*, May 8, 1920, 16. Newspapers.com.

20 "To Learn Fate Today," 16.

21 "Fountain Convicted; Is Sentenced to Hang," *Baltimore Sun*, May 9, 1920, 16. Newspapers.com.

22 "Fountain Convicted; Is Sentenced to Hang," 16.

23 "Court Gives Reasons," *Easton Star-Democrat*, May 22, 1920, 1 and 3.

24 "Court Gives Reasons," 3.

25 "Court Gives Reasons," 3.

26 "Court Gives Reasons," 3.

27 "Fountain Verdict Near," 7. "Death Decree for Fountain," 3. "Fountain's Case to Be Appealed," *Baltimore Afro-American*, May 2, 1919, A1. ProQuest.com. Isaiah Fountain v. State, April Term 1919 No. 39 [MSA S1733-530, 1/65/04/100]. Ct of Appeals: "Stipulation for Appeal," Isaiah Fountain v. State of Maryland, in the Court of Appeals of Maryland, No. 23, April Term, 1919, Appellant's Supplemental Brief on Evidence Only, at 48.

28 "Court Gives Reasons," 3

29 "Court Gives Reasons," 3.

30 "Court Gives Reasons," 1.

31 "Court Gives Reasons," 3.

CHAPTER 14

Back to Talbot County

The verdict of the Baltimore County Court was in accord with that rendered by the Talbot court.

—*EASTON-STAR DEMOCRAT*

The Trip Back to Talbot County

Sheriff Soulsby wasted no time in getting the twice-condemned Fountain back to Talbot County. He immediately had the prisoner transferred back to his custody and took him on the first boat from Baltimore to Talbot County. The boat landed at Claiborne, about fifteen miles from Easton. There Fountain was put on a train that took him to Bloomfield Station, just two miles from Easton. The final leg of his journey to the Talbot County Jail was by automobile. Fountain was in his cell before the residents of Easton knew that he was back.[1]

The *Easton Star-Democrat* received the first news of Fountain's conviction from State's Attorney Charles Butler just a few minutes after the trial ended. The paper promptly posted a bulletin in their window on Dover Street. Within minutes, hundreds of Easton citizens were crowding the sidewalk to read the news of Fountain's second conviction. The *Star-Democrat* also phoned the news to various Talbot County towns, including Trappe, where the crime took place.[2]

Word quickly spread that Fountain was back in the Talbot County Jail in Easton, but this time no angry crowds gathered there. The people of Talbot County seemed to be satisfied with Fountain's guilty verdict and death sentence. They were content with letting justice take its course; lynching didn't seem to be a consideration. However, Sheriff Soulsby wasn't taking any chances. He was determined that his condemned prisoner remain safe and secure, so he immediately placed a day-and-night watch on Fountain's cell until the governor could set an execution date.[3]

Newspapers React

It didn't take long for newspapers to react to Isaiah Fountain's conviction and sentencing. The *Baltimore Afro-American* believed that the Towson court's rejection of Fountain's alibi was wrong. The paper said this faulty verdict was ample reason for the governor of Maryland to commute Fountain's sentence to life imprisonment.[4] The newspaper cast doubt on Bertha Simpson's identification of Fountain as her attacker, writing: "She may have been mistaken as to identity and there are some circumstances surrounding her identification which indicate that she may have erred and also that undue zeal on the part of some may have caused the State to try to fasten the crime on the man [Fountain]." The newspaper also questioned some of the State's evidence against Fountain and claimed it was insufficient to warrant the death penalty.[5]

Even before his retrial in Towson, there were reports of efforts to raise money to save Fountain. One report asserted that some "well-dressed colored men from Washington" attempted to pay a Baltimore County attorney to assist in the Fountain defense, but the attorney declined the offer.[6] A call went out to churches to have their parishioners sign petitions for Governor Ritchie to commute Fountain's death sentence.[7] Such appeals for mercy for Fountain didn't get much support on the Eastern Shore.

A week after Isaiah Fountain returned to his jail cell in Easton, the *Star-Democrat* published another article in its running battle with the press of Baltimore. The article gloated about the guilty verdict despite the pro-Fountain efforts of the Baltimore newspapers. It read:

> The verdict of the Baltimore County Court was in accord with that rendered by the Talbot court, and in spite of the efforts of the Baltimore papers to prove the man innocent, in which volumes of propaganda were printed, and even slurs on the Talbot court and jury, the ablest court in the State has declared his guilt. The verdict is a refutation of all the misguided attempts to make the man out a victim of circumstances, and goes to prove how unreliable the Baltimore newspapers can be in matters of this sort, so many cheap cub reporters are employed by these papers, who see yellow every time they are assigned to a case of unusual importance. Talbot County has had its dose of this stuff and always sincerely pities the community that happens to be invaded by these raw recruits of the press.[8]

If the *Star-Democrat* was any indicator of public sentiment in Talbot County, Isaiah Fountain would get no sympathy, nor see any efforts to have his sentence commuted. Talbot County citizens had their rape conviction—twice. Now they wanted to see Fountain at the end of a rope.

Endnotes

1 "Fountain Convicted; Is Sentenced to Hang," *Baltimore Sun*, May 9, 1920, 16. Newspapers.com.

2 "Fountain in Jail," *Easton Star-Democrat*, May 15, 1920, 4.

3 "Fountain Convicted; Is Sentenced to Hang," 16.

4 "Fountain May Be Reprieved," *Baltimore Afro-American*, May 14, 1920, 2. ProQuest.com.

5 "The Fountain Case," *Baltimore Afro-American*, May 14, 1920, 4. ProQuest.com.

6 "Negroes Mad Money for Fountain Case," *Easton Star-Democrat*, May 22, 1920, 1.

7 "The Forum," *Baltimore Afro-American*, May 21, 1920, 4. ProQuest. com.

8 "Fountain in Jail," 4.

CHAPTER 15

Another Escape

The day and night watch is kept every minute, and the Sheriff is determined that nothing shall be done or undone to give the prisoner the least chance to escape.

—*BALTIMORE SUN*

Fountain Waits

While the newspapers and the public argued about whether Isaiah Fountain should be executed or have his sentence commuted to life imprisonment, Fountain endured in his cell in the Talbot County Jail with little to do but think about his fate. It was up to Maryland Governor Albert C. Ritchie to either set the date of his execution or commute his sentence.

Fountain's tedium was interrupted about a week after he returned to Easton. A Black man from Baltimore showed up at the jail office and confronted Sheriff Soulsby's wife. The man was convinced that Fountain was innocent and wanted to free him. Mrs. Soulsby became alarmed by the man's actions and called a deputy, who arrested the man, who apparently suffered from mental issues.[1]

Two "colored preachers" from Trappe who served as Isaiah Fountain's spiritual advisors regularly visited Fountain in jail. Fountain told them that he had been converted and was ready to meet his maker. The preachers told reporters that he still maintained his innocence but seemed to be resigned to his fate.[2]

Sheriff Soulsby also visited with his prisoner—often twice a day. The sheriff said that Fountain was anxious about his execution but didn't seem to fear it. Soulsby told a reporter that Fountain was a good prisoner, had a good appetite, and caused no trouble. Sheriff Soulsby said that different people stopped by each day to visit with Fountain, but the prisoner declined all the requests. In spite of Fountain's good behavior, Sheriff Soulsby remained cautious and kept up the round-the-clock guard. Soulsby told the *Sun* that he was determined that "nothing shall be done or undone to give the prisoner the least chance to escape."[3]

Another Escape (Tuesday, June 15, 1920)

While the sheriff was determined to keep Fountain in custody until his execution, the governor had yet to set the date. Since his second conviction, Isaiah had spent thirty-eight days pondering his fate. Once again, he was faced with the decision to run or die, and for the second time, he chose to run.

On Tuesday, June 15, 1920, at about 11:00 p.m.,[4] Fountain again escaped from the Talbot County Jail. The *Baltimore Evening Sun* reported that Fountain's escape scheme began several days earlier. Somehow, he obtained a metal file belonging to Sheriff Soulsby from two fellow Black prisoners named Ralph Loper and Lee Dixon, both jail trustees. Fountain gradually filed through three of the iron bars of his cell door. He filed completely through two of the bars and the third enough to bend it back to enlarge the opening. He then camouflaged the damaged areas with soap and wrapped them with "automobile tape" to temporarily hold them together. This was possible because his "day and night watch" guards were lax in their duties: instead of sitting in front of the prisoner's cell as they were instructed, they spent their time sitting on the porch of the attached sheriff's house.[5]

On that Tuesday evening, Fountain called Charles Seymour, the night watchman, and asked for a cup of water. Seymour went to get the water from the tap located in another area of the jail, but he neglected to follow proper procedure to lock the connecting door behind him. Fountain used the opportunity to quickly remove the two fully filed bars from his cell door and bend back the third. He crawled through the opening, ducked through the open connecting door, and entered the hall of the attached sheriff's house. From there, Fountain walked out through the unlocked front door.

Sheriff Soulsby and his wife were in the second-floor bedroom when they heard the front door close. At the same time, Charles Seymour discovered Fountain's empty cell and began shouting that he had escaped. The sheriff jumped from his bed, ran downstairs and into the street in his nightclothes, and rang the Easton fire bell to raise the alarm. Townspeople poured into the street, and within a few minutes another manhunt for Isaiah Fountain was underway.[6]

Another Manhunt

For the second time in fourteen months, Isaiah Fountain had managed to escape from the Talbot County Jail and was again the subject of a massive dragnet. Talbot countians were enraged that Fountain was once more trying to delay justice—justice that had already been deferred by appeals, legal upsets, a second trial, and the ongoing delay in setting Fountain's execution date. Search parties were deployed in Talbot County, across the Eastern Shore, throughout the rest of Maryland, and into other states. As with Fountain's first escape, reports of sightings and theories of possible destinations poured in. Searches were conducted almost non-stop, and the hunt for Isaiah Fountain was again making headlines.

Maryland Governor Ritchie wasted no time sending Captain George Henry of the Baltimore Police Department to "assume complete direction of the search upon his arrival." Ritchie also ordered ten motorcycle officers to Easton to join the search for the escapee.[7] The motorcycle officers had orders to stop all cars with Black occupants and to question them.[8]

Initial reports had Fountain escaping in a car driven by a pair of Black men and fleeing from Easton toward Centreville, some twenty miles to the north. Motorcycle policemen were sent in pursuit and reached speeds of "more than a mile a minute" without sighting the car. Other searchers were deployed toward the Delaware state line, believing that

Fountain would again head in that direction. Still another theory had Fountain escaping across the Chesapeake Bay in a high-powered boat, heading for "a Southern port."[9]

Other leads were investigated, but Talbot County became the primary search area, with the main effort concentrated in the Trappe district, Fountain's home. This district is essentially a peninsula connected to the northern part of the county by a two-mile strip of land that extends from Trippe Creek in the west to the Choptank River in the east. The rest of the peninsula is bordered by the Choptank and Tred Avon Rivers. For a while, the land and water borders of the Trappe district were guarded by armed patrols forming "an impassable cordon about the peninsula." The patrols then began to move toward the center of the district, hoping to surround and capture the fugitive.[10]

A pack of bloodhounds and their handlers arrived from Suffolk, Virginia, to help in the search for Fountain. The homes and farms of local Black people—especially Fountain's relatives and friends—were searched, and several were detained or arrested on suspicion of aiding the escapee. Rain and frequent thunderstorms made it difficult for the bloodhounds to find Fountain's scent, and the dogs were soon returned to Virginia. The rainy weather, thick underbrush, soggy fields, and dense woods made it uncomfortable and difficult for the searchers to maneuver.[11]

Changing Tactics

The official search efforts were conducted by sheriff's deputies, Baltimore police, and state motorcycle police, as well as additional deputies sent from Baltimore.[12] Informal posses of armed citizens were also scouring Talbot County in search of Fountain. Some of these numbered up to six hundred people and included men with ropes, "apparently hoping they would reach the fugitive before the State Deputies." The undisciplined vigilantes often intermingled with the official law enforcement searchers and created problems for the manhunt. This caused Sheriff Soulsby to adopt a policy of secrecy in deploying the official searchers. According to the *Baltimore Sun*:

> The policy of secrecy was adopted for two reasons. One is because of the fear that Fountain is being "tipped off" to the plans of the posse. The other is growing fear that Fountain will be lynched if caught. Chagrinned by the monotonous failure of each clue, many members of the posse are taking a grimmer attitude toward the fugitive. Some are even carrying ropes and openly declare that they will give the negro short [shrift].[13]

The decision to use only "official" law enforcement officers in the search was also made so that evidence wouldn't be destroyed by the untrained civilian volunteers. This decision was not well received by the civilians. Some resented being excluded, and others refused to leave the search area. Finally, the large crowd of volunteers and their 125 automobiles left the Trappe district search area to the professional searchers.[14]

As part of the reorganization of the search, the leaders of the operation, Captain Henry and Sheriff Soulsby, set up their headquarters at the Talbot County Jail. There they received and coordinated all information about the search, including new sightings and tips. Former Talbot County Sheriff James Gannon was recalled and put in charge of the prisoners who had been arrested during the search. Gannon was charged with "grilling them when occasion demands."[15] One of the fourteen Black people held in the jail and grilled was Isaiah Fountain's 55-year-old mother, Fannie.[16]

While the search for Fountain was in high gear in Talbot County, reports of sightings elsewhere continued to pour in. The fugitive was supposedly sighted in Wicomico and Somerset Counties on Maryland's Lower Eastern Shore, various places in Delaware, and even in York County, Pennsylvania. One report said that Fountain had been shot by searchers, while another said that he was cornered in a swamp.[17]

Talbot County citizens were concerned about the escaped convicted rapist and followed the news of the manhunt closely. Charles Willis Sr., a Trappe farmer, wrote in his diary about the search and rumors about Fountain's escape:

> June 21: No capture of "Fountain" yet—nor do authorities really know where he is… "The Sun" to day states that the State of Maryland has taken control of the "Fountain" case in its entirety. A rigid examination by the Atty. Gen. of Md. will be held next week in Easton of those in charge of the jail & of Fountain—as to how the man could alone have escaped. It is public talk & belief that he was furnished money by "societies" of Balto. & Wash. & that he paid his way to freedom.[18]

After almost a week of searching, the leaders of the manhunt for Fountain were embarrassed and frustrated by their lack of success. In their desperation, they even requested help from the United States Army. They contacted the Aberdeen Proving Ground army base northeast of Baltimore to request the use of an airplane and pilot to conduct an aerial search for

Fountain.[19] They also issued a printed statement admitting that Fountain might have gone beyond the established search perimeter and asking citizens and police throughout Maryland and other states to be on the alert for him. The search leaders asked newspapers nationwide to print their appeal.[20]

Fountain's Recapture (Tuesday, June 22, 1920)

Isaiah Fountain spent seven days evading hundreds of law enforcement officers and civilian searchers. He was finally captured in the small town of Queen Anne in Talbot County, about thirteen miles northeast of Easton. This time, his flight was foiled by an alert fourteen-year-old girl named Virginia Andersen. Fountain had made his way to a farm near Queen Anne that was owned by her father, Calvin Andersen, and had again taken refuge in a hayloft. Young Virginia entered the barn to get her horse and called out the horse's name. Thinking he had been discovered, Fountain jumped down and ran out of the barn. Miss Andersen notified a neighbor, who then called the authorities in Easton. The *Baltimore Sun* reported that the search teams were deployed elsewhere, and it took the sheriff some time to gather a group of about fifty armed men to send to the Andersen farm in a fleet of automobiles. When the group arrived at the farm, they were able to easily track him because of the marks he left with his bare feet.[21]

The *Wilmington Morning News* gave a somewhat different account of the capture. According to that paper, Virginia Andersen mounted her horse and rode a few miles to report that she had seen Fountain in the barn. A crowd of about one hundred men headed for the Andersen farm, the article continued, and tracked Fountain to a thick woods. The posses searched the woods for about thirty minutes and sighted Fountain. Several of the men "seized the felon, who after a hard struggle, was subdued." Four of his captors put Fountain in an automobile and quickly sped to Easton.[22]

Back at the Talbot County Jail in Easton once more, Captain Henry of the Baltimore Police took charge of Fountain and secured him in a new cell—one with no damaged bars. Additional guards were posted both inside and outside the jail, due to the "intense" feelings of the townspeople. Crowds of people continued to pass by the jail until late at night, but they made no attempt to lynch Fountain or create a disturbance.[23] Isaiah Fountain was back in custody after being free for six days and seventeen hours.

The Escape Investigation

While Isaiah Fountain was still at large this second time, Governor Ritchie ordered Maryland Attorney General Armstrong to investigate his escape and provide recommendations about what further actions should be taken. Meanwhile, Talbot County citizens demanded action from Sheriff Soulsby: They wanted him to arrest the two jail wardens who were responsible for guarding Fountain and charge them with neglect of duty.[24]

On June 23, 1920, the assistant attorney general, Lindsay Spencer, began his investigation. Spencer questioned Sheriff Charles Soulsby, Mrs. Soulsby, John Scott (the day watchman), and Charles Seymour (the night watchman who was on duty when Fountain escaped from the jail). Spencer also interviewed Lee Dixon, the Black jail trustee who provided the metal file that Fountain used to cut the bars of his cell door. Other inmates, including Joe Allison and Ralph Loper, were also interviewed about the escape.[25]

The *Wilmington News Journal* reported that the escape plot began about a week before Fountain's breakout. A jail trustee by the name of Lee Dixon took a metal file from the jail's workhouse. Dixon gave the file to another inmate, Ralph Loper, who then gave it to Fountain. Loper, who was in the cell next to Fountain, was due to be released in just a few days; he urged Fountain to escape the jail and join him in Wilmington, Delaware. Another inmate, Joe Allison, who was in the cell on the other side of Fountain, stated that he heard Fountain and Loper plotting the escape and filing the bars of the cell door.[26] After more questioning, Allison admitted that he also helped Fountain file the bars of his cell door.[27] After his capture, Fountain confirmed that Joe Allison encouraged him to escape the jail and helped to file the bars. Allison also made noise to distract the jail guard while Isaiah was filing the iron bars of his cell door. Fountain spoke freely about the aid he received from Joe Allison, who was White, but he emphatically denied that he received any aid from the Black inmates.[28] According to Fountain, Joe Allison also gave him an iron window weight to knock out the guard when he made his escape. Fountain said he had refused to attack the night guard, Charles Seymour, because Seymour had treated him well, and Fountain didn't want to harm him.[29]

Isaiah Fountain revealed to the astounded investigators that he had spent the first six days after his escape hiding in a barn just a few blocks from the Talbot County Jail. As hundreds of people searched for him on the Eastern Shore and in neighboring states, he was less than a mile from where he'd started. After leaving the sheriff's house on Tuesday night, Fountain had run behind the jail on West Street and headed south toward the hospital. He then traveled east for several blocks to the vicinity of the Baltimore, Chesapeake & Atlantic Railroad tracks (near South Aurora Street and Maryland Avenue). There he hid in the hayloft of a barn owned by Raymond Marvel. The night before his capture, he decided to leave the hayloft. He headed north to Goldsborough Street, then east on Matthewstown Road (MD Route 328). He then traveled north to Queen Anne, where he was finally captured. Once he was returned to the Easton jail, Fountain asked the sheriff's wife for some food. He said he'd had nothing to eat since his escape except for cherries and what he could find growing in local gardens.[30]

Press Reaction

From the very beginning of the Fountain case, there was a clear division of editorial opinion in the press about the story. The Eastern Shore newspapers took it for granted that Fountain was guilty and downplayed the lynching sentiment present on the Shore. The "city newspapers" of the Western Shore tended to give Fountain the benefit of the doubt and generally displayed a much more unbiased approach in reporting his trials. The city papers also showed their contempt for the practice of lynching. Almost universally, though, the newspapers printed articles expressing relief once Isaiah Fountain was captured this second time. After all, who wanted a twice-convicted rapist running loose?

When Isaiah Fountain escaped for the second time, the Baltimore *Evening Sun* changed its attitude about lynching. The date of Fountain's second escape coincided with the lynching of three Black men in Duluth, Minnesota. The three men had been arrested on suspicion of raping a White woman and were forcibly taken from their jail cells by a mob and lynched.[31] The Duluth lynching was widely publicized, and the violent incident apparently caused the *Evening Sun* to look at lynching in a different light. Whether the paper now believed that Fountain was guilty or was tiring of his dramatic escapes, the *Evening Sun* changed its editorial approach to the Fountain case.

The change came two days after Fountain's second escape, when the *Evening Sun* published a baffling editorial. On the one hand, the editors expressed naïve amazement that lynchings could even occur in Northern Minnesota. The paper reported that the state was "inhabited largely, if not chiefly, by Scandinavians and their descendants, with no inherited race prejudice and little reason or opportunity to acquire it, for the climate is too severe for negroes to live there in any great numbers." The editorial described the lynchings in Duluth and continued: "Imagine a thing like that occurring in Baltimore or Richmond, or even Atlanta or New Orleans."[32] (Apparently, the *Evening Sun's* editorial writers were unaware of the seventy-six lynchings of Black people that had occurred in the United States the previous year—the most, in fact, since 1903.[33]) After righteously implying that the citizens of Baltimore were free of lynching tendencies, the editors sympathized with the people of Talbot County over the problems caused by the Fountain case.

The *Evening Sun*'s editorial then described Isaiah Fountain's two trials, his near lynching, and his two escapes. The paper even praised the honor of Talbot County before concluding that lynchings are justifiable in cases of rape:

> It is just such things as Fountain's escapes which stimulate the fury of mobs and often lead them to take no chance with legal procedure. It is to the honor of Talbot and all of Maryland that Fountain was given all his rights under the law.
>
> Referring again to Duluth, it is curious how real white men everywhere "see red" when white women are attacked by negro men. It arouses a racial fury which no other crime quite equals. Its sudden and murderous manifestations are not confined to the South, where negroes are numerous, but appear in most unexpected places, such as Duluth, where negroes are few and race prejudice is little in evidence.[34]

The day after Fountain was captured, the *Evening Sun* again criticized his escapes, as well as the Talbot County Jail officials for allowing them. It also repeated its newfound appreciation of mob fury. It appeared that the paper had had its fill of Isaiah Fountain and his escapades. The *Evening Sun* was ready to see him die for his crime. The paper declared:

> There has been too much delay and too much carelessness in the Fountain case, but otherwise it has been a credit to the State. His crime was of the fiendish sort that too often arouses such fury in a mob that it takes summary vengeance. Yet Fountain was protected, given a fair trial in his own county in another part of the State, besides being allowed two opportunities to escape. The charge

that he is being railroaded to the gallows because he is a negro is ridiculous.

A good deal of sympathy will be bestowed upon Fountain by soft-hearted persons, who forget the innocent and terribly estranged and mutilated victim of his crime. It will be argued that he is a negro of low mentality and should not be executed for his murderous bestiality. But if capital punishment is ever justified, surely it must be in such a case as Fountain's.[35]

The *Evening Sun*'s new perspective on lynching suggested the paper wouldn't object if a mob stormed the Talbot County Jail and lynched Isaiah Fountain on the spot. The paper, like many White residents of Talbot County, wanted to see Isaiah Fountain dead and the Fountain case over.

The Death Warrant

On the day after Fountain's capture, Governor Ritchie, through his secretary of state, set the date for the execution. Sheriff Soulsby received a warrant that authorized him to hang Fountain at the Talbot County Jail on Friday, July 23, 1920—just one month away.[36] Sheriff Soulsby read the formal death warrant to Isaiah Fountain in his jail cell. Witnesses reported that after hearing the news, the prisoner appeared to be resigned to his fate.[37] Isaiah Fountain's end was near.

Endnotes

1 "Negro Stirs Easton," *Wilmington News Journal*, May 17, 1920, 6. Newspapers.com.

2 "Negro, Doomed to Hang, Calmly Awaits Death," *Baltimore Sun*, June 12, 1920, 11. Newspapers.com.

3 "Negro, Doomed to Hang, Calmly Awaits Death," 11.

4 "Bloodhounds on Trail," *Star-Democrat*, June 19, 1920.

5 "Fountain's Chase Covers All Roads of the Eastern Shore," *Baltimore Evening Sun*, June 16, 1920, 1. Newspapers.com.

6 "Fountain's Chase Covers All Roads of the Eastern Shore," 1.

7 "Chase Leads to Delaware for Fountain," *Baltimore Sun*, June 17, 1920, 1. Newspapers.com.

8 "State Police Again Urged," *Baltimore Sun*, June 17, 1920, 22. Newspapers.com.

9 "Chase Leads to Delaware for Fountain," 1.

10 "Manhunt Off on Hot Scent for Fountain," *Baltimore Sun*, June 18, 1920, 1 and 8. Newspapers.com.

11 "Bloodhounds on Trail," *Star-Democrat*, June 19, 1920, 7.

12 "Appeal Sent Out for Aid in Fountain Hunt," *Baltimore Sun*, June 21, 1920, 1. Newspapers.com.

13 "Bloodhounds at Loss in Hunt for Fountain," *Baltimore Sun*, June 19, 1920, 2. Newspapers.com.

14 "Bloodhounds at Loss in Hunt for Fountain," 2.

15 "Ask All to Hunt Fountain," *Wilmington Evening Journal*, June 21, 1920, 6. Newspapers.com.

16 "Good People in Easton Outnumbered by the Bad," *Baltimore Afro-American*, June 25, 1920, 3. ProQuest.com.

17 "Isaiah Fountain Surrounded in a Wood Near Laurel," *Wilmington News Journal*, June 22, 1920, 1. Newspapers.com.

18 Diary entry of Charles F. Willis Sr. in James Dawson's *100 Years of Change on the Eastern Shore*, 337.

19 "Man Hunt Is on in Delaware for Fountain," *Baltimore Sun*, June 20, 1920, 2. Newspapers.com.

20 "Appeal Sent out for Aid in Fountain Hunt," 1.

21 "Fountain Is Captured 14 Miles from Easton; Safely Landed in Jail," *Baltimore Sun*, June 23, 1920, 1. Newspapers.com.

22 "Catch Negro Fugitive through Brave Girl Who Rides for Posse," *Wilmington Morning News*, June 23, 1920, 1. Newspapers.com.

23 "Catch Negro Fugitive through Brave Girl Who Rides for Posse," 1.

24 "Fountain Found on Deal's Island Sheriff Is Told," *Baltimore Evening Sun*, June 19, 1920, 1. Newspapers.com.

25 "July 23 Designated for Fountain Hanging," *Baltimore Sun*, July 24, 1920, 3. Newspapers.com.

26 "Loper, Arrested Here, Suspected of Aiding in the Fountain Escape," *Wilmington News Journal*, June 17, 1920, 1 and 10. Newspapers.com.

27 "Fountain to Be Executed July 23," *News Journal*, June 24, 1920, 11. Newspapers.com.

28 "Fountain Is Captured 14 Miles from Easton; Safely Landed in Jail," 1.

29 "Fountain to Die July 23," *Wilmington Evening Journal*, June 24, 1920, 3. Newspapers.com.

30 "Fountain Is Captured 14 Miles from Easton; Safely Landed in Jail," 1.

31 "Lynched in Duluth," *Baltimore Evening Sun*, June 17, 1920, 19. Newspapers.com.

32 "Lynched in Duluth," 19.

33 Douglas O. Linder, "Lynching Statistics by Year," Famous Trials website, | University of Missouri, Kansas City School of Law, accessed June 23, 2021, https://www.famous-trials.com/sheriffshipp/1084-lynchingsyear.

34 "Lynched in Duluth," 19.

35 "Fountain Back in Jail," *Baltimore Evening Sun*, June 23, 1920, 15. Newspapers.com.

36 "Attorney General Investigates," *Star-Democrat*, June 26, 1920.

37 "Isaiah Fountain Has Cost Talbot $12,000," *Baltimore Evening Sun*, June 25, 1920, 25. Newspapers.com.

CHAPTER 16

Preparing for the Execution

Sheriff Soulsby said that Talbot County will have to make its own gallows, there being none near by which he can borrow, and he is therefore making his own arrangements accordingly.

—EASTON STAR-DEMOCRAT

Hanging Questions

As soon as Isaiah Fountain was convicted at his second trial, he knew he would die for the crime he denied committing, though not exactly when. Now—after his second escape and capture—it was announced that he had less than four weeks to live.

The question of when Fountain would die had been decided by the governor. Sheriff Soulsby was now confronted by other questions. Should Fountain's execution be public or private? And where would he get a gallows?

Public or Private

In the early twentieth century, the Maryland law left the details of every execution up to the county where the crime had been committed. The county sheriff decided if a hanging would be public or private. The *Easton Star-Democrat* explained:

> Owing to the present law of the State of Maryland, it is necessary that the condemned be executed in the county in which the crime was committed. In other states, where more modern laws have been put into effect this is not the case, but the ancient custom of localized executions still holds good here. As things stand at present, Fountain will have to be hanged at Easton.[1]

As with most topics involving the Isaiah Fountain case, opinions on the subject differed. One faction thought that the general public "deserved" the opportunity to see the convicted rapist die. An alarmingly large segment of Talbot countians supported this view. They wanted to witness Fountain's hanging, not only to see him atone for the crime of rape for which he was convicted, but because of the notoriety, embarrassment, trouble, and expense that his two trials, appeals, and two escapes had caused Talbot County. Many felt that they had been denied swift justice, since so much time had already passed since Bertha Simpson's rape on April 1, 1919. They wanted to see Fountain die in a public space.

A more conservative faction in Talbot County was against making Isaiah Fountain's execution a public event. The idea of allowing such a public spectacle raised fears that a large crowd of spectators might become unruly and demolish any

physical barriers erected to separate the mob from the condemned prisoner, "as had been the case on countless similar
occasions."[2] The leading opponent of a public execution was
General Joseph Seth[3] (the "Lost Cause" supporter mentioned
in Chapter 1), who issued this statement to the *Star-Democrat*:

> A large number of persons [...] not only in Easton, but
> all through the county and adjoining counties, are anx-
> ious that the hanging of Fountain be public. Many others,
> myself among them, prefer to have the execution done
> privately, and in as decent a manner as possible.
>
> There has been much trouble in the county because of
> Fountain, however, and the demand from persons who
> desire to see him executed has been very strong. I think
> possibly the authorities will heed this demand simply
> because of the feeling which has been aroused because
> of the case.
>
> I am opposed to making the execution public for several
> reasons. It would bring into Easton a large element which
> would be more or less objectionable. Hundreds of strang-
> ers from all over the Eastern Shore would come into town
> in their automobiles, and a crowd gather[ed] to witness
> such a spectacle would not be of the best element.
>
> There has been little discussion of the matter. Since the
> question is one of discretion and is in the hands of the
> sheriff I do not think anything has been done by those
> who would prefer a private hanging as in the best interests
> of the county. The sentiment on both sides is strong, and I
> do not believe that on the part of those who wish a private
> execution it has crystallized sufficiently to make an appeal
> to the authorities probable.

Personally I should be glad to see all executions in Maryland take place at the penitentiary in Baltimore or some other central point designated by law.[4]

Seth's opposition to the public hanging of Fountain had more to do with the "best interests" of Easton and Talbot County and how they were perceived by the public. Social or moral sensibilities about the spectacle of executing a man in public were secondary concerns for him. Others were more concerned about the damaging effects that public executions had on society and believed that they were barbaric sideshows that appealed to people's baser appetites.

The *Baltimore Sun* wrote:

There is danger that the public itself may be brutalized by making executions vulgar holidays for the entertainment of morbidly curious crowds. Public executions frequently shame the law and are a scandal to the community, because they seem to be representative of a low popular moral tone, and reveal a cold-blooded indifference to suffering and a callous curiosity that put the crown almost on a level with the criminal.

Public executions should not be permitted in Maryland. They are relics of the Dark Ages. While sheriffs are still vested with discretion in the matter, they should so exercise it as to protect their counties from the disgraceful and degrading conditions that public executions nearly always involve. Talbot has suffered enough from Fountain already. Sheriff Soulsby should see to it that the county's dignity and good name are not brought into reproach by converting the last solemn act of the law into a brutal popular picnic.[5]

The *Sun* wrote that public executions should be banned because they might be used by the condemned person as sort of a public soapbox for a cause or ideology. The *Sun* warned about glorifying the criminal and continued, "There is a sickly vein of sentimentality that would make heroes and victims out of the basest and foulest." The paper suggested that Isaiah Fountain wanted to be publicly executed "so that he may pose as a martyr and pass away with great éclat."[6]

The *Evening Sun* also reported that Fountain wanted to be executed in public. It published a front-page article claiming that Fountain had said he was being persecuted "just as Christ was persecuted." The paper reported that when Sheriff Soulsby announced that the execution would be public, Fountain asked that he die "with a crown of thorns on his brow and arrayed in purple robes."[7] There was ongoing disagreement as to whether Sheriff Soulsby even made such an announcement about a public execution, so the "crown of thorns" report also may be incorrect.

Sheriff Soulsby was pressured by the public and the press as they waited for him to decide whether he would execute Isaiah Fountain publicly or privately. The *Baltimore Sun* announced on July 1, 1920 that Fountain's execution "will probably be public." In the next sentence, the article stated that the sheriff "had not definitely made up his mind" about hanging. Finally, in the same brief article, the paper quoted Soulsby as saying, "I expect, however, the hanging will be public." Sheriff Soulsby added: "A few persons here want Fountain hanged privately. . . The great majority, however, want to see his execution."[8] Despite some reported indecision by the sheriff, it appeared that Soulsby's mindset about the execution was in line with popular sentiment for a public execution.

Just three days later, the *Sun* reported that Maryland Governor Ritchie, in San Francisco at the time, had heard about the sheriff's preference for a public hanging and ordered him to "make the hanging a private affair."[9] The *Easton Star-Democrat* declared that the *Sun* had once again published false information, that Sheriff Soulsby had never made any announcement about the execution being public, and that the governor never ordered Soulsby to reverse his decision.[10] Four days before the scheduled execution, Sheriff Soulsby finally announced that Isaiah Fountain would be hanged privately.[11]

The Gallows

The other consideration for Sheriff Soulsby was where to get a gallows. So far, all he had was a noose left over from an execution that was cancelled in 1903.[12] He still needed a gallows and a place to erect it.

Sheriff Soulsby realized that there was a gallows "problem" after Isaiah Fountain had been convicted at his second trial in May and returned to Talbot County for his execution. At that time, he told the *Easton Star-Democrat* that Talbot County would have to build a gallows because it didn't own one. Soulsby told the paper that he would be making the arrangements himself.[13]

One newspaper reported that Soulsby borrowed a used gallows from neighboring Caroline County,[14] but that report was incorrect. Soulsby knew that if he erected a gallows in the walled jail yard adjacent to the county jail, the execution would not be private. The wall surrounding the yard was too low to block the view of an execution. Erecting a screen around the gallows wouldn't provide privacy: Soulsby figured that the gathered crowd would simply tear down the screen so they could view the execution. Therefore, using an existing gallows wouldn't work for a private execution. Soulsby's plan involved constructing a new gallows in the only secure space that would ensure privacy and security—*inside* the Talbot County Jail. The gallows would have to be custom-built to fit the space.

Sheriff Soulsby decided to build the execution scaffold in the north end of the jail, in the corridor that separated the jail from his office. Reporting on how the sheriff had solved the privacy and security problems for the execution, the Wilmington News Journal provide details of the scaffold's construction:

The scaffold is made of four large white oak corner posts, from the top of which runs a cross bar, through which the rope which is to be placed around Fountain's neck is suspended. This rope is of hemp. The platform on which Fountain is to stand is about eight feet from the floor of the corridor and is seven and one-half by five feet. The trapdoor through which Fountain will fall is three and one-half feet square.

In leaving his cell to go to the scaffold Fountain will walk the entire length of the corridor, from the south end of the jail to the north end. He will have to walk up 11 steps to the platform on which he is to stand. The scaffold will be finished this afternoon, when the trap will be tried to see that the door falls all right.[15]

With the details of Fountain's execution resolved and the gallows construction nearly complete, Sheriff Soulsby was almost ready for the impending execution. He still had to plan for additional security, because large crowds were expected even though they wouldn't be able to see Fountain die. Soulsby also had to summon twenty local citizens to serve as official witnesses to the hanging, along with jail officials and a jail physician. Isaiah Fountain's family members were asked if they wanted to witness the hanging, but none responded. The sheriff told the press that he hadn't yet set an exact time for the execution and that no press representatives would be allowed.[16] Soulsby was almost ready for the hanging. Could Isaiah Fountain say the same?

Endnotes

1 "Sheriff Makes Denial," *Easton Star-Democrat*, July 10, 1920, 2.

2 "Sheriff Makes Denial," 2.

3 As noted in Chapter 1, Joseph Seth was a leading believer of the "Lost Cause" myth, as well as the driving force for the erection of the Talbot Boys Confederate monument in front of the Talbot County Courthouse a few years earlier. Seth was called "General," not because of any military background, but due to his former position as judge advocate general of Maryland.

4 "Sheriff Makes Denial," 2.

5 "Fountain's Execution," *Baltimore Sun*, July 1, 1920, 8. Newspapers.com.

6 "Fountain's Execution," 8.

7 "Fountain Requests Crown of Thorns," *Baltimore Evening Sun*, June 29, 1920, 1. Newspapers.com.

8 "Hanging of Fountain Likely to Be Public," *Baltimore Sun*, July 1, 1920, 1. Newspapers.com.

9 "Fountain Hanging Private," *Baltimore Sun*, July 4, 1920, 12. Newspapers.com.

10 "Sheriff Makes Denial," 2.

11 "Fountain Execution to Be Strictly Private," *Baltimore Sun*, July 20, 1920, 5. Newspapers.com.

12 "Fountain in Jail," *Easton Star-Democrat*, May 15, 1920, 4.

13 "Has Been Converted," *Easton Star-Democrat*, May 22, 1920.

14 Untitled, *Midland Journal*, June 11, 1920, 4. Newspapers.com.

15 "Isaiah Fountain to Hang Tomorrow," *Wilmington News Journal*, July 22, 1920, 3. Newspapers.com.

16 "Fountain to Hang Friday in Private," *Baltimore Evening Sun*, July 19, 1920, 1. Newspapers.com. Even though this article said that newspaper reporters would not be allowed at Fountain's execution, later reports mention reporters as being witnesses.

CHAPTER 17

The Death Watch and Execution

*He was in the ground before most residents
of Easton were up.*

—BALTIMORE SUN

Time Running Out

Isaiah Fountain's time on earth was running out, and he
was, understandably, frightened. According to one newspaper, he had tried to smuggle a note out of the jail to a friend
asking for poison so he wouldn't have to face the noose.
The sheriff intercepted the note and foiled the suicide plot.
This prompted Sheriff Soulsby to limit Fountain's visitors to
family members and his spiritual advisor.[1] Allowing fewer
visitors also reduced interference with the construction of the
scaffold. To ensure complete privacy, the sheriff said that the
windows in the corridor where the scaffold was erected would
be completely covered to prevent anyone from looking in. In
addition, the prisoners in the north corridor of the jail were
to be transferred to the opposite corridor so that they would
not have to see the execution.[2]

As Fountain's execution day approached, Sheriff Soulsby was also concerned about possible problems outside the jail. Soulsby certainly remembered the mob that had gathered to lynch Isaiah Fountain during his Easton trial. He also remembered the angry crowds that hunted Fountain with weapons and ropes during his two escapes and gathered around the jail after he had been captured and re-arrested. Soulsby wanted to be certain that order was maintained when Fountain was hanged. He called on the state motorcycle police to assist with security. Twelve motorcycle policemen were sent to Easton the day before the execution to bolster the force of deputies and police already assigned. They were tasked with patrolling the roads leading into Easton and turning back people who had no official business in town. The road patrols began early on the evening before the hanging and ended only after Fountain's execution.[3]

The Death Watch

Isaiah Fountain wasn't the only nervous prisoner in the county jail. He and his jail-mates had to endure the hammering, sawing, and other noises involved with building the gallows in the jail corridor, just feet from their cells. With the iron bars of cell doors providing no sound barrier, the gallows construction had to be nerve-wracking for all the prisoners. As the clamor of the scaffold construction continued to echo throughout the jail, the prisoners, most of whom were Black, complained to Sheriff Soulsby. Sheriff Soulsby told the press that the prisoners were extremely superstitious and feared that Fountain's spirit would return to the jail to haunt them after his death. The inmates pleaded with Fountain, the sheriff said, not to return as a ghost while they were still in the jail.[4]

As much as the scaffold construction noise disturbed the other prisoners, it was worse for Isaiah Fountain. He knew that the closer the workmen came to completing the scaffold, the closer he was to hanging from it. Fountain's state of mind was described by the *Wilmington Evening Journal*:

The scaffold was completed shortly before 3 o'clock yesterday afternoon [Thursday, July 22, 1920] and the trap and rope were tested with two bags of sand weighing about 200 pounds. Everything worked smoothly.

Fountain was extremely nervous yesterday and moaned continually while the workmen were completing the scaffold. He could hear the workmen discussing the scaffold and his death. At one time he distinctly heard one workman ask another if he thought the drop sufficient to break Isaiah's neck.

Shortly after noon Fountain sent for Sheriff Soulsby and pleaded with the sheriff to shoot him at once. He said the noise made by the workmen in building the scaffold was too agonizing for him and he dreaded to die on the scaffold. Long after the sheriff left his cell he continued to plead for someone to shoot him.[5]

A reporter from the *Easton Star-Democrat* had interviewed Fountain in the jail the previous week, when he once again asserted his innocence:

"They have got me in here for something I know nothing about," was the way Isaiah Fountain began an interview for publication last Wednesday afternoon. "While I am not guilty of the crime I am accused of I am ready and willing to go when the law says so. The Lord is going to take care of me, in fact I know He is." This last statement was said with much emphasis and confidence.[6]

Fountain went on to blame his wife for his situation. He claimed that if she had simply withdrawn his money from the bank and returned home, he wouldn't have gotten into trouble. He maintained, "I was in town when they claim the crime was committed." Fountain would not comment on whether he had a fair trial, but only said that it was useless to say anything about it. He had only good things to say about Sheriff Soulsby. He realized that the sheriff was only doing his duty and praised both the sheriff and his wife for their kindness.[7]

Isaiah Fountain attempted to get some spiritual comfort while he waited for his execution. He spent hours in his cell with two Black preachers, one from Trappe and the other from Easton. They sang hymns and read the Bible with Fountain to distract him from the noisy gallows construction that made it all but impossible to forget his looming execution. Fountain also told the clergymen that he was innocent of the crime for which he was to die.[8]

The overwrought Fountain continued to try to cheat the hangman's noose. With two days to go, he was placed under a deathwatch, but despite this, he tried to slash himself with a safety razor blade he found in front of his cell. His suicide attempt was foiled by the officer guarding his cell. Later the same evening, the officer heard noise in Fountain's darkened cell and shined his flashlight in to see the prisoner trying to make a noose from his bedclothes. After this second suicide attempt, the deathwatch was increased.[9]

Fountain's Execution (Friday, July 23, 1920)

Just before his hanging, Fountain met with his preacher in his cell. He reaffirmed his innocence one last time, and they said some final prayers together. Fountain's guards came for him shortly after 3:05 a.m. and took him to the sheriff's office, where his hands were tied behind his back.[10]

The *Sun* reported that Fountain "maintained his innocence to the end." It continued:

> Fountain went to pieces badly before the end. He was a-tremble and could scarcely speak coherently when he was told to get ready. It was necessary to assist him down the corridor of the jail and up the steps of the gallows. He appeared scarcely able to stand as the noose was being adjusted around his neck.[11]

Some of the witnesses expected Fountain to collapse before he climbed the eleven steps to the scaffold platform, but he made it to the top without faltering. Once Isaiah reached the platform, Sheriff Soulsby placed the noose around his neck and prepared to spring the trapdoor. At 3:13 on Friday morning, July 23, 1920, Sheriff Soulsby executed Isaiah Fountain. The *Star-Democrat* reported: "The trap was then sprung and Fountain had passed to the Great Beyond almost instantaneously." However, though the abrupt fall through the trapdoor of the scaffold broke Fountain's neck, it apparently didn't immediately kill him. He lingered at the end of the rope for ten agonizing minutes before the attending physician pronounced Isaiah Fountain dead, at 3:23 a.m.[12]

Fountain's family had refused to bury his body, but a grave had been dug for him on his farm near Trappe. His body was quickly cut down from the gallows, transported to his farm, and buried. The *Baltimore Sun* reported that "He was in the ground before most residents of Easton were up."[13]

The report that Isaiah Fountain's family had refused to bury him raises some questions. Had his family assumed he was guilty of rape and turned their backs on him? Were they ashamed because he was a convicted criminal and was hanged? Did their association with Isaiah Fountain make them possible targets of repercussions from angry Whites? Unfortunately, as was mentioned earlier, the newspapers of the time did not print articles about Black people, their activities, opinions, or feelings—unless they happened to be involved in criminal activities against Whites.

Except for some later legal issues involving Isaiah Fountain's mother and friends, I could find no other information about his survivors. Probably his wife (and children) moved to New Jersey to be with her family, as she had earlier planned. Isaac Fountain, the head of the family, had died, and the family farm had been sold to pay for Isaiah Fountain's legal expenses. The remaining family members possibly suffered shame and ostracism, due to Fountain's charges of alleged rape. Taking these factors into consideration, it's possible that living in Talbot County was no longer an option for Isaiah Fountain's survivors, prompting them to leave the area. Like many others, Isaiah Fountain's family likely just wanted to put the Fountain case behind them.

Reactions

The security measures that Sheriff Soulsby put in place out-side the jail were effective. The crowd that gathered there was far smaller than the thousands that had appeared on account of Fountain in the past. However, the *Sun* reported that three to four hundred people stayed in the streets out-side the jail all night waiting for the word that Fountain had been hanged. At one point, a group of people used a log as a battering ram, attempting to break into the jail, but they were driven away by the guards that Sheriff Soulsby had posted.[14]

The newspapers that had been covering the Fountain case from near and far all ran stories about the execution, some in greater detail than others. Many expressed relief that the twice-convicted rapist was dead, and justice was finally served.

Isaiah Fountain's hanging was, of course, an important topic with the people of Talbot County, from adults to chil-dren. A farmer living near Trappe recorded the event in his diary: "July 24: The negro, Isaiah Fountain, was [hanged] at 3.00 a.m. yesterday. The early hour to avoid any demonstra-tion by the people, if a daylight execution."[15]

Fountain's hanging was also noteworthy for Alice Gale Reddie, a sixteen-year-old girl who lived a few blocks from the jail on South Harrison Street. The hanging affected young Alice enough for her to memorialize the event in her diary:

July 23 Friday

At 3:13 this morning a niger [*sic*] [Isaiah] Fountain was hanged in Easton for the crime of assault on a white girl down in [Trappe] district. People were very well worried a niger uprising was feared and, some politicians tried to save the niger but Trappe would not stand for it.[16]

Bertha Simpson had been raped 479 days earlier and had identified Isaiah Fountain as her attacker. Since then, Fountain had been the subject of three different manhunts, two of those after he escaped jail. He was tried twice and convicted twice. He faced mobs that threatened to lynch him several times. He was hanged once, in accordance with the sentence of law, and with fatal effect. Who would have thought that Isaiah Fountain would survive sixteen months of outrage and Jim Crow "justice" to finally have a legally sanctioned execution? The Fountain case was finally over. Or was it?

Endnotes

1 "Fountain Would Secure Poison to End His Life," *Baltimore Sun*, July 17, 1920, 1. Newspapers.com.

2 "Fountain Execution to Be Strictly Private," *Baltimore Sun*, July 20, 1920, 5. Newspapers.com.

3 "Fountain Nervous as Scaffold Goes Up," *Baltimore Sun*, July 21, 1920, 2.

4 "Fountain Nervous as Scaffold Goes Up," 2.

5 "Negro Dies on Gallows: Tried Twice at Suicide," *Wilmington Evening Journal*, July 23, 1920, 17. Newspapers.com.

6 "Still Denies His Guilt," *Star-Democrat*, July 17, 1920, 1.

7 "Still Denies His Guilt," 1.

8 "Negro Dies on Gallows: Tried Twice at Suicide," 1 and 17.

9 "Fountain Pays Penalty," *Star-Democrat*, July 24, 1920, 1.

10 "Negro Dies on Gallows: Tried Twice at Suicide," 1.

11 "Denying Guilt, Fountain Goes to His Death," *Baltimore Sun*, July 23, 1920, 1. Newspapers.com.

12 "Fountain Pays Penalty," *Star-Democrat*, July 24, 1920.

13 "Denying Guilt, Fountain Goes to His Death," 1.

14 "Fountain Goes to Death; Denies His Guilt to the End," *Baltimore Sun*, July 24, 1920, 2. Newspapers.com.

15 Diary entry of Charles F. Willis Sr. in James Dawson's *100 Years of Change on the Eastern Shore*, 331.

16 Diary entry of Alice Gale Reddie, 1920, 31. Cathy Hill (Alice Gale Reddie Diary, Talbot Historical Society), in an April 4, 2020 email message to author about the discovery of the diary, said: "6 years ago a construction friend of mine who found an Easton High School girl's (graduate 1920) diary stuck inside of the walls of an Easton, Md., Harrison Street home. She spoke of hiding it before she left for college and she may have dropped it down the eaves from the attic and it ended up hidden in the wall between the basement and first floor."

CHAPTER 18

Remnants of the Fountain Case

It is inconceivable to me that such a thing could have happened.

—JUDGE WILLIAM H. ADKINS

Why the Fountain Case Was Unique

Books and articles have been written about some of the many brutal lynchings that occurred in the United States and in Maryland. The victims of these atrocities usually had no opportunity to escape their tormentors and nothing close to a legal "process" to argue their cases. Even where the targets of lynch mobs, accused of various crimes, did have trials, they were often summary shams that ended in court-ordered executions or "legal" lynchings. The so-called legal proceedings, including the executions, usually occurred so quickly that there was no time for anyone to put together a defense or even think about escaping.

The Isaiah Fountain case was unique in that Fountain took advantage of situations that allowed him to have a say in his fate. By escaping, he actively avoided being lynched by outraged mobs. Twice he ran, and twice he was captured.

Fountain and his attorneys also vigorously used the legal system to try to prove his innocence. He had a trial, an appeal of his first guilty verdict, and then a second trial. Unfortunately, except for the decision from his first appeal, the legal system of the time provided Fountain little relief. A jury trial and trial by judges both failed him. Even having a solid and compelling alibi provided by three prominent and disinterested White citizens wasn't enough to overcome the pervasive Jim Crow sentiment of the time.

Despite several close calls, Isaiah Fountain wasn't strung up by mobs, nor did he have a quick sham trial with an even quicker execution. The fight for his life and freedom lasted sixteen months—an astonishing feat for a Jim Crow Black man accused of raping a White female.

The length of time it took to prosecute and execute Fountain was an embarrassment for Talbot County. In the eyes of many Talbot countians, justice delayed was justice denied. Even more humbling for the county was that Isaiah Fountain escaped from county custody twice, generating scathing headlines nationwide. The escapes and the extended legal process were drains on the county's budget. Finally, the Fountain case generated "spin-off" controversies that extended its infamy for an additional year.

The Fountain Case Lives On

Isaiah Fountain was dead and buried on his farm in Talbot County, but his notoriety did not end with his execution. The legacy and consequences of his case lived on. The

Easton Star-Democrat had been prophetic when it called the Fountain case "one of the most noted in the State's annals."[1] Fountain continued to be an early-twentieth-century media sensation even in death. His name would be associated with trial costs, investigations, lawsuits, brutality complaints, and execution-reform legislation.

The Costs of the Case

The Isaiah Fountain case proved to be very expensive for the taxpayers of Talbot County—probably more so than anyone could have imagined when he was first singled out as a rape suspect. Not long after Fountain's first trial, Talbot County had received bills from the Baltimore Police Department for the various services provided for the trial. The county ignored the payment notices and complained about the "exorbitant charges."

Just prior to the execution, the accountants were still tallying up the final monetary costs of the Fountain case and what the county owed. At that point, the *Baltimore Evening Sun* reported that the total costs to Talbot County for the Fountain case were more than $12,000 (almost $203,000 in 2022 dollars[2]). The costs incurred by the county included Fountain's initial manhunt and return to Easton; the first trial and manhunt after escaping the lynch mob; half of Judge Adkins's reward offer; charges for the Maryland Militia, Baltimore Police, and state motorcycle police providing trial security; court of appeal costs; and costs for the search the second time he escaped, including paying for the use of the bloodhounds.[3] Other expenses included "$100 for the execution and the costs of the gallows," as well as Fountain's food and board.[4]

Finally, in December 1920, the *Easton Star-Democrat* reported: "The county commissioners on Tuesday passed for payment what is believed to be the last bill incurred because of the Isaiah Fountain trials. [...] The full amount of the costs to the taxpayers because of this case cannot be learned at this time, but [the] county treasurer will give the exact figures as soon as the press of work in his office will permit."[5]

One newspaper reported that tax rate for Talbot County citizens would have to be increased to pay for "the great expense" of the Fountain case.[6] The monetary cost of the case for each of the 18,000 Talbot County residents amounted to more than $0.67 per resident ($11.32 in 2022 dollars).[7] As with any tax hike, this increase was certainly not welcomed by Talbot County taxpayers and surely gave them yet another reason to be outraged by the Fountain case.

Execution Legislation

Isaiah Fountain was the last person to be legally executed in Talbot County and on Maryland's Eastern Shore.[8] This dubious distinction is yet another legacy of the Fountain case. More importantly, Fountain's case helped to advance execution reform legislation in Maryland. The controversy generated by his hanging was instrumental in changing where and how future executions would be performed in the State of Maryland.

The question of whether Fountain's hanging should be conducted publicly or privately was left to Sheriff Soulsby to decide. He was pressed by various factions and reportedly was directed by Governor Ritchie to have a private hanging. Although the execution went as planned, the public debate about where and how it should happen only increased support to have a centralized execution facility in the State of Maryland.

On March 8, 1922, Maryland State Senator David G. McIntosh Jr. introduced a bill in the Maryland Senate that would require all legal executions in Maryland to be conducted at the Maryland House of Correction as of January 1, 1923. Just two days after the bill was introduced, the *Baltimore Sun* published an editorial supporting the McIntosh legislation. The editorial declared:

> The scandal of county executions has been shocking to the civilized sense of the people of the State, and the brutal and morbid curiosity which they seem always to stimulate has been a source of wonder and humiliation to all humane and self-respecting minds.
>
> It is difficult to understand how, in supposedly decent communities, thousands of men and women could be found who seemed to delight in witnessing such spectacles and who flock to them as to a circus. The recent execution at Towson was characterized by this barbarous spirit, as was that some time ago at Easton. Whenever an execution occurs in the counties there is almost invariably such an exhibition of human degradation and savagery as almost makes us wonder who is the greater brute—the fiend on the gallows [or] the hardened man in the crowd who revels in the ghastly drama.
>
> This should end at once and for all. We cannot afford to pander any longer to this lingering element of hideous brutality.[9]

The time was right, and the McIntosh Bill passed both the Maryland Senate and the House of Delegates. It required the warden of the Maryland Penitentiary to establish a separate "death chamber" in which to conduct all future executions. On April 11, 1922, Governor Albert C. Ritchie signed the bill into law. After January 1, 1923, legal executions would no longer be conducted in the Maryland counties where the crimes occurred.[10] The first execution at the Maryland Penitentiary under the new law was conducted on June 8, 1923. George Chelton, a Black man, was hanged in the newly constructed chamber for assaulting a White girl in Somerset County, Maryland.[11]

Sheriff Soulsby Charged with Brutality

Just one week after Isaiah Fountain was hanged in the Talbot County Jail, his name appeared in front page headlines again. The *Baltimore Afro-American* printed a special report from the Frederick, Maryland, *Daily News* that alleged that Sheriff Soulsby had severely beaten Fountain just before his execution. Two "automobile deputies" (state policemen) from the Frederick area reported that they had been assigned as guards outside Fountain's jail cell prior to his hanging. The deputies said that Sheriff Soulsby had entered Fountain's cell about an hour and a half before the hanging and tried to get Fountain to confess to raping Bertha Simpson. The article reported that "Fountain was knocked down and beaten, and that one long gash on his head would be revealed if the body were exhumed for the purpose of conducting an investigation." The story continued:

Fountain, it is said, yelled pitifully, and declared "I'll say what you want me to say, but I didn't do it."

It is also reported that another Negro confined in the jail, who told Fountain to make a struggle when he was led on the scaffold, was also beaten.

The officers said no report of the beating had gained general circulation because no one was present at the time except Fountain, the sheriff and the two officers who witnessed the alleged affair. They did not talk about it until after they left Easton. Both discussed the alleged brutality in a matter of fact way, and told it to a number of Frederick people.[12]

The first news reports about the brutality charges against Sheriff Soulsby were confined to the Frederick newspapers and the *Baltimore Afro-American*. The American Legion post in Frederick got involved, and on August 10, 1920, the organization tried to pass a resolution to pressure Governor Ritchie to investigate Sheriff Soulsby's actions. The resolution was defeated but served to get other newspapers involved in investigating the story.[13] Soon the newspapers in Baltimore, Wilmington, Delaware, and elsewhere printed their own articles about Soulsby's beating Fountain. The *Wilmington News Journal* wrote that Sheriff Soulsby denied the reports and said that Isaiah Fountain "was given proper treatment."[14]

The *Easton Star-Democrat*, predictably, reported that Easton was "indignant" about the charges against Sheriff Soulsby. The paper again directed its ire at the *Baltimore Evening Sun*, claiming that the paper printed the charges about Soulsby as an effort to "get even" with him:

Because Sheriff Soulsby would not permit the misrepresentatives [sic] of the Evening Sun to have the "run of the jail" on the night of Isaiah Fountain's execution the Evening Sun has chosen to get even by bringing up utterly unfounded charges of cruelty to the prisoner during his last hours.

The Evening Sun has brought the matter to the attention of the governor who in turn has written a letter to Judge Adkins, asking that the charges be investigated. Just why the governor wrote as he did is a mystery, as the letter states that Motor Vehicles Commissioner Baughman and all of his deputies knew nothing of the alleged cruelty, all of whom were in the jail corridor the entire evening. The governor also called a prominent Eastonian on the phone and questioned him, and was told that there was no truth to the stories whatever.

The undertaker who buried Fountain states that there were no marks of any kind on Fountain, and several Easton physicians also testified to the same.

The Evening Sun has been such a notorious example of yellow journalism that anything it says about the Fountain case is discounted here. The only effect of this latest attack is to incense the people here more and to rally around Sheriff Soulsby.

The Baltimore Star has already added luster to its already lurid reputation by following the Evening Sun's lead in this matter. The general public here rather hope the grand jury will summon the cubs responsible for these tales, as there will then be a chance to indict them for perjury and bring home to them the consequences of promiscuous lying.[15]

Governor Ritchie was under great public pressure to act on the allegations against Sheriff Soulsby. On August 24, 1920, Ritchie sent a letter to Chief Judge Adkins in Easton, asking Adkins to empanel a grand jury to investigate the sheriff's actions. Along with his letter, the governor enclosed copies of the initial newspaper reports that were published on July 28, 1920 in the *Cumberland Times* and *Frederick News*. Ritchie also wrote that he had interviewed the head of the state motorcycle deputies and some of the members of the press who were at the execution. The governor wrote that he felt that none of the motorcycle officers witnessed or were a part of any of the allegations, and that "the charges rested too much on hearsay and inference for me to place real reliance on it." Still, Ritchie felt that the charges of cruelty were so shocking that they should be investigated. He wanted those responsible to be punished and those not responsible to be vindicated.[16]

Ritchie wrote that he had investigated the matter to the degree that he was able but had no "jurisdiction or control" over the sheriff. The governor said that since the sheriff was subject to Adkins's court, Adkins should be the one to empanel a grand jury and investigate the charges. Ritchie ended his letter to Adkins by leaving it up to the judge to "refer it to the grand jury or to let it rest."[17]

Judge Adkins replied to Governor Ritchie's letter on August 26, 1920, informing the governor that he did not feel it was necessary to call a special session of the Talbot County grand jury to investigate the charges against Sheriff Soulsby. Adkins affirmed that "it is inconceivable to me that such a thing could have happened." He then suggested that when the regular November term of the grand jury met, "there

THE ISAIAH FOUNTAIN CASE - Joseph Koper

should be a thorough investigation." Judge Adkins then
turned the tables on the governor, suggesting that Ritchie
organize the investigation. After all, if state officers had seen
and reported the alleged brutality, they should have acted to
prevent it. Adkins's letter to Ritchie continued:

> I think you would be entirely justified in having a search-
> ing inquiry made. The good name of the State is involved,
> and *if the thing charged actually happened, it must have hap-
> pened under the eyes of the State officers charged with the
> duty of guarding the prisoner and sent here by your authority.*
> [Emphasis added.]
>
> If an investigation by you of the conduct of these officers
> should develop the slightest base of truth for the [r]umor
> of improper conduct on the part of the Sheriff, I shall not
> hesitate to act on the matter.[18]

Governor Ritchie wrote back to Judge Adkins on August
30, 1920, accepting Adkins's suggestion: "I will, accordingly,
make such investigation of the matter as lies within my power
and forward the result to you."[19] The controversy that neither
Ritchie nor Adkins wanted was back in the governor's hands.

Evidently, Governor Ritchie never did investigate Sheriff
Soulsby's alleged mistreatment of Fountain—or if he did, no
results were published.

Chief Judge Adkins did charge the November term of
the Talbot County Grand Jury to investigate the cruelty
allegations. He told the grand jurors that Sheriff Soulsby
should be punished if they found the charges to be true, but
if they proved false, "he is entitled to have his name cleared
of slanderous tongues and pens and at the same time to take
away the reflection cast upon the county."[20] The grand jury

250

questioned numerous witnesses including several state motorcycle policemen, newspapermen, and other witness who were present at Fountain's execution. The panel also questioned Fountain's preacher and the undertaker.[21] On November 18, 1920, after two days of questioning witnesses, the grand jury exonerated Sheriff Soulsby of the cruelty and assault charges. The *Easton Star-Democrat* righteously proclaimed: "The sheriff was unanimously cleared of any ill treatment by the jury and Talbot County was once more proven to be not the place of lawlessness nor place of inhuman treatment, but an orderly and respectable community where every person, white or colored, receives fair treatment and impartial justice."[22] Once again, the paper's concern was more for the county's reputation and public image than whether a county prisoner had been brutalized.

Black Residents Sue Sheriff Soulsby

As noted in Chapter 15, during the week-long manhunt after Isaiah Fountain's second escape in June 1920, the searchers—under Sheriff Soulsby—were very zealous. They aggressively searched local African American homes and farms and stopped vehicles carrying Black people. Friends and members of Isaiah Fountain's family were also arrested and detained in the Talbot County Jail, where they were vigorously interrogated by the sheriff and Baltimore Police detectives. These actions and charges of physical abuse later created even more unfavorable publicity and more legal problems for Sheriff Soulsby.

During the manhunt, some of the searchers entered the homes of local Black people—including Fountain's family home itself—without warrants. They disturbed the residents and searched the homes "from top to bottom."[23] On June 16, 1920, while her son was evading searchers, Fannie Fountain was arrested for raising money to save Isaiah.[24] Almost two weeks later, the *Afro-American* newspaper reported that Mrs. Fountain, along with fourteen other Black residents of the area, was being held in the Talbot County Jail "on various flimsy charges."[25]

By the end of September 1920, while Sheriff Soulsby was still embroiled in the charges of cruelty against Isaiah Fountain, he faced more legal trouble. Six people arrested during the June manhunt for Fountain filed lawsuits against Soulsby in Baltimore City Court. The suits alleged that the people were arrested "in the hope of obtaining information as to his [Fountain's] whereabouts" and were filed by G. L. Pendleton, a Black attorney from Baltimore. He sued for $25,000 per person in damages from Sheriff Soulsby and the Fidelity and Deposit Company, Soulsby's bondsmen.[26] Seeking damages in the suits were Isaiah's mother, Fannie Fountain; two of his brothers, George and William Fountain; and three other Black women. The legal action charged:

> All alleged they were assaulted in their homes and made to spend "a black night of fear." Two of the women allege they were suspended by ropes in the jail and were swung to and fro like the pendulum of a clock; and George Fountain says he lost 66 turkeys. Most of them say they were kept in jail 10 days, although none had committed any offense.[27]

The *Baltimore Afro-American* newspaper was particularly outraged by the rough treatment reportedly suffered by the elder Mrs. Fountain when she was arrested. Even before the lawsuits were filed, the *Afro* reported details about her treatment:

> Mrs. Fountain was arrested on a night when a driving rain was falling and she was not allowed to dress. She and her son were cuffed up, as were other colored persons arrested in a futile effort to make them tell the man's [Fountain's] whereabouts. They knew nothing and, therefore, could tell nothing about the man's whereabouts. It is said that part of the household effects of the mother and son were destroyed by the invading party, trunks broken open, and the son lost 30 turkeys and over 100 fowl.
>
> Mrs. Fountain, who is an aged woman, and more bowed down than ever over the misfortune that has come to her. She was in no way connected with the crime of which her son was charged or with his escape. She declared herself humiliated at her treatment by deputies who forced her to go to jail in a driving rain without proper clothing. The aged woman broke down and wept bitterly as she told how she was cuffed about and put [through] the third degree at the jail when she was kept locked up for more than a week.[28]

According to a list of cases settled by Fannie Fountain's lawyer, G. L. Pendleton, her lawsuit for "mistreatment while in jail" was quickly dealt with, and by December 3, 1920, she was awarded $30,000 ($507,000 in 2022 dollars[29]). The list does not show the disposition of the other five lawsuits against Sheriff Soulsby, other than indicating that one of them was still being appealed as of January 21, 1925.[30] Evidently, Sheriff Soulsby's legal problems resulting from Isaiah

Fountain's case dragged on for years after the moment he sprung the gallows to hang him.

Return to Normal

By the end of 1920, news events and articles about the Isaiah Fountain case had evaporated. Fountain had been dead and buried since July. The various issues and controversies relating to his case had been investigated, the trial bills paid, and execution legislation initiated. Any remaining lawsuits were quietly litigated with little publicity. Life had returned to normal in Talbot County.

Endnotes

1 "Fountain to Baltimore?" *Star-Democrat*, November 29, 1919, 1.

2 Inflation Calculator, Saving.org Resources and Calculators, accessed March 30, 2022, https://www.saving.org/inflation/. Due to inflation, $1.00 in 1919 equals $16.90 in 2022.

3 "Isaiah Fountain Has Cost Talbot $12,000," *Baltimore Evening Sun*, June 25, 1920, 25. Newspapers.com.

4 "Fountain Case Cost $7,500, Court Officers Estimate," *Baltimore Sun*, July 10, 1920, 3 Newspapers.com.

5 "Last Fountain Bill," *Star-Democrat*, December 11, 1920, 1.

6 "Isaiah Fountain Has Cost Talbot $12,000," 25.

7 Inflation Calculator, Saving.org Resources and Calculators.

8 Juan I. Blanco, "Executions in Maryland—1876-1961," DeathPenaltyUSA website, accessed August 12, 2021, https://www.deathpenaltyusa.org/usa1/state/maryland2.htm.

9 "Private Executions," *Baltimore Sun*, March 10, 1922, 10. Newspapers.com.

10 Kevin G. Hemstock, *Injustice on the Eastern Shore: Race and the Hill Murder Trial* (Charleston: Arcadia Publishing, 2015), 177.

11 "First Hanging Is Held in State Penitentiary," *Baltimore Sun*, June 8, 1923, 28. Newspapers.com.

12 "Fountain Beaten before Execution," *Baltimore Afro-American*, July 30, 1920, 1. ProQuest.com.

13 "Motion Made to Probe Treatment of Fountain," *Baltimore Sun*, August 12, 1920, 1. Newspapers.com.

14 "Denies Ill-Treatment," *Wilmington News Journal*, August 5, 1920, 14. Newspapers.com.

15 "Easton Indignant," *Star-Democrat*, August 28, 1920.

16 "Alleged Cruelties to Fountain Taken Up," *Baltimore Evening Sun*, August 25, 1920, 22. and 8. Newspapers.com.

17 "Alleged Cruelties to Fountain Taken Up," 8.

18 "Governor to Probe Fountain Charges," *Baltimore Evening Sun*, August 31, 1920, 26. Newspapers.com.

19 "Governor to Probe Fountain Charges," 26.

20 "Bids Jury Sift Assault Rumor," *Wilmington Evening Journal*, November 16, 1920, 18. Newspapers.com.

21 "Fountain Probe Ended," *Wilmington Morning News*, November 19, 1920, 6. Newspapers.com.

22 "Sheriff Exonerated," *Star-Democrat*, November 20, 1920.

23 "Good People in Easton Outnumbered by the Bad," *Baltimore Afro-American*, June 25, 1920, 3. ProQuest.com.

24 "Fountain Escapes Again," *Baltimore Afro-American*, June 18, 1920, 1. ProQuest.com.

25 "Good People in Easton Outnumbered by the Bad," 3.

26 "Six Negroes Sue Sheriff," *Baltimore Sun*, October 1, 1920, 14. Newspapers.com.

27 "Six Negroes Sue Sheriff," 14.

28 "Fountain's Mother Roughly Handled," *Baltimore Afro-American*, July 16, 1920, 1. ProQuest.com.

29 Inflation Calculator, Saving.org Resources and Calculators.

30 "Court Decisions For Attorney George L. Pendleton." Maryland State Archives, accessed April 20, 2021, https://msa.maryland.gov/megafile/msa/speccol/sc5300/sc5339/000152/000000/000003/restricted/pendleton.xls.

CHAPTER 19

Isaiah Fountain: The Second Victim

But it seems there is serious doubts as to the guilt of the negro, in the minds of many who have read the full reports published of the trial and some who attended it. In their minds the alibi presented by his counsel was a convincing one.

—*BALTIMORE SUN*

The outcome, whatever the testimony or evidence presented, as everyone knew, was pre-ordained.

—SHERRILYN IFILL,
ON THE COURTHOUSE LAWN

The Questions

There is no doubt that Bertha Simpson was raped on April 1, 1919 and is the original victim in the Fountain case. Nonetheless, significant questions remain about Isaiah Fountain's guilt and his alleged presence at the crime scene. If Fountain wasn't present at the crime scene, he wasn't the rapist of Bertha Simpson. So who was?

After more than a century, no firsthand witnesses or participants in the Fountain case remain. However, many elements of the case beg to be re-examined. The surviving court documents and newspaper reports reveal obvious flaws in the way the case was investigated, prosecuted, and adjudicated. A reasonable person would likely agree that Isaiah Fountain would not be found guilty of the rape of Bertha Simpson if his trial were held today. In fact, he probably wouldn't even be prosecuted for the crime. A careful review of the related Maryland Court of Appeals documents and the hundreds of contemporaneous newspaper articles suggests that, far from being the scheming, manipulative, fiendish rapist he was portrayed as, Isaiah Fountain was the second victim of this case.

From the day Bertha Simpson singled out Isaiah Fountain as her attacker, no matter how questionable her identification, his fate was sealed. Talbot County reacted with almost blinding swiftness and tagged him as the rapist. There was a dogged determination in the county to prosecute, convict, and punish him with lethal dispatch. Fountain's coincidental departure from Talbot County the morning after the rape occurred was proof to many that he had committed the crime. From the beginning, the public and State's Attorney Butler believed that Fountain's trip to New Jersey to find his wife was part of his master plan to escape. There was no presumption of innocence for Isaiah Fountain.

Many residents of Talbot County, as well as some county officials, advocated and facilitated this rush to judgment. Perhaps the most noteworthy was the overly zealous Charles Butler, who allegedly was "out to get" Fountain because of a previous legal encounter. Butler abruptly took over the rape investigation from Sheriff Stitchberry, who was conducting an orderly and methodical investigation of the crime. Ignoring Stitchberry's evidence of another suspect, Butler summarily ordered the sheriff to go after Isaiah Fountain. Butler then conducted the victim's identification interview with only Simpson and her grandmother present and without the sheriff—even though he was in the same building at the time. Butler later had Simpson make the official identification of Fountain while the accused was the only Black man in the room and was surrounded by uniformed Baltimore Police officers. Reportedly, Butler even suggested that Fountain planned the rape and deliberately met with several prominent Easton citizens, including the chief of police, for the sole purpose of creating an alibi—and all this while he was nine miles from the crime scene at almost the same time the crime was taking place.[1]

At Fountain's first trial, the state's attorney failed to have Sheriff Stitchberry testify about significant exculpatory evidence, including Simpson's early statement that Fountain's horse and buggy were not the ones used during the crime. Nor did Sheriff Stitchberry get to testify that the horse and buggy that Simpson initially identified had been driven by another man during the time of her rape, and in the same area.

State's Attorney Butler, along with Chief Circuit Court Judge William Adkins, were instrumental in fast-tracking the indictment and trial of Isaiah Fountain. Butler and Adkins could have ensured that a more thorough investigation of the crime was conducted. They could have tried to "cool down" the fury of the population. However, they chose not to wait the thirty-seven days until the May term of the new grand jury to indict Fountain. Judge Adkins hurriedly recalled the previous term's grand jury to obtain a quick indictment and then scheduled the trial for just four days later. Only when the defense team requested more time to prepare their case did Judge Adkins delay the start of Fountain's trial for five additional days. Judge Adkins refused Fountain's attorney's request to have the trial moved to Baltimore—a move that would have allowed for more security and possibly a more neutral jury pool. With all these factors in place to ensure swift "justice," Fountain was declared a suspect, hunted, arrested, indicted, tried, convicted, and sentenced in just twenty-four days—including the two days he spent on the run from the outraged mob that wanted to lynch him.

To be fair to Adkins and Butler, their aim in having Fountain's legal process and trial so quickly scheduled may have been to avoid his being lynched by enraged citizens. During the days of Jim Crow, any perceived delays in the legal process were often used as excuses by the population to justify the lynching of a Black suspect—especially when a sex crime against a White female was at issue. Isaiah Fountain's life was at risk both from within the legal system and outside it.

Questionable Justice

Isaiah Fountain was twice convicted of rape. At the first trial, he was convicted by an all-White jury that heard the evidence and deliberated while the courthouse was surrounded by angry mobs and armed troops. The appeals court concluded that this threat of mob violence undoubtedly intimidated the jury and caused them to render a guilty verdict after fewer than nine minutes of deliberation. Compounding the issue of jury intimidation was Judge Adkins's announcement to the court that Fountain had escaped the previous night. Astonishingly, Adkins made the escape announcement in the presence of the jury. The announcement surely raised serious doubt in the jurors' minds about the defendant's innocence. Realizing his mistake, when the trial resumed, the judge instructed the jury to forget about his statement about Fountain's escape. The judge's action was a futile attempt to correct his judicial error.

Fountain's second trial, by a tribunal of judges in Towson, also resulted in a guilty verdict. The judges' statement about their decision-making process revealed that their verdict was significantly influenced by the only direct evidence submitted by the prosecution at that trial: the testimony of the victim, Bertha Simpson, identifying Isaiah Fountain as her attacker. The Baltimore County judges stated that all the other testimony presented to the court was circumstantial.[2]

The jury at the first trial and the judges at the second all readily accepted Bertha Simpson's identification of Isaiah Fountain as her rapist—even though her testimony was shaky and sometimes contradictory. In both trials, other very credible and objective evidence was either ignored or manipulated in order to justify the guilty verdicts.

Admittedly, other detrimental evidence was presented by the prosecution against Fountain at both trials, but the Simpson identification remained foremost. The other key prosecution evidence was the blacksmith's testimony about the wagon wheel tire and horseshoe imprints in the road, and the testimony of witnesses about seeing Fountain's wagon in the crime scene area.

The victim's direct testimony was reported as being inconsistent and tentative. Also, the method and circumstances of Simpson's identification of Fountain were regarded as being irregular and suspect. In her book, *On the Courthouse Lawn: Confronting the Legacy of Lynching in the Twenty-First Century*, author and lawyer Sherrilyn Ifill commented about the unreliability of the victim's testimony. Ifill wrote: "Simpson's identification of Fountain as her attacker was so filled with contradictions that it would not stand up in court today, or perhaps even in 1919, but for the fact that Fountain was black."[3]

What about the other prosecution witnesses who testified against Fountain? Were they lying? Were they mistaken? Were they coerced? Who knows? Perhaps they slanted their testimony or lied in response to racial bias, public pressure, or fear of mob violence. However, given the Jim Crow environment and attitudes toward Black people at the time, it seems that the possibility of false testimony *against* Isaiah Fountain was more likely than false testimony in his favor.

At both trials, the testimonies of three very credible and respected White witnesses were totally ignored. The Easton chief of police, the county assistant treasurer, and the bank teller all swore that Isaiah Fountain was in Easton at almost the same time Bertha Simpson was being attacked. If they were to be believed, there was no way that Isaiah Fountain could have traveled the nine miles to the crime scene to find, stalk, and attack the victim. These three witnesses had nothing to gain by giving testimony to support Fountain's alibi—indeed, their testimony went against the overwhelming popular sentiment in Talbot County that Fountain was the rapist of Bertha Simpson. If anything, these citizens risked being shunned and deplored by their White neighbors for their contrarian testimonies in support of the Black alleged rapist.

Perhaps the most brazen disregard of justice was the Towson judges' detailed explanation of how they added time to Bertha Simpson's own testimony of the timeline of the afternoon. The judges moved the time of her attack to as late as 5:30 p.m., effectively changing the time that the crime was committed by up to an hour and a half. They dubiously interpreted the evidence so that—in contradiction to Bertha Simpson's own testimony—Fountain had the opportunity to commit the crime after all. It is amazing that defense attorney Eugene O'Dunne did not appeal the verdict of the second trial based on the judges' admitted fabrication of the rape timeline.

The deck was stacked against Isaiah Fountain from the very beginning, as an African American during the Jim Crow era. Sherrilyn Ifill suggested that the trial's outcome was inevitable, regardless of whatever testimony and evidence was presented on Fountain's behalf.[4] Once he was arrested for Bertha Simpson's rape, only his two escapes from detention gave Fountain any real chance to avoid imminent death. Fountain's capture and return to the Jim Crow era justice system sealed his fate as the second victim of the Fountain case.

The justice system failed Bertha Simpson by not finding, prosecuting, and punishing her true rapist. It failed Isaiah Fountain by twice denying him fair trials and then hanging him for a crime that he repeatedly and steadfastly denied committing. Perhaps the retelling of his remarkable story a century later will at least provide some acknowledgement that Isaiah Fountain was denied the justice he deserved.

Endnotes

1 "Fountain Wins His Appeal for Another Trial," *Evening Sun*, July 17, 1919, 16. Newspapers.com.

2 "Court Gives Reasons," *Easton Star-Democrat*, May 22, 1920, 1.

3 Sherrilyn A. Ifill, *On the Courthouse Lawn: Confronting the Legacy of Lynching in the Twenty-First Century* (Boston: Beacon Press, 2018), 11.

4 Ifill, *On The Courthouse Lawn*, 11.

EPILOGUE

Déjà vu in Talbot County

There's an expression, déjà vu, that means that you feel
like you've been somewhere before, that you've somehow
already dreamed it or experienced it in your mind.

— NEIL GAIMAN

No Fountain News

With the arrival of 1921, the outrage over Bertha Simpson's rape and the ensuing Fountain Case had subsided in Talbot County. After months of trials, angry mobs, escapes, manhunts, and appeals, Isaiah Fountain had been hanged for the crime and had been in his grave since the previous July. Talbot County had survived an intense period of racial outrage and notoriety and endured intense criticism from its city cousins for its perceived bias and blatant Jim Crow treatment of an African American man charged with raping a White girl. The period of the Fountain case had not been Talbot County's finest season, but the county—especially its White population—managed to endure, and even prosper.

There's no doubt that the Isaiah Fountain case had negative effects for the Black population in Talbot County,
especially in the Trappe district, Fountain's home area. In
addition to the aggressive and unreasonable searches and
incarceration of Blacks during Fountain's escapes, local
Blacks suffered other forms of intimidation, harassment, and
even banishment. According to James Dawson, the author
of *Irregularities in Abundance: An Anecdotal History of Trappe
District in Talbot Co.*, Md., after Fountain's first escape from
the lynch mob outside the courthouse, the Ku Klux Klan
held a rally and burned a cross in a field behind Main Street
in Trappe.[1] No doubt, the rally was held to send a message to
the local Black population to not offer assistance to Fountain.

Dawson continued: "After the Fountain incident, black
families who had lived within the town limits were forced
to move outside of town, some lost their houses and moved
away." A then-resident of Trappe remembered that some
Whites expressed the sentiment: "we don't want n-----s on
Main St."[2] For decades after the Fountain case, there was
an unwritten rule in the Trappe district that limited where
Blacks could live. However, regardless of the strong anti-
Black sentiment, there were probably just as many Whites
in the district who bore no animosity toward their Black
neighbors.[3]

Jim Crow laws persisted, along with differing legal standards used for the prosecution and conviction of Black people
and their White neighbors. The Blacks of Talbot County
continued to be prosecuted and even put to death for crimes
that were regularly considered more serious than similar
crimes committed by White offenders. Threats of lynchings
still continued on the Eastern Shore, and some of its counties

experienced brutal lynchings as late as 1933. These vicious events made big headlines in Maryland and elsewhere, but none of them reached the same sustained, long-term notoriety as the Fountain case, becoming "one of the most noted in the State's annals."[4]

Another Outrage

Almost nine months of 1921 had passed, and autumn was about to begin when another shocking event occurred in Talbot County. Racial outrage again surged in the county and stoked the dormant coals of the Fountain case.

On Wednesday, September 21, 1921—more than a year after Isaiah Fountain's execution—a White girl named Mattie left her classes at the high school[5] in the waterfront town of Oxford, Maryland. She walked a quarter mile and then rode the Oxford-Bellevue ferry across the Tred Avon River. After leaving the ferry at the Bellevue landing, the girl walked a short distance on Bellevue Road and turned south to walk to her home on Ferry Neck Road. The girl reported that, in the vicinity of Ferry Neck Church,[6] she was accosted by a one-legged Black man who displayed a large knife. She said the man threw her to the ground and threatened to rape her. She fought back, and both parties suffered injuries. The girl escaped her attacker, sought aid, and was taken to Easton Hospital for treatment.[7]

Talbot County Sheriff Charles Soulsby was notified of the attempted assault, and with the aid of the State Police, he quickly formed a search posse. Later that night, twenty-two-year-old Perry Castle from Bellevue was arrested at his father's house. Castle, who was Black and had only one leg, was promptly transported to the Talbot County Jail in Easton. Recalling the trial delays and multiple escapes of Isaiah Fountain more than two years earlier, citizens began to express concerns about getting quick justice for Castle's alleged crime.[8]

Once again, threats of mob violence and rumblings of lynching arose in Talbot County; outside police were brought in to ensure Castle's safety. The young girl identified Perry Castle as her assailant on Thursday, September 22, as she was rolled into the room in a wheelchair.[9] Later that day, Sheriff Soulsby received the news about crowds gathering in Easton, rumored to be threatening Castle. He took the prisoner from the jail to a remote area outside Easton for his safety and returned him early the next morning, after the crowds had dispersed. He also posted extra guards, including state policemen, around the jail.[10]

Perry Castle was tried in Easton on November 25, 1921. Talbot County Chief Circuit Court Judge William H. Adkins presided at Castle's non-jury trial. The prosecutor was State's Attorney Charles Butler, and the defense attorney was Joseph Seth. During the trial, Jerry Castle admitted that he took hold of the victim but denied trying to assault her. He was quickly convicted and sentenced by Judge Adkins to eighteen years in the Maryland Penitentiary.[11]

This story and the circumstances may sound familiar. Without a doubt, it was uncannily similar to a previous Talbot County court case. Was it a case of pure coincidence?

Mattie, the victim of Perry Castle in the Bellevue assault in the autumn of 1921, was a fourteen-year-old girl whose older sister lived ten miles away, near Trappe, with their grandparents. In the spring of 1919, Mattie's older sister had experienced a similar assault when she was also fourteen years old. Her assailant was convicted of rape and sentenced to death by hanging. His name, of course, was Isaiah Fountain.

Mattie Simpson, the Bellevue assault victim, was Bertha Simpson's younger sister. Surely, the possibilities were minuscule that two sisters could have been assaulted while walking home from their schools by two different Black men in the same county within two and a half years.

Most of the published newspaper articles reported that the Trappe and Bellevue assault victims were sisters. They even published that both victims made their identifications of the Black assailants while sitting in wheelchairs. However, of all the newspapers, only the *Baltimore Afro-American* raised questions about the eerily identical circumstances of the two attacks. The newspaper also questioned the intelligence and intent of the Simpson family.[12]

The *Afro-American* wrote:

> The news of the attempted rape of the Simpson white girl on the Eastern Shore comes so close to the alleged outrage upon the sister of the same girl by [Isaiah] Fountain last year that it deserves more than passing notice.

> Fountain maintained his innocence to the last in spite of the third degree methods of Sheriff Soulsby and his deputies, but nevertheless was hung on circumstantial evidence. Now another of the same family claims to have been a victim of an alleged colored rapist.

> The first case has left such a stench in the nostrils of people who love justice and order that they have little patience with the second. There ought to be an investigation into the Simpson family to see if they have all the

intelligence of average folk, and whether these are cases of rape or cases of consent.[13]

There is no evidence that any such investigation was ever made about the bizarrely similar circumstances of the attacks on the Simpson sisters. With Perry Castle's sentencing, the news about him ended. After two and a half years, the news about Isaiah Fountain had finally also come to an end. The *Baltimore Afro-American* newspaper, however, occasionally used both the Castle and Fountain prosecutions to compare their distinctly harsher verdicts and sentences with those received by White offenders for similar or more serious crimes. In its determined campaign against the endemic two-tiered Jim Crow justice system, the paper fiercely and derisively labeled the Eastern Shore as "putrid" and stated that "there is no such thing as justice on the Eastern Shore of Maryland."[14] Despite the pleas from the *Afro-American*, there were no investigations about the legitimacy of the Castle or Fountain verdicts.

Not surprisingly, the *Easton Star-Democrat* was true to its mission of defending the reputation and honor of Easton and Talbot County when it published a response to the *Afro American*'s charges. The *Star-Democrat* asserted that the county had been "slandered in a most objectionable manner." In addition, the headline in the Easton paper stated that the *Afro-American* "Should Be Hauled Before The Court And Jailed For Contempt Of Court."[15] The media war soon ceased as all the papers lost interest in the case and moved on to other, timelier news stories. The Fountain case had exploded on the scene in April of 1919, blazed brightly for months, flickered, and finally burned out. After more than two and a half years of notoriety and fierce headlines, it faded into the obscurity of history.

What Really Happened?

With the wisdom provided by more than a century of insight and introspection, it's difficult to believe that Isaiah Fountain was treated with true justice. The outraged citizens of Talbot County, as well as the jurors at his first trial and the judges at his second, were more convinced of Fountain's guilt than we might be a century later. The passage of time has changed social mores, and federal Civil Rights legislation has changed most people's perspectives about race-related matters.

The citizens of Talbot County a century ago were products of the Jim Crow era. Many of the White citizenry too easily accepted the romantic myth of the "Lost Cause" and the system of institutionalized racism. Many readily agreed with, or put up with, the Lynch Law as a means to attain speedy "justice" while instilling terror and compliance in the Black community. Certainly, the White population's acceptance or tolerance of such practices clouded their sense of justice, morality, and humanity. That acceptance and tolerance would be alien to most Talbot countians today.

The Isaiah Fountain case leaves us with plenty of questions. Was Isaiah Fountain the scheming sexual predator and brutish villain he was portrayed as by his prosecutor and many newspapers? Did he deserve his fate of being hanged at the Talbot County Jail? Was he a handy victim of Jim Crow justice who, despite the two trial judgments against him, remained unwavering about his innocence to the very end? Was Fountain, indeed, guilty? And if so, did he get the sentence that was appropriate for his crime, or because he was a Black man living in the Jim Crow era? Did the Simpson sisters really suffer their attacks in the manner they described?

Trappe historian and author James Dawson has also expressed doubts about the outcome of the Fountain case:

> Too many years have passed to know what was true and what was not in these tragic matters. However, it seems almost inconceivable that two sisters were attacked by two different black men within two years in two different places in Talbot County.[16]

There is no doubt that the popular outrage showed by the citizens of Talbot County against Fountain was fueled by the racist laws, practices, and culture of the time. Indeed, the Fountain case would not have reached its notorious long-lived prominence without the passionate outrage that existed on Maryland's Eastern Shore during the Jim Crow era. Additionally, the Lost Cause sentiment espoused by much of the county's White population and leadership undoubtedly compelled them to maintain the status quo of keeping the Black population "in its place." Notwithstanding the few Whites who were unconvinced about Fountain's guilt and the *Baltimore Afro-American*'s crusade to save him, Isaiah Fountain was condemned by his own circumstances: He was a Black man in a Jim Crow society accused of committing "an outrage" against a White girl.

Delayed Justice

On May 8, 2021, Maryland Governor Larry Hogan made history by issuing full posthumous pardons for the thirty-four victims of racial lynchings that occurred in Maryland between 1854 and 1933. Hogan said that the pardons for the lynching victims were granted "on the basis that these extra-judicial killings violated fundamental rights to due process and equal protection of law." The governor added: "My hope is that this action will at least in some way help to right these horrific wrongs and perhaps bring a measure of peace to the memories of these individuals, and to their descendants and loved ones."[17]

Although Isaiah Fountain was not lynched, his ultimate fate was the same as that of the thirty-four pardoned victims. His execution and the dubious legal process that led to his hanging produced the same fatal result as that of the Maryland lynching victims, but under the guise of "justice." His rights of due process and equal justice under the law were denied. Perhaps—like the thirty-four pardoned lynching victims—the guilty verdict of Isaiah Fountain's second trial should be re-examined and a posthumous pardon issued. The delayed justice of a posthumous pardon for Isaiah Fountain would be a final and fitting ending for the notorious Fountain case.

THE END

Endnotes

1 James Dawson, ed., *Irregularities in Abundance: An Anecdotal History of Trappe District in Talbot Co.*, Md. (Easton, Md.: Talbot County Free Library Association, 2010), 113.

2 Dawson, *Irregularities in Abundance: An Anecdotal History of Trappe District in Talbot Co.*, Md., 115.

3 Dawson, *Irregularities in Abundance*, 115.

4 "Fountain to Baltimore?" *Star-Democrat*, November 29, 1919, 1.

5 Oxford High School was located on North Morris Street, just on the north side of the town park where the Oxford United Methodist Church now stands.

6 "Negro Attacks Girl," *Star-Democrat*, September 24, 1921, 1.

7 "Negro Attacks Schoolgirl," *Wilmington Evening Journal*, September 22, 1921, 1 and 14. Newspapers.com.

8 "Negro Attacks Schoolgirl," 14. Some newspaper articles incorrectly listed Castle's first name as Jerry, instead of Perry.

9 "Castle Admits He Seized Young Girl," *Wilmington News Journal*, September 23, 1921, 9. Newspapers.com.

10 "Negro under Guard in Jail at Easton," *Baltimore Evening Sun*, September 23, 1921, 4. Newspapers.com.

11 "Negro Gets 18 Years for Attack on Girl," *Baltimore Sun*, November 26, 1921, 1. Newspapers.com.

12 Dawson, *Irregularities in Abundance*, 115.

13 "The Simpson Case," *Baltimore Afro-American*, September 30, 1921, 7. ProQuest.com.

14 "The Putrid Eastern Shore," *Baltimore Afro-American*, December 2, 1921, 12.

15 "Shore Is Putrid," *Easton Star-Democrat*, December 10, 1921, 5.

16 Dawson, *Irregularities in Abundance: An Anecdotal History of Trappe District in Talbot Co.*, Md., 115.

17 "In Historic First, Governor Larry Hogan Issues Full Posthumous Pardon for Victims of Racial Lynching," website of the Office of Governor Larry Hogan, last modified May 8, 2021, https://

governor.maryland.gov/2021/05/08/in-historic-first-governor-ho-gan-issues-full-posthumous-pardon-for-victims-of-racial-lynching/. Other documented victims of lynchings in Maryland could not be pardoned by the governor because they had been lynched before being arrested.

BIBLIOGRAPHY

BOOKS AND PERIODICALS

Brown, C. C. *The Road to Jim Crow: The African American Struggle on Maryland's Eastern Shore, 1860–1915*. Baltimore: Maryland Historical Society, 2017.

Cep, Casey. "My Local Confederate Monument," *The New Yorker*, last modified September 12, 2020. https://www.newyorker.com/news/us-journal/my-local-confederate-monument.

Cep, Casey. "Shallow-buried Stories of Slavery Still Haunt My Home County." *Aeon Essays*. Aeon, last modified 28, 2013. https://aeon.co/essays/shallow-buried-stories-of-slavery-still-haunt-my-home-county.

Claggett, Laurence. *Easton*. Charleston: Arcadia Publishing, 1999.

Cramer, Maria, "Confederate Flag an Unnerving Sight in Capitol." *New York Times*. Updated January 14, 2021. https://www.nytimes.com/2021/01/09/us/politics/confederate-flag-capitol.html?searchResultPosition=1.

Dawson, James, ed. *100 Years of Change on the Eastern Shore: Extracts from the Willis Family Journals 1847–1951*. Charles F. Willis III, 2015.

Dawson, James. "Easton's Potter's Field." *Tidewater Times* (January 2021) 52.

Dawson, James, ed. *Irregularities in Abundance: An Anecdotal History of Trappe District in Talbot Co., Md*. Easton, Md.: The Talbot County Free Library Association, 2010.

Distinguished Men of Baltimore and Maryland. 1914, Baltimore: Baltimore American.

Duyer, Linda. *Mob Law on Delmarva: Cases of Lynchings, Near-Lynchings, Legal Executions, and Race Riots of Delaware, Maryland, and Virginia, 1870–1950*. Self-published, 2014.

Footner, Hulbert. *Rivers of the Eastern Shore*. New York: J. J. Little and Ives Company, 1944.

"Governor Larry Hogan - Official Website for the Governor of Maryland." Governor of Maryland. Last modified May 8, 2021. https://governor.maryland.gov/2021/05/08/in-historic-first-governor-hogan-issues-full-posthumous-pardon-for-victims-of-racial-lynching/.

Harrington, Norman. *Easton Album*. Easton, Maryland: Historical Society of Talbot County, 1986.

Hayman, John C. *Rails Along the Chesapeake: A History of Railroading on the Delmarva Peninsula, 1827–1978*. Marvadel Publishers, 1979.

Hemstock, G. K. *Injustice on the Eastern Shore: Race and the Hill Murder Trial*. Charleston, SC: Arcadia Publishing, 2015.

Ifill, Sherrilyn A. *On the Courthouse Lawn: Confronting the Legacy of Lynching in the Twenty-First Century*. Boston: Beacon Press, 2018.

Little, Becky. "Who Was Jim Crow?" *National Geographic*. Last modified August 6, 2015. https://www.nationalgeographic.com/history/article/150806-voting-rights-act-anniversary-jim-crow-segregation-discrimination-racism-history.

Moore, Joseph E. *Murder on Maryland's Eastern Shore: Race, Politics and the Case of Orphan Jones*. Charleston, SC: Arcadia Publishing, 2006.

Preston, Dickson J. *Talbot County: A History*. Centreville, Md.: Tidewater Publishers, 1983.

Preston, Dickson J. *Trappe: The Story of an Old-fashioned Town*. Easton, Md.: Economy Printing Co., 1976.

Seidule, Ty. *Robert E. Lee and Me: A Southerner's Reckoning with the Myth of the Lost Cause*. New York: St. Martin's Press, 2021.

Seth, Joseph B., and Mary W. Seth. *Recollections of a Long Life on the Eastern Shore*. Easton, Md.: Press of the Star-Democrat, 1926.

Wennersten, John R. *Maryland's Eastern Shore: A Journey in Time and Place*. Centreville, Md.: Cornell Maritime Press/Tidewater Publishers, 1992.

West, Teri, and Kirstyn Flood, "Legacy of Slavery, Segregation Influences Debate over Removing Confederate Statue in Maryland." Capital News Service Maryland. Last modified June 15, 2020. https://cns-maryland.org/2020/06/15/legacy-of-slavery-segregation-influences-debate-over-removing-confederate-statue-in-maryland/.

Woodward, Bob. *Rage*. New York: Simon & Schuster, 2020.

Woolever, Lydia, "Turning Tides: After Decades of Silence, the Eastern Shore Begins to Reckon with Its Difficult History." *Baltimore Magazine*, February 2021. Last modified September 14, 2021. https://www.baltimoremagazine.com/section/historypolitics/eastern-shore-begins-to-reckon-with-difficult-history-racism-slavery/.

COURT DOCUMENTS

Court of Appeals (Records and Briefs), Isaiah Fountain v. State, April Term 1919, No. 39 [MSA S1733-530, 1/65/04/100])

Fountain v. State (No. 39) (Court of Appeals of Maryland, July 17, 1919). The Atlantic Reporter, Volume 107, pages 554–557. Google Books, accessed July 21, 2020. https://www.google.com/books/edition/The_Atlantic_Reporter/Kznb7Nl_5wUC?hl=en&gbpv=1&dq=the+Atlantic+reporter,+volume+107&pg=PR14&printsec=frontcover

Fountain v. State, 135 Md. 87 (1919) (Court of Appeals of Maryland, Opinion of the Court. October 29, 1919.), *LexRoll (MD)*, last modified November 22, 2017. https://maryland.lexroll.com/fountain-v-state-of-maryland-135-md-87-1919/.

Maryland Office of the Public Defender, *et al* v. Talbot County, Maryland (1:21-cv-01088-ELH Document 1), Complaint, May 5, 2021. ACLU of Maryland. Accessed February 8, 2022. https://www.aclu-md.org/sites/default/files/field_documents/opd_et_al_v._talbot_county.pdf.

Maryland Office of the Public Defender, *et al* v.Talbot County, Maryland (1:21-cv-01088-ELH Document 11-3), Declaration, August 13, 2021. ACLU of Maryland. Accessed February 8, 2022. https://www.aclu-md.org/sites/default/files/doc._11-3_declaration_of_r._potter.pdf.

NEWSPAPERS

Baltimore Afro-American. Various articles from April 9, 1919 to October 27, 1922. ProQuest.com.

Baltimore Sun. Various articles from April 3,1919 to June 8, 1923. Newspapers.com.

Cambridge Daily Banner. Various articles from April 22, 1919 to July 23, 1920. Newspapers.com.

Denton Journal. Various articles from April 26, 1919 to July 24, 1920. Newspapers.com.

Easton Star-Democrat. Various articles from April 4, 1919 to December 10, 1921. Maryland Room, Microfilm Newspaper Archives, Talbot County Free Library, Easton, Md.

Midland Journal (Rising Sun, Md.). No Title. June 11, 1920, 4. Newspapers.com.

Washington Post. Various articles from April 25, 1919 to July 22, 1920. Newspapers.com.

Washington Times. Various articles from April 3, 1919 to April 29, 1922. Newspapers.com.

Wilmington Evening Journal. Various articles from April 3, 1919 to June 5,1924. Newspapers.com.

Wilmington Morning News. Various articles from April 4, 1919 to October 23, 1921. Newspapers.com.

Wilmington News Journal. Various articles from April 8, 1919 to September 23, 1920. Newspapers.com.

ARCHIVES

Oxford Museum, Photo Archives, Oxford, Md.

Talbot County Free Library, Maryland Room, Easton, Md.

Talbot Historical Society, Newspaper Microfilm, Photo Archives, Easton, Md.

EMAILS

Daffin, James. January 19, 2021. 'Courtroom Info.' Email.

Moore, Joseph. September 24, 2019. 'Murder On Maryland's Eastern Shore.' Email.

INTERNET RESOURCES

Maryland and local history

Digital Maryland, Maryland State Library Resource Center, Enoch Pratt Free Library: https://collections.digitalmaryland.org/digital/collection/mdph/id/1265/rec/1

Maryland Historical Trust: https://mht.maryland.gov/

Maryland State Archives: https://msa.maryland.gov/

Maryland State Archives, Biographical Series:https://msa.maryland.gov/msa/homepage/html/biographies.html

Maryland State Archives, Talbot County records: https://msa.maryland.gov/msa/mdmanual/36loc/ta/records/html/00list.html

Maryland State Archives, Special Collection, Newspapers: http://speccol.msa.maryland.gov/pages/newspaper/index.aspx

Maryland Office of Tourism website, History section: https://www.visitmaryland.org/history

Abandoned Rails, Maryland: https://www.abandonedrails.com/maryland

Save the Talbot Boys, Facebook page: https://www.facebook.com/SaveTalbotBoys/photos/1762671537220225

The Oxford Museum, Oxford Maryland: https://www.oxfordmuseummd.org/

Unicorn Bookshop (Easton, Maryland), Trappe history: https://www.unicornbookshop.com/trappehistory/trappe_history.html

GENERAL US HISTORY AND RECORDS

Census.gov: https://www.census.gov/quickfacts/fact/table/talbotcountymaryland/RHI125219.

Census records: https://www.archives.gov/research/census/about

Database of executions in the USA: https://www.deathpenaltyusa.org/

Famous Trials, hosted by the UMKC School of Law: https://famous-trials.com/

History.com: www.history.com

Legends of America: https://www.legendsofamerica.com/

Lumen learning, Boundless US History: https://courses.lumenlearning.com/boundless-ushistory/

Saving.org: Accessed March 30, 2022. https://www.saving.org/inflation/.

MAPS

Adapted from "Create Maps on Scribble Maps." Map Data @2022 Google. Accessed January 2, 2022. https://www.scribblemaps.com/create#/lat=38.57917134&lng=-75.86763379&z=11&t=custom_style

INDEX

Note: Pages in photo insert are set in italics.

C

D

Douglass, Frederick, 9, 11, *142*

E

Easter Sunday, 45–47

Easton Star-Democrat, 21–22, 172–73, 200–202, 247, 251, 270
accusing the *Sun* of lying about O'Dunne's compensation, 132
disagree with Baltimore newspaper reports, 46
exorbitant charges, 182
on final payment related to the case, 244
Fountain asserting his innocence to reporter of, 233–34
on Fountain's life in danger in Talbot County, 43
on incorrect reporting of *Baltimore Sun* during trial, 130
malicious reports in Baltimore papers, 125
denial of armed mob present at courthouse, 123
not satisfied with *Sun* portrayal of Talbot County citizens, 131
opposing the decision of Court of Appeals, 168
against other newspapers on way of reporting, 122–23
on perceived unfairness, 129
on presence of large crowds at criminal trial, 187
publication of complete judges' statement, 192
publication of false news, 226
on public execution of Fountain in Easton, 222
on public outrage in Trappe district, 37
on receipt of first news of Fountain's conviction from Butler, 199
reporting assault of Simpson, *140*
reporting on trial day, 52–53, 55, 62, 70
reporting Seth statement for private hanging, 223
reporting uniqueness of the case, 243
report on lynching threats, 39–40
report on unnecessary delay of execution, 180
responding to the *Sun's* push for new trial for Fountain, 128
restrained in reporting, 69–70
on statement of Adkins regarding Fountain escape from violence, 124

288

H

Harrington, Emerson, 80, 88
  extradition papers for return of Fountain to Talbot, 39
  notification to be on lookout for Fountain, 84
  warning to Judge Adkins about the mob, 92
Henry, George, 208, 210, 213
Hogan, Larry, 272–73
Hopper, Philemon B., 54
Hubbard, William, 38

I

Ifill, Sherrilyn, xv, xvi, 12, 257, 262
indictment, 40–43, 60, 259–60
institutionalized racism, 271
Irregularities in Abundance: An Anecdotal History of Trappe District in Talbot Co. (Dawson), 266

J

Jim Crow, 1, 3, 5–6, 114, 238, 242, 260
Johnson, Lyndon, 6

K

Ku Klux Klan, 266

L

Lawrence, Frederick, 45
Loper, Ralph, 207, 214
Lost Cause movement, 6–11, *138, 139*
lynching, 5, 11–13, 215
  attempted, 122, 157

defined, 11

gang, 131

mob, 67–70, 87

prospect of, 45

threat of, 12–13, 39, 46, 52, 69, 124, *150*

victims pardoned posthumously by governor, 272-273

M

Marbury, Ogle, 164

Marvel, Raymond, 214

Maryland Constitution, 171

Maryland Militia, 92–93

  service charges for, 243

  troops, 112

  uniformed and armed, 93

Maryland National Guard, 93, 96n27

Maryland State Guard, 93

Maryland State Police, road deputies, 95n13

McIntosh, David Gregg, 19n35

McIntosh law, 245–46

media war, 121–33

Mills, Andrew, 30–32, 34

mob violence, 13, 102

  fear of, 262

  influence on jury, 158–59

  threats of, 157, 260, 268

Mullikin, H. E., 26, 31, 41, 59–60, 159, 162, 187

  filing of appeal to Maryland Court of Appeals, 157–58

  on state's attorney's ethics and impartiality, 163–64

Mullikin, James, 44, 46, 55, 132–33, 187

Mushaw, Harvey, 32, 42

N

S

Schwaninger, Theodore "Swanaker," 60–61, 104, 108

Scott, John, 213

Second Judicial Circuit, 129

second trial, 185–96. *See also* trial

final preparations, 185–86

first day of, 186–88

fourth day of, 191–92

judges' explanation, 192–96

second day of, 188

third day of, 188–90

security of prisoner, 112–13

sentence and verdict, 110–12, 191

Seth, Joseph B., 7–10, *139,* 223

believer of Lost Cause myth, 229n3

opposition to the public hanging, 223–24

Seymour, Charles, 207, 213, 214

Shehan, W. Mason, 91

Simpson, Bertha, 27n6, 44, 109, 186–88, 194–95, 222, 238, 246, 257–58, 262, 269

assailant, 29–30

assault report in newspapers, 24–25

delayed report to the Talbot County Sheriff, 25

identification of Fountain, 42, 160, 200, 261

identification of the horse and buggy, 30, 32, 163

inconsistent reporting of assault in newspapers, 25

reported and described in newspapers, 22–23

sites associated with the assault of, *136*

testimony of, 41, 57, 58–59, 263

Trappe High School, *140*

Simpson, Ida, 22

CPSIA information can be obtained
at www.ICGtesting.com
Printed in the USA
JSHW020843060323
38441JS00001B/3